How language shapes relationships in professional sports teams

ALSO AVAILABLE FROM BLOOMSBURY

Sports Discourse, Tony Schirato
Corpus Approaches to the Language of Sports, Marcus Callies and Magnus Levin

How language shapes relationships in professional sports teams

Power and solidarity dynamics in a New Zealand rugby team

KIERAN FILE

BLOOMSBURY ACADEMIC
LONDON • NEW YORK • OXFORD • NEW DELHI • SYDNEY

BLOOMSBURY ACADEMIC
Bloomsbury Publishing Plc
50 Bedford Square, London, WC1B 3DP, UK
1385 Broadway, New York, NY 10018, USA
29 Earlsfort Terrace, Dublin 2, Ireland

BLOOMSBURY, BLOOMSBURY ACADEMIC and the Diana logo
are trademarks of Bloomsbury Publishing Plc

First published in Great Britain 2023
This paperback edition published 2024

Copyright © Kieran File, 2023

Kieran File has asserted his right under the Copyright, Designs and
Patents Act, 1988, to be identified as Author of this work.

For legal purposes the Acknowledgements on p. xiv constitute an
extension of this copyright page.

Cover design: Tjaša Krivec
Cover image © miodrag ignjatovic

All rights reserved. No part of this publication may be reproduced or
transmitted in any form or by any means, electronic or mechanical,
including photocopying, recording, or any information storage or retrieval
system, without prior permission in writing from the publishers.

Bloomsbury Publishing Plc does not have any control over, or responsibility for,
any third-party websites referred to or in this book. All internet addresses given in this
book were correct at the time of going to press. The author and publisher regret any
inconvenience caused if addresses have changed or sites have ceased to exist,
but can accept no responsibility for any such changes.

A catalogue record for this book is available from the British Library.

A catalog record for this book is available from the Library of Congress.

ISBN: HB: 978-1-3500-4424-1
       PB: 978-1-3500-4423-4
       ePDF: 978-1-3500-4426-5
       eBook: 978-1-3500-4425-8

Typeset by Integra Software Services Pvt. Ltd.

To find out more about our authors and books visit www.bloomsbury.com
and sign up for our newsletters.

For Anna, Seb and Zizzy ... my most important relationships.

Contents

List of figures ix

List of tables x

Preface xi

Acknowledgements xiv

1 How do relationships work in professional sports teams? Investigating the *performance* of relationships through a linguistic lens 1

2 Introducing our toolkit: Discourse analytical tools for locating relational dynamics in social interaction 25

3 How do coaches exercise control over players? Constructing asymmetrical power relations through language 59

4 Exercising power through questioning: How coaches *use* their questions 79

5 How does power sharing work? The interactional distribution of power between coach and captain 97

6 Power dynamics amongst players: Establishing flatter social structures in on-field problem-solving talk 117

7 Bonding before battle: How the captain fosters togetherness and belonging in *pre-match team-talk* rituals 135

8 Maintaining professional distance in interaction: The nature of solidarity between coaches and players 155

9 Criticism and solidarity between coach and players: Variation in critical feedback practices 175

10 Widening the linguistic lens: Identifying cultural belief systems underlying how relationships work in professional sports teams 193

Appendix 1: Technical rugby terms explained 215

Appendix 2: Contextual information about individuals in the team 218

References 221

Index 233

List of figures

1.1 Conceptual lens for unpacking how relationships work 18

List of tables

1.1 Overview of the team by name, nickname, role and group 6

2.1 Outline of the type and amount of interactions recorded 30

2.2 Transcription conventions used in this book 33

2.3 Important interactional tasks evident in training sessions, team meetings and on match days 35

2.4 A list of core speech actions being performed through speaker utterances in our data 39

2.5 Grammatical subsystems of language for unpacking how speech actions are being designed 43

2.6 Analytical tools for studying turn-taking patterns in our data 46

2.7 Interpretive mechanisms for making sense of the interactional practices we saw in our data 51

Preface

In this book, we aim to build an understanding of *how relationships are actually working* in a professional sports team. We will do this by shining a light on the actual dynamics of relationships as they are being enacted by professional athletes and coaches in the real-life, authentic settings and social interactions of a team.

The source of data collected and analysed to perform this more dynamic analysis of relationships is language or the authentic linguistic practices sports professionals (coaches, captains, support staff and players) deploy in their everyday social interactions with one another. Language is arguably the most central tool humans draw on to manage the complex realities of their interpersonal interactions with others. Without language, many of the complex tasks we need to perform or accomplish with others, particularly in our professional lives, would be difficult if not impossible. For example, in the course of a normal working day, people may rely on language to give instructions to others, negotiate decisions with others, develop strategy, coordinate groups of people, convey technical information, give feedback and motivate others. All of these tasks are central to the accomplishment of workplace tasks and all are ritually accomplished with at least some need for language. What's more, *the way* they use language to perform these tasks will say a lot about how they are making their relationships work in the process. Language, therefore, provides a rich, naturally occurring source of data to probe questions about relationships. As we will see throughout the chapters of this book, patterns in the way sports professionals use language when engaged in their everyday (professional) tasks with one another are capable of revealing a great deal of insight about how they ritually shape their relationships with one another.

While this book is a book about language, it is simultaneously a book about what language helps humans do and what human language patterns can reveal. The main role our language analysis plays in this book is to help shine a light on the mechanics or dynamics of relating – how sports professionals actively construct, manage or shape their relations with others in the course of their real everyday interactional activities. However, in illustrating and unpacking these everyday relational dynamics we also have a valuable source of empirical data upon which to do deeper, more abstract theoretical work that can advance discussions about how relationships work. While the empirical illustrations of relationships in action are revealing in their own right, they also offer us a chance to question what lies behind these dynamics in terms of abstract sociocultural knowledge and belief systems that are giving rise to and being reconstructed in everyday relational dynamics. Social scientists from many disciplines concern themselves with the goal of locating the often abstract, taken-for-granted ways people in different (cultural) groups do things. For sociolinguists and discourse analysts (the subdiscipline of linguistics we draw on in this book), language practices evolve in particular sociocultural contexts to help their members do the things they need to do with language and attend to the social structures evident and important in the process. The language patterns people use, then, offer a naturally occurring source of data from which to locate or reverse-engineer cultural premises that are alive and evident in the (interpersonal) behaviour of people in particular groups. While at this broader, more abstract level claims are put forward tentatively (considering we take a case-study approach in this book), it is our goal to use the empirical analyses we conduct to derive a set of hypotheses or principles that underlie or explain the culture of relating in high-performance sport for future researchers to build on, challenge, revise and/or consolidate.

It is hoped that this research agenda provides food for thought for the wider research and practitioner community interested in learning more about relationships in professional or high-performance sports teams. However, ultimately, it is hoped that this book displays the value of a linguistic lens on relationships and the affordances this grossly underutilized theoretical and methodological toolkit offers to our understanding of this important topic for high-performance sports teams. Very few social science toolkits are capable of unpacking and exploring the interconnectedness of ritual social practices and the deeper underlying ideology or cultural knowledge systems that they reflect and/or give rise to. A large amount of knowledge about relationships in this professional domain has been built upon methods that ask sports professionals for their reflections and insights about relationships. By using a linguistic lens, one that looks for deeper meaning in the everyday practices of language, we look at what people do as they actually shape their relationships rather than what they say they do. This linguistic turn in the social sciences has yet to have a significant impact on research practice and knowledge development in the domain of professional sport. As readers work through the chapters of this book, it is hoped that they come to appreciate the value of a linguistic lens and the power it offers for locating and unpacking the relational significance of even the most ritual and mundane linguistic practices of sports professionals' interactions.

One final note to make in this foreword concerns what this book is *not*. It is important to bear in mind from the outset that discourse analysis is a qualitative research endeavour. What this means at its core is that we are more interested in *reporting* on what the participants themselves do and less interested in *evaluating* the suitability, reliability or validity of these practices. This more evaluative dimension is important and can be informed by linguistic data and analyses of the kind we offer in this book (we tentatively raise potential issues or points for consideration as we work through the chapters). However, we feel that this is ultimately something practitioners, and researchers who use research tools that are specifically designed to evaluate social practices, are better placed to consider. We do hope the discussions we have in this book stimulate additional discussions at a more evaluative level; however, it is not our intention to foreground these in this book. Instead, in line with the qualitative epistemology adopted in this book, the goal is to help inform those discussions by pinning down specific practices that are significant for shaping relationships and presenting in-depth accounts as to how these practices shape relationships in this professional domain. Readers from different contexts may view the practices they see in this book in very different ways; some may see them as largely unacceptable in light of their context or their philosophical standpoint, while others may find them perfectly acceptable. However, regardless, the work outlined in this book should give these discussions greater focus and clarity by highlighting ritual linguistic practices and their relational implications, so researchers and practitioners are better equipped to evaluate or more thoroughly consider practices in their own (or other) contexts.

In sum, it is hoped that the work presented in this book helps to raise new questions, opens up additional directions for relationship research, provides illustrations of additional tools researchers can draw on to develop a better understanding of the more dynamic reality of relationships or relating in high-performance sporting contexts, and gives practitioners a framework through which to engage in more targeted reflection.

Acknowledgements

This book would not be possible without the help and support of a number of people, groups and institutional bodies for which I am truly indebted. First and foremost, I want to extend my thanks to the professional New Zealand rugby team and the support staff who welcomed me and my audio and video recorders into their sacred spaces. While they remain anonymous throughout this book, they know who they are and I speak to them directly here when I say that without you this book and the insights generated would not have been possible. Very special thanks to the head coach of this team and to the team's personal development manager, who has been a constant source of support for all my crazy ideas and projects.

I would also like to extend my thanks to the Economic and Social Research Council (ESRC) which funded an allied impact project that allowed me to connect with this team and provide impact support on a particular communication issue the team was having. This ESRC-funded project helped provide the basis for the work I report on in this book.

A very special thank you to Dr Elaine Vine for all of her amazing, patient support over the years. From the early days in the functional grammar module to present-day chats about language use in sporting contexts, I have really appreciated and valued your guidance.

Finally, I need to express my gratitude to my family, particularly my long-suffering wife, Anna, who has picked up the slack especially in the final stages of writing this book. Writing a book, at least in my experience, is an all-encompassing affair, and I want to say thank you (in print!) to my wife for giving me the space I needed to get this done. Apparently, I am never allowed to write another book, and I can understand why.

1

How do relationships work in professional sports teams?

Investigating the *performance* of relationships through a linguistic lens

Outlining the mission

This book is concerned with one overarching question: *How are relationships actually working in professional sports teams?* While research into relationships in high-performance sports teams has grown in recent years (Azadfada et al., 2014; Bennie & O'Connor, 2012; Burke, 2001; Davis & Jowett, 2010; Jackson et al., 2010; Jowett & Cockerill, 2002, 2003; Jowett & Ntoumanis, 2004; Kassing & Infante, 1999; Lafrenière et al., 2008; Sagar & Jowett, 2012), studies that attempt to understand how relationships are actually working, or perhaps more to the point, how coaches and players shape their relationships in their authentic professional contexts, are few and far between. In this book, we make this more dynamic question of how relationships work our central concern, as we attempt to provide illustrations and empirically grounded accounts of the everyday, taken-for-granted practices that shape relationships in a professional New Zealand rugby team (introduced later in this chapter).

Our goals for writing this book are threefold. The primary goal is to offer the research and practitioner community **empirical** illustrations of relationships (of power and solidarity) as they are actually being enacted. To do this we deploy the tools of discourse analysis (G. Brown & Yule, 1983; P. Brown & Levinson, 1978; Drew & Heritage, 1992; Fairclough, 2003a; Gee, 2018; Hyland & Paltridge, 2013; Jaworski & Coupland, 2006; Liddicoat, 2022; Schiffrin, 1994) and sociolinguistics (Beeching, 2006; Blommaert, 2007;

Boxer, 2002; J. Holmes, 2014; Jaspers, 2012; Vine et al., 2008) to mine the everyday linguistic exchanges between coaches, the captain and players of our professional New Zealand rugby team for evidence of how they are enacting or constructing relations of power and solidarity with one another. These insights provide us with some direct evidence of how relationships are working or are being made to work in this professional domain in and through language.

The second goal, one that derives from these empirical insights, is more **theoretical** in nature. From these empirical illustrations, we have a body of evidence to ask deeper, more abstract and theoretical questions about how relationships work. Here we ask what the empirical insights of coaches, captains and players interacting and relating suggest about the unwritten, deeper, cultural principles that appear to underlie relating and relationships in this professional domain. What shared, taken-for-granted, cultural knowledge is being talked into being in the everyday interactional and relational practices of our team? Asking these questions allows us to add more theoretical hypotheses or claims about relationships to ongoing discussions that can be consolidated, revised or challenged by the findings of ongoing and future research.

A final and perhaps more indirect goal pursued in this book is **methodological**: to illustrate the value of a linguistic lens for drawing out insights about relationships in high-performance sports teams. As we will argue immediately below, empirical insights of the kind presented in this book are largely missing from debates and discussions about relationships in sports teams. The lack of direct insight regarding how sports professionals actually enact, perform, manage, negotiate and construct their relationships with one another has ultimately left us blind to some of the realities of relating in this professional context. A linguistic lens offers the research community a useful toolkit to help address these more dynamic questions of relationships as they are actually being enacted in real, high-performance settings. It is hoped that through the work presented in this book, readers will come to value the insights a linguistic lens can provide and consider linguistics in future interdisciplinary research endeavours in this topical domain.

In the remainder of this introduction, we expand on the above mission statement, outlining a number of key dimensions of the linguistic lens deployed in this book. This includes insights about the central elements we are bringing together to derive insights about relationships: language, **interactional dynamics**, **relational dynamics** (of power and solidarity) and **interpersonal ideology** (Poutiainen, 2015). However, before we outline this conceptual framework, we need to dedicate some attention to motivating the work we do in this book by positioning it amongst the wider, interdisciplinary research into relationships in high-performance sports teams.

Motivating this work: Analysing the *performance* of relationships in a high-performance sports team

The topic of relationships is clearly one that is important for professional sport. A keyword search of the word *relationships* on a popular sports news website revealed a number of news articles and headlines that reflect a concern with relationships. Even without delving into each of the articles, the headlines point to the perceived importance of relationships to the success and failure of sports teams and their individual members (i.e. coaches and managers). *Strong* relationships are desirable and can be *key* to teams achieving positive sporting goals and bad relationships can *cost* sports professionals (particularly coaches) their jobs. In fact, the issue of relating or relationships can be seen as central to the sporting endeavour, with some headlines above highlighting this centrality.

Researchers have also solidified this causal link between good relationships and a range of positive sporting outcomes, from better results to personal satisfaction of the individual members of the team (Davis & Jowett, 2010; Duda, 2013; Jowett & Ntoumanis, 2004; Lyle, 2002; Poczwardowski et al., 2006). In search of a formula to establish positive relationships, researchers have, by and large, engaged in an agenda of locating and testing out practices that can help practitioners establish the positive relationships they covet. In such work, the relational concept of cohesion has been a frequent target for analysis and understanding as researchers test out the impact of greater cohesion on team success and seek to evaluate particular methods of cohering (Brawley et al., 1987; Carron et al., 2002; García-Calvo et al., 2014; Heuzé et al., 2006; Kozub & McDonnell, 2000; Pescosolido & Saavedra, 2012; Prapavessis & Carron, 1997; Turman, 2003, 2008).

While work is well underway in testing practices that help to establish positive relations, researchers have rarely asked what people are actually doing when they engage in the process of relating or building and managing relationships in high-performance sports teams (File, 2019; Groom et al., 2012; Schnurr et al., 2020; Wilson, 2011; Wolfers et al., 2017). Most of the research into relationships in high-performance sports teams has been conducted through the lens of psychology which has concentrated on understanding *cognitions* – or interpretations and assessments of individual's behaviour in relationship dyads. The methods employed to understand relationships from this perspective have been surveys and interviews which typically ask participants to reflect on relationships and what they value more generally rather than looking at the processes through which people actually relate in situ. This has left us somewhat blind to the actual practices that establish working relationships and social structures in sports teams and the complex realities that sports practitioners negotiate on a daily basis.

Additionally, one of the more pertinent issues the research community needs to confront is the extent to which they are actually studying *the relationship* or offering more of an individual's perception on the relationship. Because psychology-informed studies, which have dominated the research landscape in this topic area, typically ask individuals within a relationship dyad (like the coach in the coach–player dyad) to reflect on the behaviour and practices they prefer or value, we have a range of interesting, but ultimately one-sided, accounts of relationships. In other words, we have little knowledge of how the relationship itself, as a jointly constructed phenomenon, is being established or co-constructed in and through the behaviour of two or more people. Relationships are, by their very definition, social accomplishments which are *performed* – enacted, negotiated, managed and established – in and through social interaction with others. To draw on psychological notions, relationships might best be understood as inter-psychological accomplishments that people carry out, enact and accomplish *together*. Relationships are certainly constructed by individuals making decisions about how to behave and how to act. However, what actually happens when these individuals come together and put their knowledge into action to shape, act on and negotiate their relationships has not been a key area of research, despite arguably being more representative of the notion of a relationship. This is something the current book attempts to address.

The view from the field: Time for a focus on relationships in action?

As well as expanding the theoretical and methodological toolkit for exploring relationships in high-performance sport, there is also direct evidence from the field that closer attention to the way relationships are actually playing out or working in high-performance sport might be timely. A growing number of reports from the domain of professional sport have called into question some of the go-to practices of relating in high-performance sports teams and organizations. For example, at British Cycling, accusations of bullying by coaches led to a full-scale review of coaching practices in this sporting body (Ingle, 2017b; Roan, 2016). Reports of bullying, racism, sexism and discrimination against able-bodied and Paralympic athletes have also been raised and investigated in British Rowing, British Bobsleigh, British Gymnastics, British Canoeing and British Swimming (BBC Sport, 2017a, 2017b; N. Hope, 2017; Ingle, 2017a, 2017c, 2017d; Roan, 2017). Similar issues were also raised in professional and national football teams in the UK. High-profile cases in this instance were the England women's football team, the

Newcastle Football Club under-23 squad (C. Hope, 2019b) and the Cardiff Football Club under-18 squad (C. Hope, 2019a, 2021) where coaches were stood down while investigations took place. Outside of the UK, the national women's football teams in New Zealand (Australian Associated Press, 2018) and Australia (T. Holmes, 2019) also went through similar investigations which resulted in coaches being fired or resigning.

In many of these cases, the actual practices of coaches and athletes used in their contexts were reported on and laid bare and were often cited as reasons for breakdowns in relationships or evidence of the establishment of 'toxic' cultures. Coaches 'communicating in an abusive manner' or making 'inflammatory comments' were cited as contributing to relationship breakdown and establishing cultures of fear. These included the use of derogatory terms of address, the use of adjectives like 'fat' and 'lazy' to describe athletes, the use of language that athletes deemed sexist, racist or that undermined other identity categories of the athletes, including the mobilization of stereotypes in interaction like 'black people do not make good bobsleigh drivers'. There were also reports of strong unmitigated criticism being directed at athletes, accusations by coaches of their players throwing races and threats and 'aggressive warnings' being issued. There was even an alleged instance where a fake Caribbean accent was put on by a white coach and directed at an athlete of African heritage, presumably as a humour attempt. Other complaints drew attention to the communication processes and unclear communication channels and included accusations of withholding of information (and data), not explaining decisions and a general lack of transparency.

Ironically, the intention behind many of the above actions, at least on the part of the speaker, may have been to attempt to shape positive relations. Humour, for example, is a well-established strategy for attempting to build rapport between people, and direct and aggressive language is also anecdotally linked to the encoding of motivational properties in messages in sports teams. However, these intentions were perhaps misread, not fully picked up or considered completely inappropriate by one of the participants, leading to breakdown in relationships and the initiation of disciplinary actions and procedures.

These reports from the field (so to speak) lend support to the agenda we pursue in this book. Any research that can put the everyday practices and processes of interpersonal communication by sports professionals under the microscope has the potential to contribute to practitioner discussions regarding this important aspect of professional life. While we do not concern ourselves directly with the cases outlined above in the current book or with the issue of bullying, we do make it a central mission to shine a light on taken-for-granted interactional practices in our professional rugby team and the way these shape their relationships with one another. By illustrating and pointing to the practices that establish relationships, we can better inform discussions by the practitioner community about the interconnections between language use and relationships.

Our context: How relationships work in a professional New Zealand rugby team

In this book, we ground our analysis of how relationships are working in a case study of a professional New Zealand rugby team, which we have named *The Rhinos* to help protect their identity. The Rhinos play in New Zealand's regional professional competition.

In studies where there is a greater concern for understanding the fine-grained processes of relating, case studies offer researchers a chance to engage in in-depth analysis, drawing on aspects of the case study context that may be important for understanding the complexity underlying how relationships are working or being made to work.

Over the course of this book, readers will become more familiar with our team and their context, particularly the ways in which members of this team are constructing their relationships with one another. However, to begin orienting readers to this case study context, Table 1.1 provides an overview of the team membership and the various formal or institutional roles they were assigned.

As Table 1.1 illustrates, the Rhinos had a coaching team of four coaches – one head coach and three assistant coaches. There were also specific technical coaching staff, (the scrum coach) and a number of other support staff that

Table 1.1 Overview of the team by name, nickname, role and group

Group	Title or role	Name (pseudonym)	Name (in nickname form, if used)
Coaching staff	Head coach	Tane	Tane
	Assistant coach (forwards)	Greg	Greg
	Assistant coach (backs)	Terry	Terry
	Assistant coach (temporary)	Kaipo	Po
	Technical coach: Scrum	Joseph	Red

Players	Captain	Sebastian	Seb
	Players (forwards)	Jason	Jase
		Harvey	Hook
		Tamati	Tee
		Chase	Cherry
		Jayden	Jay
		Michael	Mickey
		Thomas	Topper
		Phoenix	Phony
		Nixon	Nixon
		Matthew	Rocky
		Steve	Stevie
		Gary	Gaz
		Jesse	Jez
		Arthur	Arty
		Ashton	Ash
		Terrance	Beef
		Abel	Abel
		Henare	Henny
		Grayson	Grayson
		Aaron	Azza
	Players (backs)	Flynn	Fly
		Timothy	Timmy
		Kingston	Kingy
		Mark	Maz
		Salu	Salu
		Liam	Leaf
		Nikau	Nikau
		Sione	Sione
		Lima	Lima
		Lagi	Lagi
		Rangi	Rangi
		Manu	Manu
		Fetu	Feefi
		Brian	BJ
Support staff	Head fitness trainer	Daniel	Danny
	Assistant fitness trainer	Lloyd	Lloyd
	Team doctor	Tony	T-bone
	Team physio	Daryl	Dazza
	Team analyst and videographer	Eric	Eric
	Kit man	Phillip	Phil
	Team logistics manager	Martin	Marty

took care of the team's fitness regime, their strength and conditioning and warmups, managing the kit and equipment, performing important technical analysis of game footage, managing the logistics of the team and looking after the health and safety of the players. These official titles or roles were documented on the team's official website giving them formal status. All names in this book are pseudonyms.

The researcher spent a month with the Rhinos during their pre-season campaign. Serendipitously, this allowed for the study and analysis of the early stages of relationship building. This aspect of the case-study context is arguably useful considering our broader research goals. While a great deal of the analytical work we carry out in this book will concern the question of how this team are constructing their relationships, the fact that the team have not had that much time together, to establish a unique or specific style, arguably provides a window on the general cultural knowledge concerning how relationships should work in high-performance sports teams. Having not spent a great deal of time together, the practices on show in our data may reflect the player's and coach's orientation to more general cultural knowledge about relating in a high-performance sporting context that members have picked up in and across the other teams and contexts that they have played in.

What is a relationship? Using the notion of professional role to ground our analyses

A key issue we need to resolve before going further is what exactly counts as a relationship in this context? How do we organize the above membership of the team into relationships or dyads that are valid to this cultural community? While relationships can be defined and approached for study in various ways, in our particular context, the **roles** people adopted in the team provided us with a useful, ready-made and relevant way to frame our analysis of how relationships are working in this team. Institutional contexts are at least in part defined by people adopting particular roles within the institution (Drew & Heritage, 1992), which makes the notion of role an important and defining feature of professional or working environments. When we step into our professional working contexts, we are usually doing so with some awareness of our role, function or position within the institution vis-à-vis others and any similarities or differences in the rights, responsibilities and obligations we have vis-à-vis other people in different roles. And, whenever we configure into **role-relationships** to work through the tasks of our professional activity, we make this understanding evident by acting and reacting in accordance with our cultural knowledge of how to behave in our role vis-à-vis those in other roles.

As Table 1.1 highlights, there are a number of roles that contribute to the smooth running of a professional sports team and any of these roles and the role-relationships they regularly configure into would be interesting to unpack. However, in this book, we focus on three recognizable roles within the institution of sport: **coach**, inclusive of the sub roles of head coach, assistant coaches, technical coaches, the **captain** and the **players**, not only as a whole group but also as individuals, some of whom have distinctive claims to experience, important team positions and other important claims to social status. This decision to narrow our focus to three roles was based primarily on the sheer amount of data we were able to collect that showed people in these three roles in (inter)action. Reference is made in the book to other roles in the team (i.e. physios, trainers, water carriers, the team's logistics manager, the kit, the team's technical advisors). However, we did not have enough data of their speaking roles to be able to provide a rich account of how their role-relationships with others were being constructed in our team.

It is important to note here that we did not orchestrate or artificially create situations in which the people in these roles configured into role-relationships. Instead, we located natural settings where coaches, the captain and players would get together in their various **relationship dyads** and perform their everyday professional business. The main dyads we saw being enacted regularly across the settings of our team were the **coach–player** dyad, the **coach–captain** dyad and the **captain–player** and **player–player** dyads. The analysis we present in this book will provide readers with insights into how these different role-relationships worked in our professional New Zealand rugby team.

In this book, then, we approach the question of relationships (and what a relationship is) very much from the perspective of professional roles, using these more static categories to help us ground our finer-grained analysis of how relationships are being enacted. However, there is additional information that we collected about the people adopting these roles that we also draw on to refine our analysis further. This is particularly the case for the rather monolithic category of **player**. We introduce this information and the process through which we implemented these insights into our analysis in the next chapter.

Framing our study conceptually: Studying relationships in action

Having motivated the work we do in this book and having outlined the context in which we do it, we now need to ground this work theoretically. The conceptual basis for the research we report on in this book lies in the groundbreaking work of social scientists like Goffman (1970, 1976, 1979, 2006), Gumperz (1982, 1999, 2015), Hymes (1967, 1972, 1974), Sacks, Schegloff and Jefferson (Sacks et al., 1974) and others who claimed that society could be better understood if we studied the behaviour of people engaged in their authentic, everyday activities. For social scientists of this ilk, the study of individuals in mundane, typical, everyday activities would provide the basis for a deeper understanding of society by providing evidence of the ways in which societal constraints and social structures were influencing or being reflected and reconstructed in behaviour. Such an idea spawned an increasingly influential stream of research activity concerned with locating or reverse-engineering society (as people understand it and perform it) in the everyday behaviour, including an emphasis on the social practices individuals deploy in their authentic contexts to constitute society.

At the heart of social scientific work of this kind is the analysis of authentic, naturally occurring episodes of social interaction. It is in social interactions where people negotiate their worlds, positioning themselves vis-à-vis others as they jointly manage the tasks and activities that constitute their personal and professional lives. Through language and other semiotic resources (i.e. body language) deployed in social interaction, people can actively shape their encounters with others in ways they perceive to be socially appropriate, normative, relevant and/or suitable to the context in which they find themselves. Social interactions, then, provide a naturally occurring source of data to study in order to locate everyday social practices and develop an understanding of the shared knowledge systems that are being talked into being in and through these practices.

Disciplines such as sociolinguistics and sociology that have an interest in the relationship between language and society, and that have tools capable of locating how social actors behave in social interactions – primarily through a close analysis of their language – have become particularly valuable source of insight, helping to build knowledge about how people operate in and constitute the different domains of society as we know them.

In this book, we use this conceptual model to guide our study of how role-relationships work in our professional New Zealand rugby team. In studying the performance of role-relationships in the course of everyday social interactions we aim to locate patterns in the way people are behaving vis-à-vis one another – their **interactional dynamics** – and use these patterns to build an understanding of the **relational dynamics** or structures they are constructing in the process. These interactional and relational dynamics evident in our data can in turn be used as an evidence base for locating and putting forward claims regarding the ideas and beliefs about relationships in this cultural context – **interpersonal ideologies** – that are in play and are being reconstructed by members of our professional New Zealand rugby team.

To engage in this more performative analysis of relationships in our New Zealand rugby team, we need social interaction data that is capable of showing us how people are behaving in and through language. By social interactions (or texts as they are known in discourse analysis circles) we mean the whole, complete interactional events in which members of the team come together to work through the professional business of their team. Examples, in a sporting team context, of particular social interactions might include pre-match huddles, half-time team talks, talk during training drills, match evaluation meetings (where the team review footage and discuss issues) and other social interactions where members of the team carry out their professional business. For the analyses we present in this book, we have collected and analysed a range of everyday professional interactions from our professional New Zealand rugby team. We outline specific details about how this data was collected and analysed, including more specifics about the data set of social interactions we collected and analysed, in the next chapter. In the next section, we go deeper into our conceptual toolkit to introduce discourse analysis – the specific theoretical toolkit we used to analyse and process authentic language use in social interactions for insights about relationships.

Applying a linguistic lens to relationships: Using the theoretical tools of discourse analysis

In this book we draw on the tools of discourse analysis, specifically the fine-grained approaches to analysing language in use linked to sociolinguistics. We use these linguistically informed approaches to discourse analysis to help us analyse language use and social interaction in our professional New Zealand rugby team and use it to illustrate and build theory about how relationships are working in this professional domain.

For discourse analysts, language is more than an abstract set of sounds, signs or symbols that we organize in grammatically correct ways to make understandable sentences. It is a functional toolkit, something we deploy to transmit information and manage relationships in our everyday personal and professional contexts. When analysing language, discourse analysts emphasize an account of the functions that language is performing over the forms (although the forms are important, as we will see).

Importantly for the work we do in this book, discourse analysts have been particularly active in trying to understand the role language plays in accomplishing relational goals (or relational work), attempting effects to relationships or shaping relationships in particular ways (J. Holmes & Marra,

2004; J. Holmes & Schnurr, 2006; Locher, 2013; Mirivel & Fuller, 2017; Spencer-Oatey, 2011). Additionally, the location of underlying social structures as they are reflected and (re)constructed in language dynamics and practices of people in everyday life has been very much at the heart of the discourse analytical research agenda (Blommaert, 2007; G. Brown & Yule, 1983; Coulthard, 1992; Fairclough, 1992, 2003a; Gee, 2018; Hyland & Paltridge, 2013; Johnstone, 2008). What discourse analysts bring to this wider theoretical agenda is an ability to pin down or locate language practices that matter and systematically use language practices to generate social theory.

Underlying this functional view of language are a number of important assumptions and interlinked ideas about what language does and what language is capable of revealing. These ideas have become taken-for-granted principles of the work discourse analysts do and are often left largely unspoken in research reports. However, considering the broader audience we are targeting for this book, it is perhaps worth paying some attention to these here, especially considering they will be central to the analyses of language that we present in this book. Below, we have outlined three important ideas about language that are crucial to understanding the work discourse analysts do and that will further acclimatize readers to the way language will be mobilized as a source of data in this book.

Idea 1: Language makes meaning and performs actions or functions

The first, perhaps all-encompassing, idea about language we need to adopt is that language does things – it is used by people to perform actions and functions. We touched on this above when we said that language is more than a set of abstract forms and is, instead, a toolkit humans draw on to perform social actions or functions in social interactions with others. In more technical terms, language (discursive practice) is in a dialectical relationship with social practice (Fairclough, 1992), allowing humans to have a material effect on their environments in and through the use of words. Popular wisdom often places language in an inferior position to action (i.e., actions speak louder than words). However, for discourse analysts, words are actions and people use words to perform an array of important actions or functions in the management of their interactions with others.

When analysing language, discourse analysts are drawn to the meanings a speaker is making in a collection of words. For example, analysts might ask what speech actions (Searle, 1969, 1985) a speaker is performing (i.e. thanking, directing, eliciting, promising, criticizing, congratulating) in and through their language. However, as discourse analysts have illustrated, function is a multifarious concept and there may be many functions a speaker is attempting in and through the shaping of their message that go beyond a neat and tidy semantic or performative function being accomplished in their utterance of talk. For example, a speaker may be trying to belittle someone, claim expert status, disagree respectfully (or not), indicate displeasure with someone, attempt to convince others their course of action is right, build togetherness and so on. Language helps people perform these and other functions (that can be conceptualized on many different levels) in the course of their everyday social interactions and discourse analysts aim to locate and bring into focus these sometime opaque functions.

Two particularly relevant concepts we draw on in our analysis of the functional properties of language are **transactional** and **relational** meaning (J. Holmes, 2013). For discourse analysts, language is not just a tool we use for transmitting information from one person to another (the more **transactional** functions of language). It is *a*, if not *the* most, central tool that humans themselves draw on to actively perform, enact or manage their relationships with others (the **relational** or **interpersonal** functions of language). This distinction acknowledges the fact that when engaged in most types of interaction with others, people are broadly concerned with two key functions: transmitting information to one another as they pursue their shared tasks and appropriately managing or shaping their relationships with those they are interacting with.

This simple, but important, distinction between two higher-level functions humans are trying to achieve in and through language is particularly relevant for the work we do in this book. The category of relational meaning is also a flexible and malleable category, allowing us to look for relational functions (in particular) that speakers might be trying to accomplish on a number of levels as they shape their contributions to ongoing social interactions. In the next chapter we outline some of the well-established discourse analysis tools that we drew on to locate relational meanings or functions being performed in and through language.

Idea 2: The rights to perform particular actions through language are socially distributed

In tracking and locating the transactional and relational functions speakers perform in and through language, we can begin to map out how certain people are behaving vis-à-vis others. Put more technically, we can locate the social distribution of particular actions and start to build a profile of the rights, responsibilities and obligations that particular people in their specific roles (in our case, members of our professional New Zealand rugby team) are claiming and performing over others, in and through language, in and across the various situations in which they interact.

What this idea implies is that language choices and the actions people perform in and through language are not necessarily innocent, random, free or consequence free. Rather, they are socially distributed, often unequally, with the social rights, responsibilities and obligations to perform particular actions patterning in often socially and culturally predictable ways. This predictability is in large part what makes the fluid communication we experience on a daily basis possible, as socialized members of particular communities and organizations come together often with a shared understanding (at least on a broader level) about how to go about their activities together.

We use this theoretical idea about language to guide our analysis of language patterns by mapping actions performed in and through language onto the roles speakers have or adopt in the team, to reverse-engineer an understanding of how role-relationships are working. With respect to sports teams, for example, do some individuals in particular roles in the team claim exclusive rights to give instructions, lead team talks or provide feedback to others, and, if so, what do these more social-level patterns (enacted through language) suggest about the nature of the relationship these individuals are constructing with one another?

Sociolinguists and discourse analysts have repeatedly shown how language varies according to who the speaker is, who the addressee is and their relative status to one another (Bell, 1984; Bell & Gibson, 2011; Bell & Johnson, 1997; Buchstaller, 2006; Coupland, 1980; Giles, 2016; Hultgren, 2011). By paying close attention to who does what with their language to whom and how, discourse analysts can generate sociolinguistic facts about how language rights are being socially distributed. They can then use these facts as the basis for a deeper, more interpretive analysis of the social relationships and underlying norms and ideologies that are being communicated (often indirectly) through these claims to linguistic rights (a point we expand on below).

Idea 3: Language makes, reveals and is constructing meaning at micro and macro levels

Connected to the above point, discourse analysts see language as performing functions and making meanings at both micro and more macro levels (Alvesson & Karreman, 2000; Fairclough, 1985, 1992, 2003b; Gee, 2018). By micro and macro here, we refer to a distinction between the meanings people make in the specific or immediate context or interaction (the micro) and the more abstract meanings they simultaneously make at a broader level with respect to the institutional context or culture to which the participants are also connected (the macro).

Any stretch of authentic language can be studied at both of these levels. Analysts can study how language is being used in the more local interactions people are involved in to, for example, solve problems, give or receive feedback, or deliver a rousing motivational team talk. At this level, discourse analysts can help to better understand the way people are using language to perform and shape their local, goal-driven encounters. Simultaneously, the patterns unearthed in these local-level interactions can also be analysed at a higher, more macro level as analysts try to develop insights about how these (and other) activities are done normatively in the institutional culture. Put in a more academic way, our local-level surface structures and interactional practices in everyday personal and professional interactions reflect deeper social structures (Frey, 1996, p. 19; Richards, 2006, p. 51). For discourse analysts, a key, but complex, question that drives analysis of language is what are the patterns telling us at a micro, local or surface levels about how the participants are managing the interaction at hand and what are these patterns communicating at a more macro, societal or cultural level about the beliefs and ideologies members of this culture share and that are being talked into being.

Readers of this book, then, need to prepare themselves for analysis of language at multiple levels: (1) detailed analysis of the micro level or local management of interactions by social actors (i.e. coaches, players, the captain) as they shape their task-based, interpersonal encounters with one another, and (2) analysis of the macro-level realization of deeper cultural or ideological meaning about the relative rights, responsibilities and social relations these individuals in their roles are constructing with one another. Pinning these micro-level and macro-level meanings down and considering the interconnections between the two is a strength of discourse analysis and offers us a chance to comprehensively address the question of how relationships are working in our team.

The above three ideas outline how we will mobilize or use language in this book to study how relationships are working in our professional New Zealand rugby team. However, there is one more piece of the puzzle we need to integrate into our conceptual model that will help us with more of the interpretive work we engage in as we turn language patterns into insights about relationships. At this level, we need concepts – more social and non-linguistic ones – that are going to help us process the patterns in our team's interactions more directly at a relationship level. The concepts we have drawn on to help us in this book are power and solidarity, and we outline these briefly below.

Dynamics of power and solidarity: How can we interpret patterns of language use for insights about relationships?

To make sense of the patterns we see in our team's social interactions at a relationship level, we need conceptual tools that can help us interpret the language behaviour. Two such concepts that are core to the discussions we have in this book are **power** and **solidarity**. Power and solidarity are pervasive features of human relationships in any context (Schulze, 2014), with all relationships arguably involving negotiations of power and solidarity. Whenever people enter interactions with others, they will be drawing on, confirming and/or adjusting their understandings of the relative degree of **power** they share with or have over others and the degree of **solidarity** they have (or do not have) with those others.

Defining power and solidarity is not a particularly easy task but one that is necessary if we are to mobilize these concepts as interpretive tools in this book. While there are many facets to it, **power** can be broadly defined as the capacity or ability to direct or influence the behaviour of others or the course of (future) events ('Power,' 2015). Applied to our context, such a definition conjures up notions of particular rights, responsibilities, obligations that some individuals (i.e. coaches, the captain and players) may claim over others because of the greater degree of institutional power they have or perceive themselves to have. Power can be located in taken-for-granted ways in which people, for example, claim and exercise influence or **control** over any shared agenda or activity a group of people are involved in. It may also be accomplished in and through practices that establish a speaker as having greater **expertise** or knowledge vis-à-vis others. Both of these aspects of power were relevant in the analytical work we carried out in this book.

While power and solidarity are not linguistic concepts per se, linguists, sociolinguists and discourse analysts have frequently made locating the practices of control and (expert) power, as they manifest in ritual language practices, a focus of their work (R. Brown & Gilman, 1960; Fairclough, 2001; J. Holmes & Stubbe, 2003; Thornborrow, 2014; Vine, 2004). What can make these analyses particularly valuable is that they often illustrate how these different types of power are enacted ritually in the very taken-for-granted interactional practices of members of the cultural group being studied. Power can hide in plain sight, often manifesting itself in mundane linguistic practices that frequently escape critical attention, perhaps because of their mundaneness. In this book, a major component of the analytical work we carry out aims to locate meanings of control and expert power difference in the mundane practices of our team's social interaction.

Solidarity is perhaps an even more complex concept to pin down and one that has multiple dimensions and aspects. Solidarity, or situations in which there is high solidarity, are likely to conjure up notions of a **belonging** or **togetherness** between individuals, unity or alignment on issues, actions and feelings ('Solidarity,' 2015), the establishment of equal degrees of social status amongst individuals, or lower degrees of **social distance** (or higher degrees of closeness and familiarity) between individuals. In a professional sports team context, solidarity is often seen as a value that is desirable (Halldorsson et al., 2017), perhaps because it has at its foundation the coordination of individuals and a unity or purpose, togetherness and belonging.

As with power, the practices of solidarity – where solidarity is oriented to or where social distance is created by participants – hide in plain sight but can be located from a close analysis of the interactional practices in authentic social interaction (R. Brown & Gilman, 1960; Chimbwete-Phiri & Schnurr, 2017; Daly et al., 2004; Lipovsky, 2008; Ostermann, 2003). Through a range of linguistic practices, people can, for example, make, accept or deny efforts to establish solidarity with others in their social interactions. Discourse analysts have been particularly active in illustrating how the everyday and taken-for-granted linguistic and interactional practices in social interaction can encode and reveal the understandings people have and are actively constructing about the relative degree of solidarity they have or are attempting to have with their interlocutors.

In the next chapter, when we present our analytical toolkit, we will outline further details about how we operationalized these concepts of power and solidarity as interpretive resources in our overall endeavour to illustrate how relationships are working in our professional New Zealand rugby team. However, conceptually, with power and solidarity discussed above, we now have the key interrelated dimensions of our study laid out. In the final section of this chapter, we pull everything together and outline the discussions to come in the findings chapters of this book.

Pulling together our linguistic lens on relationships

At this stage, before we close the chapter, it may be worthwhile consolidating the various concepts, elements and dimensions of the linguistic lens we are applying to relationships in this book. Figure 1.1 attempts to present the key layers or dimensions of analytical work we are carrying out in this book but also presents them in an interconnected relationship with one another.

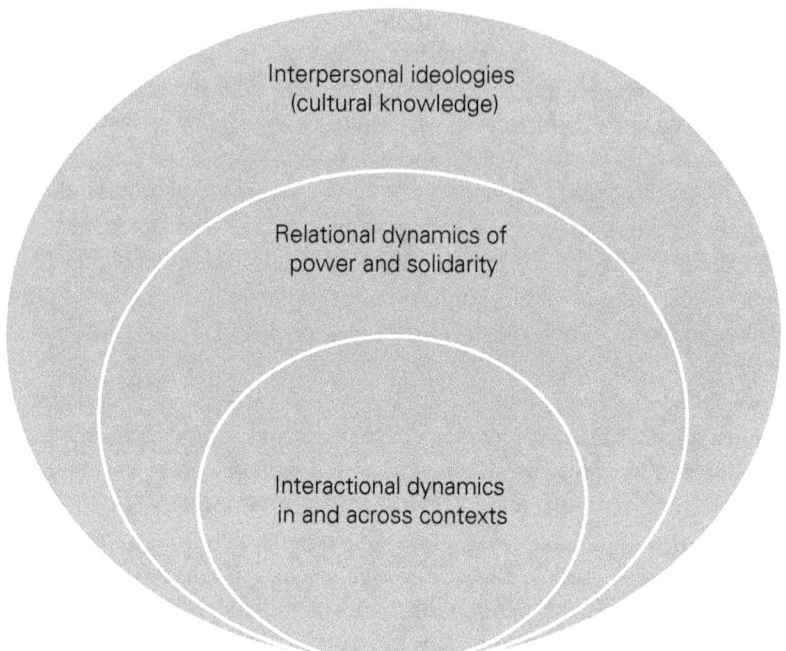

FIGURE 1.1 *A conceptual lens for unpacking how relationships work.*

This model depicts how we will use a close analysis of the **interactional dynamics** (the linguistic practices and meanings evident in social interactions in our team) in order to develop data-driven accounts of the **relational dynamics** (of power and solidarity) that are being constructed between individuals in particular roles in and through language in our team. We can then use these accounts to engage in the deeper, more theoretical work of identifying cultural principles and **interpersonal ideologies** that underlie and explain the dynamics we see in our data.

The interconnection of these three dimensions is important to model if we are to provide a complex account of how relationships were working in our team. However, in order to reach these complex understandings, we need to do a significant amount of analytical work within each layer of dimension. This is particularly the case for the description of the interactional dynamics which provide the raw data and therefore the basis for our complex accounts of relationships. To help the readers understand what this involves, we have provided the following questions as indications of what drove our inquiries at these three different levels.

In addressing Question 1, we will build an understanding of the everyday language use patterns in our team's interactions. We have used the term

Interactional dynamics	1. What interactional practices and dynamics can be located in the social interactions of our professional New Zealand rugby team, that show how those in specific institutional roles are communicating and using language with one another, in their everyday professional activities?
Relational dynamics	2. What role-relationship dynamics (or meanings) of power and solidarity are being constructed (performed, attempted, accomplished) and reflected in and through these interactional practices?
Interpersonal ideologies	3. What insights can we put forward for further testing and reflection about how relationships work in high-performance sports teams, specifically with respect to a more macro-level interpersonal ideology (i.e. underlying assumptions, ideologies, beliefs and shared social knowledge) that underlies, frames, explains and is being signalled in the patterns we see in the interactional practices of our team?

interactional dynamics to focus our observations of language in use. This means focusing on language as a discourse analyst would, highlighting the functions people appear to be performing in their interactions with others. By doing this, we have made sure to foreground not only individual's use of language but also the way two or more people use language to jointly achieve the goals of a particular interaction (like a half-time team talk). Everything we concern ourselves with in this book emanates from these very important descriptive or empirical accounts of the patterns of meaning making in interaction, and readers will encounter the results of this unpacking work in the findings chapters to come.

Question 2 helps to direct a process by which we interpret or make sense of the linguistic practices we have identified at more of a relational level, using them to generate accounts of the **relational dynamics** that are being constructed by people in and through their linguistic practices. The notions of **power** and **solidarity** are recruited here to help guide and narrow this process and build conclusions about the power and solidarity dynamics being constructed in and through interaction in our team.

Question 3 asks the bigger and more abstract question of what underlies the relational dynamics we have located in our team, or, perhaps more to the point, what underlying values and ideologies appear to explain them. By asking this question, we engage in the task of trying to locate deeper cultural knowledge systems of professional sport that are being talked into being in the interactional and relational dynamics of members of our rugby team. In this book, we borrow the term **interpersonal ideology** (Poutiainen, 2015) to help locate this deeper 'subset of cultural premises' that help to explain the relational dynamics and linguistic practices of the members of our team. These subsets of ideological premises can be brought together to inform broader claims about the **relational culture** or **relational context** of high-performance sport, a goal we pursue in the final chapter.

Outline of the book

With the agenda and conceptual framework of this book mapped out, we can now outline the specific chapters in more detail. In the next chapter, we outline the analytical toolkit we used to locate patterns of interaction and language use by the members of our professional New Zealand rugby team. Then, in Chapters 3 to 9, we present a series of accounts of how different role-relationships are working in this team, by illustrating and discussing the relational dynamics of power and solidarity we observed in the team's interactions.

In Chapters 3 to 6, we concentrate on dynamics of power, illustrating how power worked in a range of everyday coach–player, captain–coach, captain–player and player–player interactions in our team. In Chapter 3, we illustrate how coaches claim and exercise control over players through some of the most mundane, taken-for-granted but also widespread interactional practices we saw in our sports team's interactions. In Chapter 4, we focus specifically on questioning patterns and how the way questioning appears to work in coach–player interactions. The patterns we illustrate in this chapter highlight how questions are a key resource for coaches allowing them to perform a number of power-laden dimensions of their coaching identity. However, they are perhaps also a favoured resource of coaches because of the degree of control they allow coaches to maintain over the interaction and, by extension, the players. In Chapters 3 and 4, the findings are clear evidence of the often-cited asymmetrical power relationship between coaches and players (Groom et al., 2012; Rylander, 2015) being constructed in our team. However, by illustrating power in action, we pin down the subtle, taken-for-granted linguistic practices that establish that power difference.

In Chapter 5 we focus on how power works in settings where coach–captain and captain–player role-relationships are in play. These analyses allow us to explore the way power is shared (if at all) by coaches and the captain – two roles in the team with claims to institutional authority. In Chapter 6, the last chapter dedicated to power dynamics, we shift our focus to player–player relations, presenting an analysis of how power worked within playing groups when they were on the field of play and free of the influence of the coaches. The findings in this chapter will show how power structures can flatten significantly in player–player interactions, but that there are still subtle markers in the linguistic practices of more informal hierarchies in play.

In Chapter 7 we shift our focus from power to solidarity, analysing player–player solidarity work in the interactional practices in pre-match team addresses delivered by the captain. Through this chapter we highlight how captains attempt to foster belonging in these important bonding interactions, highlighting a range of linguistic and interactional practices that both represent the group as united and encourage the assembled players to contribute to and acknowledge those united representations. In Chapter 8, we look at coach–player solidarity, trying to locate evidence in the interactional practices between coaches and players that can give us clues about how solidarity works in this role-relationship. As readers will have already seen in previous chapters, coach–player relations are characterized by asymmetrical power difference. However, in our data we found subtle linguistic practices in the speech of coaches that could be read as attempts to foster bonds and solidarity between coaches and players. Nevertheless, we also show that reaching the stage of being true equals was not something the coaches oriented to or appreciated suggesting that coach–player solidarity is a particularly complex matter.

Finally, in Chapter 9, we stay with coach–player solidarity and explore the extent to which coach–player solidarity was (or was not) managed in episodes of critical feedback delivered by coaches to the players. Criticism, theoretically at least, provides a challenge for solidarity between the criticizer and the target of criticism. In this chapter we look at how coaches shaped episodes of critical feedback and what these patterns further illustrate about the nature of solidarity between coaches and players in our professional rugby team.

In Chapter 10, the final chapter of the book, we bring our findings together and use them to engage in our deeper search for underlying cultural knowledge systems and ideologies that are being talked into being in the team's interactional and relational dynamics. We will present six what could be considered underlying cultural principles that are being oriented to across the team's different settings and relational dyads. At this level, we are primarily concerned with the task of putting forward claims about the culture that our team appear to be constructing in and through their social interactions. These broader claims about the interpersonal ideology in high-performance sports teams are provided not in an attempt to offer a generalizable picture of cultural knowledge underpinning relationships in this cultural context. Instead, they are an attempt to provide hypotheses for testing by future research and for reflecting on by practitioners as the research community seeks greater clarity in this endeavour.

Our audience: An interdisciplinary research community and practitioners of high-performance sport

One final note to make in this introduction concerns the target audience for this book. As with many discourse analytical and sociolinguistic projects, insights are developed to contribute to theoretical discussions about how language use shapes and is shaped by society, but also to provide a means for generating important critical reflection processes for the communities that linguists study.

In this book, we take on this tricky challenge of writing for a specialist and non-specialist audience simultaneously. Readers from a linguistics background will hopefully find the insights presented in this book to be an opportunity to look at how language is working in a hard to access speech community. We also hope to attract an interdisciplinary audience of researchers interested in the broader topic of relationships in a professional sports team. However, this book is also intended to be a resource for practitioners in sport and the book has been written with this broader audience of practitioners and non-linguists in mind.

One of the key functions we hope this book performs for practitioners is the chance to reflect on their own practices or the practices of those they train and educate. By providing illustrations of language use in specific but recognizable contexts (i.e., during team meetings, match reflection sessions, half-time team talks) of a high-performance sports team, practitioners have concrete examples, albeit from another team context, to guide their own critical reflection processes. The ability to reflect critically on language use and the role it plays in shaping social life is becoming increasingly important. As we noted in the foreword, we do not critically reflect on the practices we observe ourselves, as we are not professional coaches, athletes or sports advisors. However, we hope by pinning down practices and applying a set of concepts and terminology to a specific case study context, practitioners will be able to have similar discussions and engage in critical reflection of the way their practices are shaping relationships in their own context.

Finally, regardless of who the audience is, many may find the technical details of rugby somewhat hard to fathom. In the extracts we present in this book, rugby professionals will often use technical details that are specific to the rugby community. Readers can take solace in the fact that our main interest in this book is not so much what people are saying but how they are saying it, interacting and performing their turns at talk. However, we have provided a brief set of definitions of key terms in rugby in Appendix 1 to help readers wishing to familiarize themselves with some of the technical details of the sport that pop up in the transcripts and in our analytical commentary.

Chapter conclusion and looking forward

In this chapter we have argued for more research into how relationships are actually working in the real-life settings where they are in play, and we have laid out the theoretical toolkit we have used to house this research agenda. A major part of this introduction involved introducing and mobilizing language and social interaction as valuable sources of naturally occurring data for studying relationships as they are working in their natural settings. We also introduced the familiar and pervasive relationship concepts of power and solidarity, which we draw on in this book to process or make sense of the interactional dynamics we see in our team.

In the next chapter, we turn our focus to more methodological and analytical matters, outlining the process of conducting a discourse analytical study and the tools we drew on to help locate and unpack linguistic behaviour in social interactions for insights about how relationships were working.

2

Introducing our toolkit

Discourse analytical tools for locating relational dynamics in social interaction

Introduction

In this chapter, we focus on methodological matters for our analysis of how role-relationships work in our professional New Zealand rugby team. This will involve outlining in greater detail the data set and the analytical tools and processes we used to locate relational dynamics of power and solidarity in patterns of social interaction in our professional New Zealand rugby team.

As discourse analysts, our analytical work is grounded in the micro-level analysis of language use and the social actions language is performing in its context of use. Therefore, the bulk of our attention in this chapter is dedicated to introducing the tools we used to describe, code or process the interactions (or raw interactional data) in ways that help us to locate what people in their professional roles are doing with their language (i.e. how they behaved vis-à-vis one another) in and across the team's interactional contexts. However, we also dedicate some space to outlining how we move from (or between) our analysis of the micro-level linguistic features of our team's interactions and the more macro-level features of power and solidarity that are evident in these micro-level linguistic patterns.

An overview of our analytical process

However, before we get into the specifics, we have provided a brief overview of the key components of our analytical process. As we have made it our goal to write for both a specialist and non-specialist audience, we hope having this overview of the analytical process will facilitate greater comprehension of the remaining sections of this chapter and ultimately the analytical activities we engage in and report on in this book.

Regarding that process for generating insights about how relationships are working in our professional New Zealand rugby team, we need to:

1. **Collect recordings of authentic interactions**: if we are to learn more about and from the way people enacting, shaping and managing their relationships with one another from the way they use language with one another, we need to collect recordings of real language being used in authentic interactions. As we will illustrate below, we have collected authentic recordings of the typical, recurring and ritual interactions of our team during training sessions, team meetings and on match days to build a data set to support our linguistic lens on relationships.

2. **Locate patterns in the way people are using language to do things (their linguistic practices) in these interactions**: we need to process the raw language (or interactional) data we have collected so it can be used to help generate meaningful insights about how relationships are working. To do this we need tools that can help us capture what people (or social actors) are doing vis-à-vis one another with their language in their everyday interactions. We apply a series of well-established discourse analytical tools that aim to locate the sometimes-complex social actions or functions people are attempting or the relational functions or meanings they are making in and through their linguistic practices in social interaction. This involves looking at language but ultimately looking at language users (roles like the coach, captain and players in the team) and studying how these different members of the team use language to shape their contributions to the team's interactions (i.e. half-time team talks or team meetings). The tools we deploy can help us locate social actions or meanings in the fine-grained decisions speakers make as they design their messages and the way they carve up the interactional floor as they take turns in unfolding team interactions.

3. **Locate (or interpret) relational dynamics of power and solidarity in the linguistic practices**: if we are to take the patterns of social action we have located in our team's interactions and learn from them, in our case use them to shine a light on the relationship dynamics that are being constructed, we need concepts to help us with this process. As we have outlined in the previous chapter,

we draw on the concepts of **power** and **solidarity** to help map out and describe the relational dynamics we see in our team. In some instances, we also draw loosely on other concepts like *identity* and *interactional role* to bring together and discuss our linguistic analyses at this higher-level (of relational dynamics). We discuss how we do this further below.

4   **Account for (or explain) these relational dynamics more broadly by considering what they tell us about the culture of relating in high-performance sports teams**: while the illustrations of relational dynamics in action are the primary contribution of our work, we can also consider these findings more broadly and look to locate underlying cultural ideas that are being signalled or indexed in the relational dynamics. At this level we are putting forward tentative, but ultimately empirically grounded, hypotheses about the high-performance sports team culture for confirming, reworking or discarding as researchers and practitioners collect and analyse more data and/or consider the dynamic realities of relating in their own or other professional sports team contexts. This more macro-level work can connect to and help to drive the more theoretical discussions about how relationships work (or should work) in high-performance sports teams.

5   **Refine these accounts by considering additional contextual information we have, particularly about the people**: however, we also need to ensure that we are open and clear about the features of the local-level context that might explain some of the patterns we see in our data. We therefore need to draw attention to important features of the specific context as we present our analyses and accounts, particularly when they appear relevant or significant to understanding the meanings of the linguistic practices we see in our data. We outline some of the additional contextual information we have collected and drawn on further below.

The above five components provide a snapshot of the different, integrated steps or stages of our linguistic lens on relationships. They should, however, not be seen as a linear analytical process as many of these steps converge into a single sense-making exercise that is ultimately informed by what patterns practices we see in the behaviour of, in our case, the professional New Zealand rugby team. We expand on each of these five stages, providing important details from our study design, in the remaining sections of this chapter.

Collecting and using authentic interactions as data

In this section, we provide details about the authentic interactions we collected from our professional New Zealand rugby team that served as the raw data for our linguistic lens on relationships. From a practical perspective, this meant venturing into the natural sites and settings where the members of our team were interacting with one another, armed with a video or audio recorder, and recording these interactions for closer examination.

We approached a professional New Zealand rugby team we were acquainted with to enquire about our study. Upon being granted access to the team, and after ethical clearance was also granted, we set about the task of collecting examples of authentic, everyday, naturally occurring and (where possible) complete interactions between the members of our professional New Zealand rugby team. To do this, we immersed ourselves in the environment, as a fly on the wall, and collected recordings using a GoPro camera and additional audio recorders, primarily as backup in case the video recorder failed (which it did on occasion).

The researcher was fortunate enough to be given permission to collect audio and video recordings in all of the sites and settings where the team conducted their professional business (these have been outlined further in the next section). The camera and audio recorders were attached to the researcher so as to provide the least amount of distraction to the coaches and the playing group. As others have noted, adding recorders to coaches and players can prove distracting and may negatively impact the goal of trying to blend into the environment and collect as natural a source of data as possible (Wilson, 2011). In some situations, and where consent was given, recorders were positioned in meeting rooms or changing rooms. However, most data were recorded by the researcher who shadowed the coaches and the players as they went about their everyday activities. Additional field notes support the data collection and analysis process, but the primary form of data is the recorded interactions and the language and interaction patterns the people are exhibiting in these interactions.

Our data set of interactions

In this book we concentrate on three settings where the team carried out the bulk of their professional business. These three settings were *team meetings*, *team training sessions* and *match days*. There were also other smaller subsets of data we were able to collect from other team settings. For example, we collected observations (unrecorded) of team interaction patterns on the team bus and when travelling by plane and in airports to matches. These interactions were not recorded due to perceptions by the researcher that such an action might be too imposing on the interaction taking place. We also collected interactions from the team's gym when they were engaged in gym sessions and physio-led activities. However, to concentrate on role-relationships in the team where we had amassed the most data, we have not reported on recordings from these other settings in this book.

Specific details of the interactions that we did record and use for analysis in this book have been provided in Table 2.1.

To facilitate recording of data on match days, the researcher was given the responsibility as one of the team's water carriers, shadowing other water carriers, trainers and physios. These water carriers sat on the bench near the players during matches. Importantly, though, they also had permission to run onto the field during the match to provide water and assistance to players when there was a stoppage in play and to deliver messages to the team from the coaching staff (that were communicated via audio channels). This provided an opportunity to collect examples of social interactions between players on the field, albeit during stoppages in the match.

Some important limitations in our data set

There are some important limitations we need to highlight here in outlining our data set. First, because the researcher could only be in one place at a time, we were not able to collect all of the interactions that took place in our team. In most cases, this was not an issue as the team were often together as a group when performing their business. However, during training sessions and match days, the team would sometimes split into groups (forwards and backs) to run group-specific training drills or to reflect on the first half of the match (during half-time team talks on match days). In these instances, the researcher would follow one member of the coaching staff around as they observed and interacted with players during these drills, trying to collect a balance of recordings from these different subgroups.

The feelings of discomfort recording personal interactions, i.e. on the team bus, should also be seen as a limitation, particularly considering we are dealing with relationships in this book. These more private interactions are undoubtably settings where relationships would have been attended to, particularly with respect to solidarity. Future work may find a way to navigate this level of discomfort we felt. However, in our study, it was this issue in large part drove our decision to focus on how professional role-relationships worked in our team, as the bulk of our data came from settings where people were enacting their role-relationships.

Table 2.1 Outline of the type and amount of interactions recorded

Sites and settings where talk took place	Activity types of the team	Brief description of the role of talk in this activity	Amount of audio/video data
Talk at training base during team training sessions	Warm-ups	• Sequences of talk where the team were led through warm-up drills to prepare for the training session	386 minutes (6 hours: 26 minutes)
	Setting up training drills	• Sequences of talk where training session activities were laid out and instructions were given	
	Training drills	• Sequences of talk that took place while the team were engaged in the physical training drills	
	Reflecting on training drills	• Sequences of talk that involved reflection on recently completed training drills	
	Huddles: to open or close training sessions, or in break between activities	• Sequences of talk that opened or wrapped up the training sessions or particular stages of a training session	
Talk at training base during team meetings	Pre-training briefs	• Sequences of talk that laid out the broader agenda for the upcoming/imminent training session	116 minutes (1 hour: 56 minutes)
	Match evaluation sessions	• Sequences of talk where performance in previous matches (often accompanying with video clips) was reflected on	
	Team strategy sessions (for upcoming matches)	• Sequences of talk where the team's strategies for upcoming matches were communicated	
	Team administration meetings	• Sequences of talk when the team's selection for upcoming matches was communicated usually run by the logistics manager, naming team, giving details of where to be and when	

INTRODUCING OUR TOOLKIT: DISCOURSE ANALYSIS

Talk at stadiums during match days	Match-day warm-ups	• Sequences of talk before, during and after warm-up routines	551 minutes (9 hours: 11 minutes)
	Pre-match team talks	• Sequences of talk in the changing sheds immediately before the beginning of a match	
	Half-time team talks	• Sequences of talk in the changing sheds at half-time during a match	
	Post-match team talks	• Sequences of talk in the changing sheds at the conclusion of a match	
	Talk during the match	• Sequences of talk on the field as the match is in action • Sequences of talk in the coach's box between the coaching team as the match is in action • Sequences of talk on the team bench as the match is in action	
	Talk during stoppages in the match (on-field huddles)	• Sequences of talk amongst the players on the field during stoppages in a match. • Sometimes punctuated by talk between trainers and the players.	
		Total data set in hours and minutes	**1,053 minutes** (17 hours: 33 minutes)

Finally, recording interactions in a sports team, as others have noted (Wilson, 2009, 2011), did prove difficult and we encountered more than our fair share of challenges. Sports teams communicate in a range of settings, many of which are outdoor, leaving recordings susceptible to wind noise, rain and other atmospheric conditions (in the middle of a New Zealand winter). There were also noises that impacted the quality of the recording, one of the main ones being the stadium noises during matches, where the stadium announcer or the crowd noises would occasionally impact the quality of recordings. The echo in changing rooms and the sound of boot studs or sprigs on concrete floors were also an issue in achieving a clear recording at times. The video interactions were also limited on occasion by the inability to capture what could be a large number of individuals in a single frame at the same time. This meant we were not always able to locate who said what, although these cases usually involved minor speaking contributions.

However, by and large, we were able to collect a large amount of video and audio data from our four-week immersion period with the team that gave us a sufficient base to be able to draw conclusions about how the members (i.e. the different roles) of our team behaved in the team's recurring and everyday professional interactions.

Transcribing language and social interaction

While the recordings themselves are the primary source of data that we consult during analysis, discourse analysts also produce detailed transcriptions of these recordings to facilitate the micro-level look at language. This practice distinguishes then from other social science disciplines that regularly draw on language data to support their empirical and theoretical work. These transcriptions make it easier to home in on the finer details of interactions that are often important for understanding social life is working but can be missed or fly under the radar when taking a broader look at communication patterns. They also allow for the more effective comparative analysis across interactions and variation in the contexts of use.

For our purposes in this book, it is important to note that these transcriptions, as readers will see, do not just capture what people say. They also capture (as best as possible) all manner of other conversational realities and, in some cases, features that might are frequently considered imperfections of conversation. For example, in transcripts compiled by discourse analysts, it is common to find representations of silence, observable body movements and gestures, volume and tone of delivery, overlapping talk (as multiple speakers compete for the floor), interruption, repeated words, false starts and all manner of other interactional realities of human interaction. Many of these interactional phenomena are often overlooked in broader studies of communication or put down as conversational imperfections. However, they all have the potential to signal or cue important meanings or functions that can be useful for developing an account of how interactions are working and, by extension, how relationships

INTRODUCING OUR TOOLKIT: DISCOURSE ANALYSIS

Table 2.2 Transcription conventions used in this book

Symbol	Explanation for key
?	Rising intonation noted when delivering an utterance
word-	An abrupt cutoff or a false start and correction of a word
word	Stressed or accented words or utterances
word::::	Stretching or elongation of the sound of a word
WORD	Word or utterance delivered with loud volume
/word\	Co-occurrence and overlapping of speech between two or more individuals
word==	Latching between utterances (where an utterance is added on to another in quick succession)
(word)	The word transcribed in parentheses is the transcriber's best guess due to poor audio quality
(unclear)	Words are unclear and inaudible due to poor audio quality
{word}	Notable non-speech activity, body movement, gesturing actions
+/++/+++	Short pauses or silences of less than a second
{2.0}	Longer pauses or silences, noted in seconds within the parenthesis

are working. Table 2.2 outlines the transcription conventions we used in this book to capture the range of interactional phenomena that were prevalent in the interactions of our team.

As alluded to above, the quality of recordings was not always clear, and features of the surrounding environment did at times impact the clarity of data captured. In these cases, sections of the talk that were unclear were not able to be transcribed and have been documented as *(unclear)* in the transcripts. Readers may also find transcripts representing natural speech to appear disorganized, with repeated words, false starts and all manner of other features of unplanned spoken speech. This should not be read as an indictment on the speaker but more of a reality of human speech and the unpolished feel it can generate when we transfer it to written form.

In the chapters of this book, readers will encounter a number of transcripts from the data and all discussions presented in this book will emanate from specific transcribed extracts of the data. Presenting transcripts of the authentic interactions for readers themselves is the cornerstone of discourse analytical efforts of reliability and validity. By presenting transcripts of the authentic interactions in the context being explored, readers have the opportunity to scrutinize the interaction themselves and critically consider the explanation being offered by the researcher in the process.

Identifying a primary unit of analysis: Locating purposeful activities in the interactional data

With our data set outlined, we can now turn to matters of analysis and how we processed the raw interactional data for insights about relationships. One way to start processing the interactional data is to identify the purposeful activities of the team's interactions and the important professional tasks or activities the group are performing in these interactions. Discourse analysts often refer to whole, bounded events or activities mediated by speech as genres or texts (Carter et al., 2001; Fairclough, 2003b). Texts are (usually) long stretches of talk or written communication that are deployed to perform some general purpose and/or a series of finer-level purposes or goals. As a unit of analysis, whole texts (or in our case whole interactions, like a half-time team talk) provide a frame of interaction activity where people are attempting to accomplish or achieve some purposeful activity. By adopting this view of texts or interactions, we can then look more closely at the role particular individuals play in the process of working together towards achieving the goals or purposes of the text at hand. These purposeful activities or frames of activity help to ground the finer-grained analysis we do subsequently and provide the frame for reporting on the actions of individuals. By identifying particular frames of activity, we have already taken a big, meaningful step towards processing the language by directing our attention to how language is being used by people as they pursue a purposeful task.

In Table 2.1, we already started this process of identifying purposeful activities or frames of activity we used in this book to organize our analysis, by providing details of the settings where talk was used to accomplish some task or tasks (in training sessions, team meetings and on match days). These interactional settings also involve configurations of roles and role-relationships, or **participation frameworks** (Goffman, 1981; see also Chovanec, 2016; Dynel, 2014; Hutchby, 2014 for illustrations of discourse analytical work in this space), to help us ground our analysis of the different relational dyads in our team (i.e. the coach–player or player–player dyads).

However, we can also frame these interactional activities at a finer level where there is more emphasis on the actual social (or interpersonal) actions people are performing within these activities. A label like half-time team talk, for example, does not tell us much in terms of the actual activities or tasks that the group are performing or accomplishing. For some readers, a setting like the *half-time team talk* will likely conjure up finer-grained communicative actions like giving instructions, motivating, solving problems or giving feedback. As readers will see, there are less of these tasks than there are activity types and many of them we see being enacted and accomplished in and across a range of different activity types. However, they provide a more specific social activity to help frame the analysis of interpersonal communication in our team and allow us to report on how different individuals in different roles behave when pursuing these important joint or shared tasks.

To capture and label these finer-grained purposes, so they can be part of our analytical process, we have drawn on the label **interactional task**, as a finer-grained category for capturing what is going on in an interaction. In Table 2.3, we have provided an indication of key interactional tasks that we will draw on to help house our analyses of the relationships in our team.

The process of locating these finer-level tasks is an analytical one in its own right, and it should be noted that we arrived at these labels based on preliminary analysis of the interactions we collected. We accept that there may be other ways of labelling these interpersonal tasks and there may be additional interpersonal tasks performed in and across the various activity types of a sports team. The above list of interactional tasks, which will become central in our analysis of relationships in action in this book, should be read as an account of the tasks that talk was regularly used to accomplish in our team context and should not be read as an exhaustive or generalizable list of all tasks that talk performs in high-performance sports teams. Additionally, the assigning of tasks to specific interactions can be a messy one and we frequently saw multiple tasks being performed in,

Table 2.3 Important interactional tasks evident in training sessions, team meetings and on match days

Solving problems	Sequences of talk that set out to identify problems and solutions to them
Giving feedback	Sequences of talk that set out to provide feedback or a positive or corrective nature
Giving instructions	Sequences of talk that set out to give people or persons directions
Motivating	Sequences of talk that set out to provoke, arouse or encourage people or persons

for example, a half-time team talk, and often in ways where they intersect with one another. In these half-time team talks, members may engage in sequences designed to solve problems and other sequences designed to motivate. At times, these tasks may be pursued simultaneously making them hard to clearly extract and pin down.

However, the labels do help to orient our analyses to what people are doing as a group and allow us to see how different people in different roles are contributing (or not) to the team's interactional activities. While the labelling process of interactional activities is an imperfect and imprecise one, providing these labels gives us an important and authentic contextual frame through which to interpret the linguistic behaviour insights about how relationships are working in our team. By looking at the way individuals in our team behave linguistically as they pursue these interactional tasks – i.e. who does the directing, who gives the feedback, how is feedback given by particular individuals, who claims responsibility to motivate the group – we can advance our understanding of the kinds of rights and responsibilities (power) certain individuals are claiming vis-à-vis others and the degree of social distance that is being heightened or reduced (solidarity) in the important professional activities of the group.

Making sense of raw interactional data: Using discourse analysis to locate people's social actions in language patterns

With our raw data prepared, we can now outline the tools we used to unpack the specific language use patterns *within* these interactions and locate how people in particular roles used language as they pursued the interactional tasks of their team's professional activities. For discourse analysts, these tools amount to a metalanguage for systematically locating, processing and describing the linguistic forms we see in the team's interactions in terms of the social actions, functions or meanings speakers are making in and through their language choices.

This toolkit is larger and broader than the one traditionally used to talk about language forms (i.e. nouns, verbs, split infinitives) which can make it somewhat daunting for non-specialists. However, while the simpler, more traditional, formal categories for classifying language tell us a lot about language itself, but very little about how language is functioning in people's interactions and, importantly, how particular linguistic actions by particular individuals are shaping the social interactions and interpersonal relations of

INTRODUCING OUR TOOLKIT: DISCOURSE ANALYSIS

the individuals involved. The multiple levels and types of tools we outline below allow us to look at the language people are using in multiple ways and generate deeper insights about the functions people are performing through their selections of linguistic form.

To categorize language according to the actions it performs, we draw on the notion of an **utterance**. An utterance – a stretch of speech produced by a single speaker (Johnstone, 2008) – is perhaps most easily understood as the spoken equivalent of the sentence. However, an utterance is perhaps a broader category that captures any contribution to an interaction, regardless of whether it is a fully formed sentence or not. When people speak with one another, they do not always speak in grammatically complete sentences, with many utterances being non-clausal in nature (Biber, 1988, 1999). However, this does not make these utterances any less meaningful and, as we will show, the smallest and least grammatically full contributions to an interaction are meaningful and are capable of performing important social actions or functions in an ongoing interaction.

When analysing utterances, we can apply a number of different levels of attention. We can look at **the content** of the utterance and *what* is being spoken about. However, ultimately, our primary interest is in *how* questions, particularly how a particular utterance is functioning, what we have labelled in this book **the (speech) action**. Speech acts (Searle, 1969, 1985) or speech actions are a central feature of discourse analytical work and represent a view of language as a performative tool humans use to act on the world (Aarons & Mierowsky, 2017; Rosaldo, 1982; Yates, 2010). We can also look at how certain utterances or speech actions are being designed to make, for example, more subtle meanings, mitigate or boost the strength of an action or to be more or less direct/indirect. At this level, we are interested more in **the design of the speech action**, and any effort a speaker has gone to shape the meaning of their action in particular ways.

However, ultimately, discourse analysts are not just interested in categorizing utterances of talk into speech actions, nor do they seek to study the speech actions or the design of speech actions in isolation. Instead, they are interested in how these actions are deployed by speakers across interactions, as people act and react to one another (and one another's actions) in unfolding activities, texts or stretches of talk. At this level we are interested in **turn-taking patterns** and tracking how people take turns, the turns they take at particular moments in interactions and the design options they deploy in shaping their turns at talk as social interactions unfold.

We briefly expand on these four integrated levels of analysis below, drawing attention to some of the specific classification tools and analytical processes we used at each of these levels.

The content of the utterance

Most utterances encode some informational content. Locating this layer of information involves identifying the topics an individual is talking about, whether it is particular people, events, activities, technical details or feelings a speaker is recounting. The topical information, or the *what* of an utterance, is one aspect of the meaning of an utterance that we paid attention to in our analysis and is typically the most obvious feature of talk that non-specialists might gravitate to when they seek to classify language.

However, this layer of analysis, while it was integrated into our wider sense-making job, was secondary in focus to the more performative actions people were performing through their talk. Any utterance that construes content is also simultaneously doing something in an unfolding interaction, and it is at this level where we can locate richer insights to help us our overall task of understanding how relationships are working. Therefore, we did not deploy any specific and systematic analytical process for studying the content of utterances in our data and mainly refer to content when and where it helps us to illuminate what is going on in a particular extract.

The speech actions of an utterance

The most central analytical work we did on the utterances of speakers was to try and understand what action(s) or function(s) they were performing in an unfolding interaction. An utterance like *get your shoulders tighter*, for example, is arguably performing the action of **directing** or **instructing** an individual to do something. It may, indirectly, be performing a range of other meanings or functions as well, like **giving critical feedback**, and we may be able to make a case for these more indirect functions as we unpack the language use in an interactional context more extensively. However, more broadly, this level of analysis is concerned with identifying what appeared to be recognizable speech actions or functions a person was performing in and through their utterances of talk.

There are a vast number or potential speech actions or functions a speaker may perform in and through language (i.e. greeting, eliciting, offering, commanding, apologizing, promising, reminding, insulting, assuring, hinting, boasting or explaining). However, there are, in the English language at least, a relatively stable set of core speech actions that we can locate in speaker utterances. In this book, we use this core set of speech actions (in the left-hand column of Table 2.4) as a key point of departure for unpacking the utterances and identifying meanings and social actions speakers are performing in and through their utterances.

However, it is important to note that these core speech actions are often used as a starting point – a point of departure – for a deeper look at the more nuanced ways particular speech actions are functioning. For example, if we look more closely at the design choices speakers make (which we discuss further below) when they shape their utterances, we may notice an attempt by the speaker to make more subtle meaning or perform a more nuanced function through their utterance. For example, a directive to *get your shoulders tighter* might come across more as a suggestion if it were shaped as *you could get your shoulders tighter*, and such a decision in a particular context might reflect or construct a different relational dynamic in the process. In our analysis, therefore, we also paid attention to these nuances in the design of speech actions and much of the work we do in our analysis will involve making sense of and illustrating our claims about what actions speakers are performing in their interactional moves. Some of the more nuanced speech actions we identified and comment on in our analysis are registered above in the right-hand column of Table 2.4.

Identifying the function of an utterance is by no means an uncontroversial task, largely because the functions of an utterance are not always transparent and clear from the set of language forms uttered by a speaker. For example, the phrase *is it cold in here* (and often cited example in discourse analytical work) might be functioning explicitly or **directly** as an observation or it might

Table 2.4 A list of core speech actions being performed through speaker utterances in our data

Core speech actions	More nuanced versions
Stating (i.e. making statements)	Informing Criticizing
Eliciting (i.e. asking questions)	Asking for unknown information Eliciting confirmation Seeking compliance
Directing (i.e. making some attempt to tell someone to do something)	Instructing or commanding Suggesting Proposing Offering Motivating
Assessing (i.e. making some form of evaluative assessment)	Blaming Criticizing Giving warnings Praising Thanking

be functioning *implicitly* or **indirectly** as a request for someone to get up and shut the window. Discourse analysts rely on their own perceptions of the actions being performed, as native users of the language, to classify utterances according to their function. However, they also look for clues as to how the addressees are interpreting an action (what are sometimes referred to in speech act theory as the perlocutionary effects of the message). For example, if someone gets up and shuts the window after hearing the phrase *is it cold in here* and the original speaker says *thank you* in return, we have a warrant to label this action as a request, or at least as potentially functioning as a request.

There is another layer of action that needs highlighting: how a speaker's utterance is functioning in the overall management of the interaction. For example, is a particular utterance functioning to **initiate** a discussion, **close** it down, **add** to an ongoing discussion or **shift** the topic. We will speak more about this level of speech action when we discuss the turn-taking patterns further below.

The design choices of speech actions

While assigning utterances a function or action is an important analytical task for unpacking how people are using language and making their interactions work, discourse analysts can also look at how these utterances (and the speech actions they perform) are being shaped or designed through more micro-level considerations and choices. This involves looking within utterances and assessing the significance of finer units of language being chosen by the speaker to realize their speech actions.

In this book, there were two reasons why we looked closer at how speech actions were being designed. First, we look at these micro-level choices speakers make to help us with the process of identifying the topics of talk and the (sometimes more nuanced) function an utterance (as discussed above). Some speech functions, particularly those that are direct in nature, can take a particular shape grammatically and these grammatical forms can give us a clue as to what the utterance is doing in the interaction. For example, a directive like *get your shoulders tighter* is at least partially recognizable as a directive due to the imperative grammatical syntax structure. This grammatical information within the speech utterance, then, can provide an aid for us as we attempt to classify utterances according to the speech action they are performing.

The other reason we look within speech actions is to identify specific stylistic choices speakers are making as they style (design) and deliver their speech actions in more or less direct/indirect or nuanced ways. At this level, we look at all manner of micro-level linguistic (lexical and grammatical) systems that speakers make choices from to help them encode subtle meanings to their messages or to perform messages in more or less direct ways. Humans are faced with many choices from our linguistic subsystems when they design their messages, and these different choices can shape the message in more nuanced and interpersonally different ways. For example, issuing an assessment of a bad match result by calling it a *disaster*, for example, construes it in quite different ways compared to the choice to construe it as *learning opportunity*.

However, beyond topic words, there are a number of other linguistic subsystems that can be significant in the shaping of the meaning of a message. The *pronoun* subsystem (*he*, *she*, *it*, *we*, *they* or other ways speakers marked who or what they were speaking about) is a particularly important one and was a frequent target for our finer-level analysis. While, on a content level, the choice of pronoun might be viewed as a simple signalling of who (i.e. the subjects) the speaker is talking about, it can at times be a particularly significant one on an interpersonal level. For example, in post-match media interview research, File (2018, 2019) and File and Wilson (2017) found that managers and coaches would use the pronoun *we* instead of *they* when reflecting negatively on the team's performance in their post-match interviews (i.e. *we* didn't perform well today instead of *they* didn't perform well today). In this case, both *we* and *they* are references to the team, but the choice to use *we* instead of *they* encodes quite different meanings regarding the way the coach positions themselves vis-à-vis the team. By using *they*, the coach is clearly positioning themselves as distant from the players when commenting on their performance as a group, whereas by using *we* the coach may be constructing or attempting to construct themselves as more of a member of the playing group. In any case, the use of *we* hints at a more inclusive construction. This strategy was particularly evident when commenting critically on negative aspects of performance, perhaps to strategically temper the strength of these critical acts and minimize public interpretations of managerial anger and discord with their players as such meanings can be blown up in the media as indications of unrest in playing groups.

Another important lexicogrammatical system we will focus on a lot in our analysis was the system of modality (Biber, 1999; Halliday & Matthiessen, 2014). When we speak about modality, the words and phrases we are referring to are ones like *could*, *might*, *may*, *should*, *will*, *need to*, *have to* and others. These words help speakers to encode a degree of certainty to a message (or proposition) and/or a degree of obligation or necessity to a proposal. These systems provide speakers with a number of ways to encode their messages in ways that can signal, reveal and/or construct interpersonally significant meanings. Sociolinguistic concepts like obligation, for example, are not just linguistic in nature but also social in nature. Requiring someone to do something through an obligation marker like *will* (as in *you will do this*) creates meanings that the speaker has (or is claiming) the right to require something of the person they are speaking to. This system of modality, then, is a particularly significant one for understanding how relationships are being enacted. It is also one of several features that researchers have used to connect to higher-level concepts like expert power (epistemic authority) and coercive power (deontic authority) and build accounts of the interpersonal relationships and social structures individuals are constructing for one another (Landmark et al., 2015; Nanouri et al., 2022; Stevanovic & Svennevig, 2015).

Directness and indirectness, or the finer-level choices made by speakers as they shape a speech action in more or less direct or indirect ways, is also a fruitful feature of utterance design to target when studying interpersonal relations. As an illustration, there are many different ways to design the speech action of a directive – i.e. *do it, please do it, would you mind doing it, has not this been done yet, this needs doing*. Speakers that shape their directives to others in more direct ways are arguably enacting and constructing their rights to do so and may be heightening status differences between them and the person they are directing. Speakers that shape their speech actions in more indirect ways, in some cases hiding the directive or shaping it in such a way that it comes across more as a request, may be signalling or attempting to construct a different status relationship with their interlocutor. How speakers encoded their speech actions was a frequent target in our analysis particularly because it provided empirical evidence of how individuals were constructing their rights vis-à-vis others.

Finally, the finer level analysis we conducted on utterances also focused suprasegmental or prosodic features such as tone, intonation and volume of a speaker's utterance. How loud was an utterance or series of utterances and/or what intonation patterns were recognizable? These prosodic features can help speakers to convey a great deal of meaning about and how it is being intended. The design choices speakers make at this level can be a particularly valuable target for analysts looking to understand how a speaker is shaping the message for their audience and the constructing interpersonal relations in that moment of time. For example, a message shouted at a group of people in a small room encodes very different meanings to one delivered at a more reasonable level.

In the analysis presented in this book, we draw out a number of micro-level choices speakers made for closer attention and consider the potential interpersonal meanings and/or implications being conveyed in and through these often subtle, but very important, choices. It is hard to provide an exclusive list of all of the fine-grained linguistic features we concentrate on when we unpack speaker utterances for more delicate levels of meaning design. However, several of the more common finer level lexicogrammatical subsystems we probed in our analysis have been included in Table 2.5.

Table 2.5 Grammatical subsystems of language for unpacking how speech actions are being designed

	Functional meaning systems	Illustrative examples	Analytical questions
Grammatical design of clauses	*Clause structures*	Declarative, imperative, interrogative, non-clausal	What clause structures are speaker messages realized by?
	Interrogative forms	Y/N interrogative, Wh-interrogative, double-barrel interrogative,	What interrogative structures are used to realize elicitation messages?
	Polarity	Positive polarity (can, will, did), negative polarity (can't, won't, didn't)	Are messages shaped as positive or negative constructions?
	Mitigators or hedges	May, might, could, a little bit, not quite, just	What grammatical tools are used to soften the strength of messages?
	Boosters	Really, massively, hugely	What grammatical tools are used to boost the strength of messages?
People and reference encoding systems	*Pronouns*	I, he, she, it, we, they, them, me	What pronouns do speakers use when shaping messages?
	Terms of address	First names, formal titles (Sir, Mr, Mrs), formal title + last name (Mr Jones), nicknames (Jezza)	How do people address each other when exchanging messages?
	Deixis markers		

Table 2.5 Grammatical subsystems of language for unpacking how speech actions are being designed *(continued)*

Phrase-level and lexical choice systems	*Lexical choices*		What vocabulary items do speakers choose to use to shape messages?
	Technical language items		Is technical or lay vocabulary used to shape messages?
	Colloquialisms		Are colloquial vocabulary items being used to shape messages?
	Expletives	Fuck, shit, cunt	Are expletives being used to when shaping messages?
	Vague language	Something like that, stuff like that, and stuff	Are vague language and vague phrases being tagged onto messages?
Phonological encoding systems	*Volume*	Whispering, shouting	How are messages amplified?
	Tone and intonation	Rising intonation, falling intonation, monotone delivery, sarcastic tone	Are there intonation patterns or recognizable tones?
Other message encoding systems	*Laughter*		Is laughter a feature of these interactions?
	Pauses	Short pauses, long pauses	How are pauses in messages and interactional sequences functioning?
	Body language	Walking away, putting hand on shoulder, linking arms into a huddle	How is body language being utilized when shaping and delivering messages?
	Fillers	Ah, um, you know, I mean	How are speakers using fillers in their interactions?

Turn-taking patterns: The distribution (back-and-forth) of speech actions in social interaction

While the two levels of analysis presented above were significant for our work in this book, perhaps the most revealing insights came from the analysis we carried out on the turn-taking patterns in our team's interactions (see Brown & Yule, 1983; Liddicoat, 2022 for accessible introductions to turn-taking analysis). At this level, we are still interested in the actions speakers perform and the design work they put into their contributions. However, we try to track these and how they work across unfolding interactions as speakers act and react to each other in the back and forth of social interaction. From this we can generate a picture of how particular speakers are managing their own and each other's contributions and rights to contribute to ongoing texts, and how the actions taken by particular people shape relations of power and solidarity in the group.

One of the easier focal points of turn-taking analysis centres on understanding who does what speech actions with their turns at talk. At this level, we connect our analysis of speech actions to the specific interactions and see which people in which roles perform particular speech actions (like directing, eliciting, assessing) in unfolding interactions. However, the analysis of turn-taking does get much more dynamic and complex than this. What we are primarily concerned with when we analyse interactions at this level is tracking how turns are ritually being taken by people in unfolding interactions. By generating a picture of the way people take turns in their interactional activities, we can build an understanding of the way people are performing their roles vis-à-vis one another in real time as they deliver, receive and act on messages from others in their social interactions.

Turn-taking patterns have been a key target for discourse analysts, especially those from the schools of Interactional Sociolinguistics (Gumperz, 2015; Jaspers, 2012; Schiffrin, 1996; Vine et al., 2008) and Conversation Analysis (Clayman & Heritage, 2002; Drew & Heritage, 1992; Jefferson, 1988; Sacks et al., 1974; Schegloff, 1995). Because of this, there are a number of well-established tools that we can draw on here to study how social interactions in our team play out over longer stretches. Some of the key aspects of turn-taking that we target in our analyses have been briefly outlined in Table 2.6.

The human turn-taking system is incredibly intricate and complex, integrating multiple choices a speaker needs to make as they negotiate and sustain their entry to an interaction. The outline provided above of the tools we use in this book will hopefully help readers to see how complex and integrated these choices are. And, as readers work through the chapters of

Table 2.6 Analytical tools for studying turn-taking patterns in our data

Turn-taking patterns	Description	Analytical questions
Turn type	See above sections on speech action and speech action design.	• What turns are individuals in particular roles claiming rights to perform on, to or with others? • Do speakers take different turns to shift their interactional footing and establish different interactional sequences?
Turn length	Here we are interested in seeing how much talk individuals in particular roles engage in and how dominant a given speaker is in or across the team's interactions.	• Who speaks a lot? • Who does not speak at all? • How long are speaker turns? • Who dominates speaking opportunities in the team's interactions?
General floor management	Here we are interested in patterns concerning the overall management of the floor and the rights speakers in particular roles claim to be able to manage the interactional spaces of the team.	• Who initiates interactions in the team? • Which interactions do particular individuals initiate? • Who closes interactions in the team and which interactions do these individuals close? • Who keeps interactions going and takes charge of where they go?
Turn entry management	Linked to the above category, here we are interested in locating how speakers in different roles negotiate their entry to the interaction. Do they select themselves to speak? Do they wait to be selected? Are certain people selected to speak?	• Do individuals in particular roles claim the right to self-select themselves to speak in team interactions? • Do individuals speak without being invited or do they only speak when invited? • Do individuals take up an invitation to speak or refuse it? • When the floor is offered to others, is it offered to everyone or anyone, or is it offered to a particular individual? • Is access to the interaction floor being restricted by dominant individuals? • Is the floor released by dominant speakers and, if so, when is it released to others?

INTRODUCING OUR TOOLKIT: DISCOURSE ANALYSIS 47

		• Do those who release the floor reclaim it? • Do speakers need to push their way in when they are going to speak? • Does the floor pass from one person to another in an orderly fashion, or is there interruption and overlap? • What do these overlaps and interruptions mean? Are there signs of competition for the floor or are floor rights clearly and unambiguously assigned, taken up and/or afforded?
Turn continuation management (the sequential management of turns across longer stretches of interaction)	At this level, we are interested in studying patterns in how people are acting and reacting to each other across sometimes long stretches of talk.	• How does the floor pass from one person to another across long sequences of talk? • What conditions (if any) are attached to taking up the floor by a previous speaker? • How are individuals in particular roles being positioned by speaker turns and how do they respond to these attempts to position them? • Are there recognizable interactional routines being deployed in interactions between individuals in particular roles (i.e. a recognizable question–answer routine in the coach–player interactions)?
Topic management	Here we focus on turn-taking at more of a topic management level, exploring how individuals claim rights to introduce (new) topics, how and whether they contribute to ongoing topical discussions, or whether they seek to change the topic.	• Are certain individuals claiming the right to introduce new topics for discussion? • Are speakers elaborating on, expanding on or extending topics raised for discussion? • How are topic shifts negotiated or managed?

this book, it is also hoped that they will see how significant these choices can be for the shaping of interpersonal relations.

These tools are particularly useful for our work in this book on understanding how relationships work as they provide us with a way to account for the dynamic management of the people in and through social interaction. By focusing on turn-taking, we can directly assess the way people are behaving vis-à-vis one another and vis-à-vis the tasks they are conducting. In presenting extracts of authentic interaction from our team, readers will be encouraged to look meticulously at these taken-for-granted patterns of turn-taking that are deployed, often ritually, to accomplish the tasks at hand.

Like other levels of linguistic analysis we carry out, these patterns of turn-taking reflect and reconstruct the culturally significant taken-for-granted social structures of the team (and perhaps of the culture of professional sport). We can use these tools to locate, for example, who claims or is afforded rights to the interactional floor, who claims rights to initiate or close interactions, and what other rights people in particular roles are claiming through their turns and how are these rights met (i.e. are they accepted or not) by others. Insights from this level of analysis show us how the interactional floor is being carved up and, by extension, how people in the team carve up social rights and responsibilities and act and react to one another in and across their professional interactions.

Non-verbal actions

One final level of analysis we carried out on the interactional data was to identify any **non-verbal** or **non-linguistic behaviour** that accompanied speaker utterances (i.e. high fives, embraces, eye contact, gesturing, nodding), especially if it appeared significant to understanding what the utterance or utterances were doing or how they were functioning. One of the most important non-verbal actions we focused on in our analysis was the act of silence. While silence is marked by the lack of linguistic items (i.e. words), it is by no means a non-linguistic or non-communicative action. Silence is capable of communicating a lot of meaning that can be significant for understanding interpersonal relationships.

While not technically linguistic in nature, non-linguistic modes of communication are being increasingly targeted by linguists as these actions can both create meaning on their own or help a speaker shape the meaning of their utterances (Asmuß, 2015; Clifton et al., 2018; Jewitt, 2014; O'Halloran & Smith, 2011). *Putting an arm around someone* while giving them critical feedback, for example, has the potential to shape the meaning of that act of criticism differently, in more nuanced ways, by mitigating the strength of it, perhaps characterizing it as more constructive in nature and shaping the relationship between the two individuals in particularly close fashion. Utterances accompanied with *laughter*, for example, can be used as evidence to label turn actions prior to the laughter as functioning as joking or humour acts. The analysis we present in this book will integrate these ancillary actions like high-fives, laughter, gestures and other forms of body language that accompany speaker utterances so as to bring into focus potential meanings this level of semiotic action can make.

Integrating these levels of analysis: Sense-making and the analytical process

With all these different levels of analysis, an important question to address is, how were they all applied to the data and in what order? For discourse analysts, this process is usually quite messy but certainly systematic. While these different levels may all be applied to the data simultaneously and in a somewhat messy fashion, they offer a range of different layers to direct researcher attention to features of importance at different levels of communicative action of choice. In other words, they provide us with a set of tools to draw out intricacies in speaker choices at a range of different, but meaningful, levels so as to capture the nuanced ways people engage in their everyday interactional tasks with one another.

We have mentioned above that the wider analytical process might best be characterized as sense making or riddle solving (Alasuutari, 1995). The riddle we are trying to solve is how are relationships working or being made to work in and through language. Our multilevel analysis of speaker utterances gives us a series of levels upon which to draw out significant linguistic choices and illustrate how they are functioning in the overall construction of interpersonal relationships in our professional New Zealand rugby team.

Moving from interactional dynamics to relational dynamics: Drawing semiotic links between language use and power and solidarity

Above we have outlined the tools we used to locate **interactional dynamics** in our team. We now need to outline the tools and process we used to draw conclusions about, make sense of, interpret and comment on these interactional dynamics in ways that shine a light on patterns at a more social or relational level. At this level, we collate and interpret features in the texts at a higher level, attempting to locate socially distributed patterns evident in the way language is being used. By doing this we can more directly address our primary research question in this book – how are relationships working?

As we outlined in the introduction, to help with this interpretation process, we have drawn on the conceptual tools of **power** and **solidarity**. By applying the lenses of power and solidarity to the speech action, speech design and turn-taking patterns in our data, we can attempt to provide empirically informed insights about how language is being used to enact relations of power and solidarity in our team. In interpreting patterns in language use through these notions of power and solidarity, we can illustrate the **relational dynamics** of our team and present accounts of how relationships are working or being made to work in and through the team's ritual and recurring linguistic practices.

As we outlined in the introduction, power and solidarity are complex and multidimensional concepts. In this book we embraced this multidimensionality as an analytical asset and used it to help locate different dimensions of power and solidarity that we saw being enacted by our team in their interactions with one another. Our analyses will centre on five particular dimensions of power and solidarity that were evident in the interactional practices of our team and proved helpful in shining a light on the relational dynamics we saw being constructed in and through the team's ritual interactional practices. Table 2.7 provides a brief overview of these five dimensions to orient readers to the discussions that are to come.

Again, these different dimensions should not be seen as an exhaustive list and each of these dimensions should also not be seen as clear-cut, distinctive categories – there is significant crossover. Even within the field of discourse analysis, where these concepts are often central to much of the analytical work by researchers interested in social relations, relational work (Locher, 2010, 2010, 2013; Locher & Watts, 2005), relational practice (J. Holmes & Marra, 2004) and rapport management (Spencer-Oatey, 2011, 2015), these concepts can be understood and approached differently.

We will not discuss these dimensions of power and solidarity further here, as we spend the bulk of the chapters of this book introducing, extracting, discussing and illustrating how these dimensions of power and solidarity work in our team's interactions. It is likely to be easier at that stage for readers to understand more about how these concepts have been applied once they start to see examples of the data and explanations as to how particular semiotic links were drawn between the interactional dynamics evident in our team's data and the processes of controlling others, exercising expert power over others, accepting the influence and control of others, or establishing belonging and togetherness, for example.

Table 2.7 Interpretive mechanisms for making sense of the interactional practices we saw in our data

	Dimension	Social processes we identified in the interactional data
Power *the capacity or ability to direct or influence the behaviour of others or the course of (future) events*	Control	Exercising control over others, imposing on others, accepting the control of others. Sometimes referred to as the amount of deontic authority or status a person is claiming.
	Expertise (or knowledge)	Claiming and exercising greater amounts of expertise or knowledge over others, accepting the expertise claims of others. Sometimes referred to as the amount of epistemic authority or status a person is claiming.
Solidarity *the expression or signalling of belonging/ togetherness, closeness (or distance), unity or alignment on issues, actions and feelings, and the degree of concern shown for one another's plights or misdeeds*	Cohesion (togetherness or belonging)	Establishing togetherness or belonging amongst a group of (two or more) people. Sometimes this is referred to using concepts like (group) cohesion, alignment or unity.
	Social distance	Getting closer or maintaining (personal or professional) distance with individuals.
	Rapport	Managing threats to rapport or boosting them. This could also be seen to reflect efforts by individuals to ensure other notions like cohesion and unity are not adversely affected by particular (socio)linguistic practices.

However, there are two more general principles we need to outline here in order to set up this more interpretive phase of the analysis. First, regarding the process of drawing links of language patterns to these more conceptual notions of power and solidarity; discourse analysts can, on the one hand, look for explicit markers or references to one's power or authority or the degree of closeness or social distance between speakers. Here utterances that explicitly mark a power-relationship like *I'm the boss*, or utterances that make reference to the nature of the social distance between individuals, like *we're friends* can be useful in this regard. However, the vast amount and array of meanings of power and solidarity we make in our everyday personal or professional interactions with others are rarely, if ever, communicated in such an explicit fashion. Rather, these meanings are signalled or established more indirectly or implicitly through other interactional actions that people deploy in and across particular contexts, in the course of their everyday interactions. As analysts, it is our task to draw semiotic links between linguistic practices, social actions (enacted through language) and the more social dimensions and dynamics of power and solidarity that people are signalling and (re)constructing in the process. This process of making and illustrating claims regarding evident links between recurring and ritual linguistic practices and the meanings about power and solidarity they are constructing is the central driving force of each of the findings chapters that follow.

Second, it is important to state that while we have separated this section on the process of interpreting dynamics of power and solidarity from the more descriptive task of understanding social actions in language patterns, that is solely for clarity and simplicity's sake. In truth, these two analytical activities are, at least in the process of making sense of the data, carried out simultaneously. The language people use and the social context they use it in are inextricably linked. In other words, when people are using language, they are sending signals about *their* understanding of how power and solidarity work in the context they are communicating in. It is this understanding that we are actually trying to explicate, locate, pin down or reverse-engineer when we analyse interactional patterns, and we can only really do this by approaching the analysis of both of these levels simultaneously.

Refining our accounts: Drawing on additional contextual information to help explain behaviour

One final practice we deployed in our analytical process was to consider the impact that specific features of the local New Zealand rugby context might be having on the functions and interpretation of linguistic practices in our data. In this book, we have mainly drawn on quite general contextual information to shape our analysis. We are, for example, looking at how people in generic roles (coach, captain, player) are speaking (or behaving) in generic interactional tasks or activities (like half-time team talks). This approach is in part to allow readers to consider the practices and relational dynamics we will highlight in this book in relation to other contexts where there may be similar roles and role-relationships being enacted and similar interactional tasks being performed. However, where it was possible, we also drew on additional and more specific contextual information to feed into our process of developing claims about how relationships were working in and through language. This contextual information helped to provide a layer of additional information to help refine the claims we were making, demarcate interpretive boundaries and draw reader attention to important features from the local context that might be conditional to or influential on the behaviour we are seeing.

One of the most important factors from our context was the time in the season that our recordings were made. As we mentioned above, the four-week period we spent with the Rhinos was during their pre-season campaign. On the one hand, this contextual factor provides a boundary for any claims we make. Readers need to consider the fact that our analysis was conducted on interactions from the early stages of the team coming together when some players were still on trial which may help to explain some of what we are seeing. However, at the same time, this early stage of relationship building, whereby players are less accustomed to one another, may have heightened and activated awareness of the more general ideological cultural knowledge systems, precisely the kind we are hoping to shine a light on in our analysis.

As well as more general contextual information about the team, we also collected information about the individuals in the team, particularly those individuals to whom we assigned the role of **players**. The label 'player' is uncritically assigned and amorphous, somewhat conveniently lumping every playing individual in the team. Therefore, we collected additional information to feed into the analytical process to help provide a more nuanced explanation of the linguistic practices we saw from particular players in our data. The details we collected about the players in the team included the members' ages, their experience level in the team, their playing position, playing histories and their accolades. A full list of additional information we collected about players (where it was possible) is provided below.

- Age
- Ethnicity
- Playing position
- The individual operating units they belong to
- How long they have been part of this team
- Amount of experience working with this specific coaching group (in this team or other)

- What other teams they have played for or professional honours they have achieved
- Their contractual status in the team (support player, contracted player)

These factors are socially relevant or contextually significant in professional sport, based on our informal interactions with the team, amongst others, and could theoretically be influential in the shaping of relationships in our team. For example, the amount of experience a person has, their contract status (permanent or squad player), whether they are regular starters or bench players, whether they have higher honours playing for club teams above this level of competition or representing their country may contribute to their standing or social status in the team which, in turn, may influence and be reflected in varying interactional behaviour we see from particular players in our data. If we find, for example, that two players are talking a significant amount and controlling the agenda in player–player interactions, and neither of these players are the captain, then this additional contextual information about those players' ages or experience levels might help to draw conclusions that could explain this more dominant interactional and relational behaviour and help us build a more nuanced account of how relationships work in our team.

Much of this additional information was collected through a short, structured interview with the members of the team. We also recorded some of this information during our observations and in more informal conversations with members of the coaching staff and team. The information we were able to collect on individual members of the squad has been compiled in Appendix 2. This information will also be introduced when presenting some of the analyses in this book and were particularly relevant when unpacking player–player relationships in Chapter 6, where the generic label of player does not allow us to explain the power dynamics we see in player–player interactions with much sophistication.

We have now established the different aspects of the linguistic lens we are applying to the data to reveal more insight about how relationships are working in our team. The interactional dynamics can in their own right provide a revealing account of how a group's interactions play out. However, in this book we use these interactional dynamics to build knowledge about the relational dynamics of power and solidarity that are being exhibited, oriented to or constructed in our team context. It is through this more inferential process, of locating relational dynamics being constructed between coaches and players, between captains and coaches and between members of the playing group, that we can advance our understanding of the dynamic realties of relating in high-performance sports teams.

Identifying cultural belief systems about how relationships work in high-performance sports teams

The final process we need to outline in this chapter concerns the level of interpersonal ideology and cultural knowledge. While it is a primary goal of this book to offer largely missing empirical illustrations of relating in action in sports teams, we also use these illustrations as empirical evidence for more theoretical purposes. For discourse analysts, one of the central purposes for accumulating illustrations of language in use is to probe underlying, abstract and taken-for-granted cultural belief systems or social norms that give rise to and/or are being signalled or (re)constructed in the practices we see in interactional data (Alvesson & Karreman, 2000; Fairclough, 1985, 2003a; Gee, 2018).

This more macro-, overarching layer of information or knowledge is often intangible, can be quite abstract, but hides in plain sight, always being oriented to and reinforced by individuals as they navigate their social interactions with others. From our accounts of the relational dynamics in a professional sports team, we reverse-engineer and pin down these taken-for-granted knowledge systems that people appear to be reflecting and establishing in their everyday interactional practices. In the process, we can put forward claims that might help to account for (and, in essence, make more tangible) the established belief systems that underlie how relationships work in the high-performance sporting culture.

To do this, we take the empirical illustrations of relational dynamics in our team and ask broader, more abstract and far-reaching questions about what these patterns suggest about how relationships work in high-performance sports teams. The discussion at this level will centre on locating what we might term abstract, unwritten rules or norms that appear to govern and that help to explain the social and interpersonal behaviour in this context. We have employed the term 'interpersonal ideology' (Poutiainen, 2015) to help separate the discussions we have at this level. Another useful label is meta-messages (Tannen, 1993a, 1993b, 2008), in our case about how relationships are working in the team, that are being communicated at higher levels and often indirectly in and through the behaviour people exhibit in their real-life interactional contexts. This level of analysis will be confined to the final chapter of this book, suitably providing a broader look across the individual findings chapters.

In developing claims at this level, we will again draw on the concepts of power and solidarity to put help organize the claims we make. The claims we put forward at this level are probably the closest discourse analysts get to putting forward anything that could be read as generalizable. As we are presenting the results of a deep and detailed look at a specific case, we cannot and do not claim generalizability, certainly not in any quantitatively understood sense of the word. Rather, the claims we put forward should be read as tentative cultural principles or cultural hypotheses that we offer to the interdisciplinary research field interested in relationships in high-performance sports teams that we hope will be tested, refined, challenged and revised in subsequent work as we continue to advance our knowledge of relationships in sporting contexts. As well as functioning as a point of departure for further research, we also hope these hypotheses function as useful points of reflection for our practitioner audience. Together with the more fine-grained analyses illustrated in the findings chapters, it is hoped these cultural hypotheses provide practitioners with the tools to better understand and critically reflect on the nature of relationships in their own contexts.

What can readers expect to encounter in the findings chapters?

With the integrated components of our analytical process outlined above, we are now ready to start our journey towards understanding the relational dynamics of our team and how these are being constructed in and through language. Before we close this chapter, though, a few notes on what exactly to expect in the findings chapters that follow might help prepare readers less accustomed to discourse analytical work. Within each findings chapter, readers will see:

- A sample of typical (unmarked) interactional dynamics exhibited in the interactions of *our* team, or, in some cases, patterns that showed interesting variation (marked) from the more typical practices,
- Verbatim transcripts of these interactional dynamics that help to illustrate how the activity types and interactional tasks of our team were enacted by people in and through language,
- Detailed analysis of the social actions particular individuals were performing as they worked towards the goals of these interactional activities/tasks. This includes close discussions of the turn-taking and turn-design features,
- Interpretive accounts of the relational meanings of power and solidarity that are evident and being constructed in and through the linguistic actions of speakers,

INTRODUCING OUR TOOLKIT: DISCOURSE ANALYSIS

- A discussion summarizing the relational dynamics observed in the data concerning the way particular relations of power and solidarity are being talked into being in our team

Readers should expect to see detailed transcriptions of our team's interactions and to read fine-grained accounts of the sociolinguistic (i.e. social action performed linguistically) behaviour of individuals in these interactions. The degree of detail linguists go to in order to unpack linguistic activity in transcripts can at times be a disorienting experience for readers less accustomed with discourse analytical work. However, this is not something discourse analysts are likely to apologize for, as it is perceived as a key strength of the work they do. Often the devil lies in the details and the detail that discourse analysts can provide into the sociolinguistic practices of people can make the taken-for-granted dynamics of social life more visible.

Wrapping up and looking forward

In this chapter, we have outlined the data set and analytical tools and processes we have drawn on to investigate how relationships work in high-performance sports teams. We have detailed the data set of authentic interactions between members of our professional New Zealand rugby team which will ultimately provide us with a source of naturally occurring data to study how relationships are working in our team. We have also introduced the analytical and conceptual tools we use to process this data, locating interactional dynamics between the coaches, captains and players that were evident in the ritual and everyday interactions of our team and the relational dynamics of power and solidarity that are being constructed in the process. We have also alerted readers of our intention to use our empirical findings to build an account of the underlying cultural values that are being reflected and (re)constructed in these interactional and relational dynamics.

In the next chapter, we begin our journey towards a greater understanding of how relationships are working in our team by starting to share the results of our analysis of the coach–player role-relationship. More specifically, we look at some of the ways power works or appears to work across the range of interactions between coaches and players.

3

How do coaches exercise control over players?

Constructing asymmetrical power relations through language

Introduction: Setting the scene

In this first findings chapter, we begin looking at patterns across the coach–player interactions of our team, paying particular attention to what these patterns tell us about power in the coach–player relationship. As we will demonstrate, an asymmetrical power relationship is being talked into being in our team, which sees the coach claiming and exercising power over players across all manner of interactional contexts. While such a power dynamic is frequently associated with coach–player relations, our goal in this chapter is to illustrate *how* that asymmetrical power relationship is being constructed by shining a light on some of the more mundane and taken-for-granted interactional practices in coach–player interactions.

We focus our attention in this chapter on the interactional practices that showed coaches exercising **control** over their players. Many of these practices show coaches dominating team talk spaces, enacting their own non-negotiable agenda, managing who (else) contributed to team interactions and leading players to particular decisions or conclusions on important team matters. We will also draw attention to the practices of players who through their contributions to team interactions co-construct this asymmetrical power relationship between coaches and players by establishing themselves as respectful followers of the will of the coach.

Coaches controlled the team's interactional floor

One of the most obvious interactional practices we observed across coach–player interactions was the overall right coaches claimed to control *when* interactions of the team were carried out, *how* they unfolded and *when* they were brought to a close. Whether it was training sessions, team meetings, match evaluation sessions or talk in the changing sheds on match days, coaches claimed the right to **initiate** interactions that were had at a team level, **deliver** their messages in these interactions unimpeded and uninterrupted, and **close** these interactions when they saw fit. They also restricted or offered limited opportunities for involvement from the players.

Extract 1 is a particularly clear and typical illustration of how control works or manifests itself in coach–player interactions. It comes from the beginning of a training session where the assistant coach/forwards coach (Greg) is outlining the training drill the team are about to engage in.

1.	**Greg**:	*come on* team *come in come in*
		{forwards assemble around the assistant coach}
2.		hey ah just a quick welcome to Red also
3.		so through his injury he's going to be aligned as part of the scrum coaching group
4.		so welcome to him
5.		so tonight's little brief *we're going to* split straight away front row and locks
6.		so *front row with Red*
7.		only apart for about four minutes or so
8.		then *we're going to come together and work* through the connections of ah prop lock and ah *just get to* a stabilized ah build a platform from being stable
9.		okay?
10.		and *that's our only go to for tonight*
11.		tomorrow night *we'll ah hit* the machine half a dozen times and *trigger in*
12.		alright?
13.		so *we'll have* locks loosies on the sled
14.		ah *front row over by the machine* please
15.		**{coach walks towards the scrum machine}**

Extract 1: [training session data] issuing instructions for a team training drill

One of the more obvious features of Extract 1 is that the coach is the only speaker. No one else was invited to contribute or took the opportunity of their own volition to contribute. This **amount of talk** is arguably a further illustration of the coach's power over players.

However, it is not until we look inside this interaction that we can reveal some of the more taken-for-granted interactional mechanisms of control. In line 1, we see the assistant coach **self-select** himself to speak, asks the team to assemble around him, before **initiating** an interaction that addresses the whole team. By implication, he asks them to cease the other activities they are engaged in (in this case, the unstructured warm-up activities or informal conversations they are having with others in the team) and come together as a group around the coach. He then uses the interaction to perform his agenda, in this particular instance welcoming a new coach to the team setup (in lines 1 to 4) and outlining the programme for the training session and drills he wants the team to do (in lines 5 to 11). He then **closes** the interaction by giving instructions to the different subgroups about where they need to be in order to start the first drill (in lines 13 and 14). He also indicates the interaction has finished by walking away from the group towards the scrum machine where he will lead a drill for a particular subgroup of the team (the locks and loosies).

These largely unremarkable interaction management practices are arguably one of the most taken-for-granted and unquestioned ways the coaches' control over players manifested itself in our team's interactions. Those in power enact their power over others by claiming exclusive rights over when an interaction needs to happen, how that interaction will proceed from start to finish and when it is finished. They bring the interaction to a close, shutting down opportunities to contribute to the interaction or, in this case, the activity being negotiated within it.

Through this process of tightly controlling the interactional floor, coaches were able to dominate the team's interactional spaces, using them to perform their agenda which becomes, by extension, the team's agenda. They offered minimal opportunities for involvement from the players in the interaction or in the development of that agenda, other than to invite them to indicate their comprehension of the instructions. Such actions, performed ritually in training sessions and across other interactional settings, perhaps imply that player involvement is unnecessary.

We do see some moves by the coach in Extract 1 that might be read as an attempt to offer the floor to the players, primarily in the form of **question tags** *okay* and *alright* in lines 9 and 12, respectively. Questions and question tags are ways in which the floor can be passed from one speaker to another as questions can function to invite contributions from others to the ongoing interaction. However, arguably, the question tags in this extract do not function to invite players to contribute to the ongoing interaction in any significant way, and instead function to elicit from the players an acceptance of what is a non-negotiable agenda being presented to them by the coach.

Based on their responses, as well, we could argue that the players do not appear to interpret these as invitations to contribute to the floor, perhaps to challenge, question or shape the agenda being outlined by the coach. Based on the *nodding* they do in response, they orient to these question tags as comprehension or confirmation checkers and duly indicate that they follow (and potentially accept) the agenda that is being laid out. In none of the agenda-setting episodes reviewed in our data, did players take up the **floor transition potential** provided by a question tag to take the floor from the coach and contribute or question the agenda.

Players, therefore, play their role in these recurring and ritual interactional addresses by the coach, supporting the coach's claims to control over their actions. They do this largely through their *silence* and by indicating their understanding and approval of the coach's instructions through *nodding* (not visible in the above transcript). In doing so, they co-construct these sequences of talk as instructional in nature – instructions from the coach to the players – and not as spaces where an agenda is negotiated or developed together. Their behaviour indicates an understanding that it is the coaches who have the rights to dictate and enforce an agenda on the players.

These practices, arguably, serve a very practical purpose in a sports team context of helping to coordinate the physical activities of twenty-plus individuals in the team, informing and organizing all individuals so they can arrange themselves as a group to prepare for and conduct, in this case, a training drill. However, interpersonally, such patterns and practices across the team's interactions leave no doubt as to who claims the power to decide what the wider group will do. The coach also uses floor restricting moves to impose his agenda on the players, a process that, in essence, interactionally establishes his authority over the players. As we will see in other extracts in this chapter and across the chapters of this book, many of these interactional practices permeate coach–player interactions in a number of other settings, helping the coach to control all manner of team activities, including situations like assessing performance, solving problems and making playing strategy decisions.

Coaches controlled who else contributed to the floor and when

Another way coaches controlled the interactional floor was by selecting who could contribute, when they could contribute, and, typically, the nature of that contribution. In Extract 2, we see an example of this practice in action from the closing stages of a training session. In this extract, we see the head coach (Tane) dominating the interaction but also inviting or offering the floor to the captain to address the team (in line 10).

HOW DO COACHES EXERCISE CONTROL OVER PLAYERS?

1.	**Tane**:	um any questions
2.		so we'll run through our we'll run through our more of our maps tomorrow night ah at six o'clock
3.		um I'll name the reserves tomorrow night when we come in
4.		but um some good learnings there boys==
5.		==the main thing is that when we when we play on Wednesday the main thing is that we're looking just to stay into our shape and bring into all the all the clean up drills that we've that we've just worked on with [coach 1]
6.		okay + so if we can stay in our shape take care of our ruck um + get lightening quick ball we should be able to um get them to edges and and moving their defensive side around
7.		{2.0}
8.		very good
9.		happy with tonight
10.		<u>um + anything from Seb</u> [**the captain**]
11.		<u>nah?</u>
12.	**Seb**:	oh just when ah + like we know tonight's about learning + obviously getting to know each other and shit
13.		but ah when we're doing the changeovers and stuff let's just get there you know
14.		straight change over run to- get to where we need to be so we just get straight into it get to the what we need to do and go home aye right?
15.		not this walk around change over bibs walk over alright?
16.		let's get into good habits aye
17.		we're into a professional environment now
18.		so changeover get there + rest there + and go again
19.	**Tane**:	<u>very good point</u>
20.		so when you're standing on the sideline boys you're actually learning and watching what's happening
21.		you're not there just having a break
22.		<u>{2.0}</u>
23.		<u>that's us</u>
24.		<u>well done</u>
25.	**Players**:	shot boys
26.	**Seb**:	hey hey
27.	**Players**:	ho

Extract 2: [training session data] closing a team training session

In the early stages of this extract (in lines 1 to 9), we see the head coach wrapping up the training session, outlining the process in the lead up to the next match and summarizing some key work-ons for that match. In lines 8 and 9, he provides his own summative evaluation of the training session, finishes his turn and then **offers** the floor directly to the captain, asking whether he has anything to add. The captain **takes up** the space offered to him by the coach and provides what appears to be a critical evaluation of the team's attitude and emphasizes the need for the group to develop professional habits in this environment (lines 12 to 18). In line 19, the coach re-claims the floor and **legitimizes** the captain's message. He then **elaborates** on this message, providing another way the players can demonstrate a professional attitude when waiting and watching team drills on the sideline (lines 20 to 21). Then, after a short period of silence, the head coach **closes** the training session (in lines 23 to 24). The captain then leads the team in their team chant and the players head to the changing sheds.

In this extract, while we do see another voice other than a coach contributing to the overall governance of the team, that voice is selected by the coach and therefore subject to coach control. In other words, the speaker did not self-select themselves to take a turn and address the group; rather, he was called upon and/or sanctioned by the coach to address the group. This practice was the most frequent way that other voices in the team were heard in team-wide interactions, particularly those interactions between coaches and players. We do see another, more general way players were invited to take the floor in line 1, where the head coach asked the players if they have *any questions*. In this instance, as was often the case, this more open invitation to ask questions is not taken up by the players and the coach reclaims the floor and continues to address the group. These two tightly controlled methods of offering the floor specifically for questions or selecting a particular individual to speak were the most frequent ways players accessed speaking turns in team-wide interactions in our data.

While these practices, particularly offering the floor to the captain free of any specific restrictions or requirements, indicate a willingness by the coach to share the floor with the players, the rules for addressing the team appear to vary between the coaches and the players. Coaches appear to sanction contributors to the floor, further constructing an understanding that it is the coach who controls the floor and, by extension, who contributes to governance of the team. Also, importantly, the person that is selected to address the group is not just anyone, but a specific member of the group – the captain – and one that also has a notional leadership role in the team. This may further establish an understanding that the team's interactional spaces are primarily occupied by those with legitimate and/or obvious claims to authority.

Additionally, by directing someone to take the floor, the coach may be further indexing his power and authority over the players. Being able to make impositions of this kind has long been shown to reflect and reconstruct institutional power and control, with those doing the imposing claiming rights to call on people to contribute as and when they see fit (J. Holmes & Stubbe, 2003; Vine, 2004). Even though the floor is passed to the captain in ways that imply it is offered and not necessarily imposed, the captain may feel obliged to speak having been called upon by the coach. One reading of the **false start** in line 12 of this extract may be that the player was not expecting to be called upon, and when he was he felt obliged to come up with something to say quickly.

There are other features in this extract that may be read as further evidence of tight control being exercised by the coach over the interactional floor. The timing of this invitation to speak is worth reflecting on in this instance. The invitation in Extract 2 is reserved for the closing stages of the training session, once all of the significant business of the training session has been completed and after the coach has made his own evaluative remarks and outlined the business for the next training session. Additionally, after the captain delivers his own message, it is **legitimized** by the coach (lines 19 to 21). This move could be read as an attempt by the coach to construct alignment between himself and the captain, a move which could function to positively manage his own relationship with the captain or to reinforce the leadership identity of the captain with the rest of the playing group. However, by explicitly sanctioning the message offered by the captain, the coach is also indirectly establishing his authority by adopting the position of evaluating the merits of the captain's message. No one else but the coach performs these message-sanctioning moves in the data we have collected, especially in these team addresses.

Taken together, the practices in Extract 2 further illustrate how coaches exercise control over the interactional floor and, by extension, exercise control over the players. By selecting particular speakers, the coach indirectly signals that access to the floor is not only restricted but that speakers who can address the team need to be sanctioned by the coach.

Coaches frequently used their talk to instruct or tell players what to do

In addition to controlling the floor and who else could join, much of the coaches' talk appeared to exhibit rights to directly control the players and their (future) actions. One of the most frequent speech actions that was deployed by coaches in coach–player team addresses was the **directive**, functioning to tell players what to do in ways that impose upon their future actions.

In Extract 1, there are **explicit directives** in line 1 (*come on* and *come in*) where players are told to stop their interactions and assemble around the assistant coach. He also gives instructions to players throughout the interaction about what they need to do in the ensuing training drill. Many of these instructions were shaped more indirectly. In lines 5, 8, 11 and 13, the coach issues instructions using statements (i.e. *we're going to split straight away* and *we'll have locks and loosies on the sled*). We speak more about the meanings and functions of this stylistic choice by coaches in Chapter 8. However, for our purposes here, the prevalence of directives (whether direct or indirect) further illustrates the coach claiming a taken-for-granted right to tell players what to do.

In Extract 3 we see another, perhaps clearer example of head coach (Tane) attempting to tell players what to do, this time from a team strategy meeting. In this extract, the team are gathered in the meeting room and are viewing diagrams on a PowerPoint presentation on the big screen showing where players are to assemble for kick-offs.

1. **Tane**: so just firstly just for our kick-off set up
2. {*starts projector and PowerPoint*}
3. so if we're kicking off
4. we've got two right footers on our team
5. so our eleven **will** always case the kick
6. um and our calls are {**strategic information withheld here, outlining short and long kick off strategies and the calls for these different options**}
7. okay? +
8. so um we**'ll** be kicking to {strategy name} mostly tomorrow unless um unless something happens
9. so on that eleven goes and um everyone else chases and connects
10. um fifteen **will** come in and take the high ball for the ah return kick
11. eight **will** be in the middle to carry and ten **will** drop and tackle right side
12. so fourteen if you just um go maybe half way and um either fetch or go back into the line ++ Joey +++
13. is that clear? +++
14. so the reason why we've done this is that um if they kick back um two can get through there straight away

15.	eight might um might come to that edge as well and six and seven might go back to that edge
16.	and the um the big fellas just just track up back down down to the middle
17.	okay?
18.	so make sure that you're + you're (nutting) your roles out
19.	{4.0} {coach moves the PowerPoint forward}
20.	just on our kick off receive
21.	{2.0}
22.	um we've got our + our wing **will** be up... [**meeting continues**]

Extract 3: *[team meeting data] outlining kick-off strategy for an upcoming match*

In this team meeting setting, we see similar interactional management practices to those witnessed in Extract 1 from the Assistant Coach. The coach initiates the interaction and uses it to pursue and achieve his agenda (or the agenda he sees as pertinent for the team). The practice of restricting player involvement in the interaction to acknowledging their understanding and/or compliance through the use of confirmation-checking question-tags is also evident again (see, for example, lines 7, 13 and 17). In some of these cases in this extract, we see the coach leave more space for the players to respond than we saw in the first example, perhaps to signal to players that there is space to ask questions if they are not sure or space to challenge strategic decisions being laid out, should they wish, but players did not take up these opportunities in the interaction.

However, what we were mainly drawn to in this extract was the degree to which the coach attempts to control the player's actions on the field. What is clear in this extract, as it was in Extract 1, is the degree of control the coach enacts over players actions, this time telling them where they need to be for the various kick-off sequences of the match. The coach again draws on **statements** to deliver these directive or instructional utterances, but he arguably adds further imposition on the players by using the **modal verb** *will* to impose on players their responsibility to be in a particular position (i.e. *fifteen will come in* and *we'll be kicking to* {strategy name}). While, on the one hand, the use of *will* encodes the future match that the coach is referring to (i.e. *in the upcoming match we will do this*), in this instance they simultaneously encode a strong obligation from the speaker (the coach) on the addressee (the players in question) to assemble in a given position and leave little room for player optionality. We also see present simple tense being used to function in similar ways (i.e. eleven *goes*, everyone else *chases*), appearing to express the habitual actions the coach expects to see from the players. Again, the imposition is strong and the implication is that the players need to follow these instructions that the coach is outlining for the team's kick-offs.

These actions are again likely to be viewed first and foremost as a way that teams can achieve clarity and coordinate the actions of multiple individuals for the benefit of the group. A clear strategy at kick-offs is going to help ensure multiple individuals do not bump into each other when going for the ball. However, again, we are left with little doubt as to whose responsibility and right it is to make, in this particular case, strategy decisions that impact the whole team. Player's actions on the field, in this instance, appear to be being controlled down to the finest degree. The ideological basis for this behaviour by coaches may lie in beliefs about the greater degree of expert power coaches can and do lay claim to. With their greater amounts of experience, coaches may feel they have earned the right to impose upon players strategy decisions they consider to be the best course of action for the group. We pick up themes of expert power difference between coaches and players in the next chapter.

The players accept this degree of control over them by the coaches, at least publicly, performing their acceptance of the coach's control by *remaining silent* and *nodding* when receiving the coach's instructions. In one instance from our data, we saw a player encoding the coach's wants or demands over their actions when asking a confirmation-checking question to confirm the coach's instructions. Extract 4 comes from a match evaluation session where the head coach (Tane) has been discussing footage from a previous match with the view to addressing a particular issue (not shown here). In lines 1 and 2, Tane checks that the players have comprehended his commentary and, in line 4, offers the floor to players for *comments*. At this stage, a player (Mickey) takes up the invitation and clarifies a point, explicitly marking the head coach's authority over the player's on-field actions in the design of his questions (see underlined utterances).

1. **Tane**: okay
2. does that make sense to everyone
3. [2.0]
4. any comments
5. **Mickey**: just um
6. **Tane**: Mickey
7. **Mickey**: just um just last night how <u>you said we shouldn't</u> get into their fifteen
8. on that one <u>do you want</u> the half to hit us and then tank

9.		or <u>do you want</u> us to tank and then /(unclear)\
10.	**Tane**:	/yeah I think\ if we get into that fifteen then that's a lot more
11.		work that you have to come + come to

Extract 4: [team meeting data] reviewing footage from a prior match

As well as being one of the few occasions where this space offered by the coach was taken up by a player, the way the player shapes his confirmation-checking questions clearly marks the coach as powerful and in control. The actual strategy being articulated by Mickey may not be clear (if you are not familiar with rugby) but what is clear is that the player constructs the coach's power or control over players by asking him what the coach *wants* (in lines 8 and 9). He also makes reference to another instruction from the previous night's meeting in line 7, again marking the coach's authority over the players' decisions and actions on the field. Such choices arguably make the meaning that coach control over players and their actions on the field is seen as an accepted and normative and perhaps functional aspect of the coach–player relationship.

Coaches controlled decision-making sequences

Linked to the above imposition on player actions during the match, it also was apparent in coach–player interactions that coaches exercised control over many of the decisions that needed to be made. In Extract 3, we saw an illustration of this where the head coach outlined the kick-off strategy, effectively making the decision on behalf of the players and without involving them. With this pattern in mind, Extract 5 grabbed our attention largely because it was one of the few occasions when there was some involvement by the players in a decision-making episode. Ultimately, though, as we will see as this extract unfolds, the coach still exercises the ultimate control over the eventual decision.

Extract 5 comes from the middle of a training session in which the forwards and the temporary forwards coach (Kaipo or Po) are running lineout drills. In this extract, Po is laying out instructions for the players regarding how they should position themselves as they perform lineouts (lines 1 to 10). However, he then engages the players in a decision-making episode regarding how they should position themselves when they have received the ball from a lineout (whether to go *inside* or *outside*). Red, the team's scrum coach, is also present during this interaction. We spend time unpacking the way this decision-making sequence unfolds, particularly lines 12 to 27, further below, as it is quite intricate and complex, but ultimately provides us with an interesting example or instance of how coaches exercise and are afforded control over decision making in the team.

1.	**Po**:	good
2.		okay we'll go with the second movement okay==
3.		==everyone happy with the number one
4.		okay good
5.		number two we've got two bailouts + okay
6.		so the prop bailout
7.		yeah we'll just walk through guys
8.		come forward NAME bail out
9.		right to the front on the five + okay==
10.		==only two calls
11.	**Players**:	{players start talking amongst themselves}
12.	**Po**:	happy
13.		{2.0}
14.	**Red**:	{to coach 3} go inside?
15.	**Po**:	yeah go inside
16.		{1.5}
17.		do you guys want to go inside or go out
18.	**Jase**:	whatever
19.	**Po**:	ah well this is your team baby
20.		what do you want to do
21.		**{players and Coach 2 discuss amongst themselves}**
22.	**Abel**:	we'll just go in + yeah
23.	**Po**:	okay if we drive + what's the best scenario for us
24.	**Players**:	**{some players answer}** out
25.	**Po**:	go out
26.		okay let's go out
27.		okay + good
28.		okay on you NAME

Extract 5: [training session data] making a technical decision

This interaction gets particularly interesting from line 12 onwards where the coach checks if the players are *happy* with what he has just laid out. This is met with some inaudible discussion amongst the players, some of whom appear to be discussing an aspect of what has been outlined by Po with the scrum coach (Red). From that discussion emerges a technical point or a decision that needs to be made about how the players should organize themselves once they have received the ball from the lineout jumper – inside or outside.

In line 14, the scrum coach (Red), perhaps summarizing the discussion with the players, asks the forwards coach to confirm whether the players should *go inside*, a move which positions Po (the forwards coach) in this instance as the primary decision maker for the team. In line 15, the forwards coach confirms that the players should *go inside*, making the decision for them. However, after a short pause, he then effectively takes that decision off the table and asks the players what they would like to do (line 17). In line 18, one of the players answers the coach indicating that either option is fine (*whatever*). This frames the decision-making episode as again down to the coach and sends the decision back to Po. However, the coach again sends the decision back to the players, telling them that it is their *team baby* and that *they* should decide what they *want to do*. We detected that Po may have been unhappy with the lethargic response from Jase and the lack of ownership after he had offered the players the opportunity to make a decision.

At this point, and after being pushed for a second time by the forwards coach to make a decision, the players discuss amongst themselves (in line 21), also consulting with the scrum coach again, and in line 22, one of the players provides an answer to the coach (*we'll just go in*). Having made the decision, and one that the coach originally also made, the matter is technically addressed. However, at this point, the coach retakes the floor in line 23 and problematizes the decision that the players have made. He uses a particular scenario, presumably to help draw attention to an issue inherent to the decision they have made. At this point, in line 24, the players quickly change their decision and the coach accepts this decision in lines 25 to 27 (*let's go out, okay, good*) before resuming the training drill.

This extract is more complex than others we have looked at in this chapter and other coach–player interactions we will look at in subsequent chapters, largely because there is a greater amount of back-and-forth interaction and negotiation between coaches and players. It may also be seen on the one hand as a good example of joint negotiation and learning taking place, as a decision is reached in and through interaction as multiple individuals consider the circumstance underlying a particular decision. However, ultimately, it also shows the coach again exercising overall control over the outcome of the interaction, in this case a decision-making episode. While the players are involved in this decision-making sequence and are even temporarily positioned as owners of the team and primary decision makers, their authority to make decisions appears to be contingent on their ability to make the right decision in the eyes of the coach. Such practices, despite being more dynamic in nature, are arguably a further exhibition of the power and control coaches exercised over players in our team.

Coaches controlled how performances were evaluated

Finally in this chapter, we also found evidence throughout our data of coaches exercising control over the collective assessment of performances in the team's important performance evaluation and problem-solving interactions. They did this again by claiming rights to dominate and control the interactional floor, which, in these performance-evaluation settings, saw them imposing *their* interpretations or **assessments** of performance on players and issuing their own directives designed to solve problems *they* found concerning.

Extract 6 comes from a half-time team talk in the changing room where assessments of performance were a central activity. In this extract, a subgroup of the team, the forwards, has assembled in one half of the changing room. As the players are coming in, taking on water and finishing their unstructured conversations, the assistant/forwards coach (Greg) takes the floor and initiates the group's more structured interaction. While there is a great deal of technical information in the extract that may puzzle readers (and researchers!) unfamiliar with rugby, talk in these half-time interactions is clearly geared towards identifying issues and outlining solutions or corrective actions for the group to implement. It is also clear how the labour in these interactions is distributed, with the coaches again claiming (and being afforded) the rights to dominate and control these interactions.

32.	Greg:	we've got to load the pressure first and then we can release it
33.		we're just fucking happy to sit there
34.		I wanna get us to lock up turn the knob everyone get the tension on the gun we explode + okay
35.		we're just fucking sitting there and hovering around and letting them do a couple of fucking rolls under us
36.		let's just lock it up and then explode alright
37.		extend out
38.		um {1.5} and just make sure that that quality's at the base +
39.		Topper you're coming into eight now anyway alright just so we can fucking launch from it + okay
40.		ah lineout time?
41.	Seb (captain):	our tempo's not (unclear)
42.	Abel:	just clarity of roles as well
43.	Greg:	yeah
44.	Players:	{echoing in agreement} yeah

45.	Greg:	we've gotta get the call early on everyone acknowledging that that's the call like==
46.		==we've fucking looked so disconnected + alright
47.		get it in your mind fucking sign off on it and then fucking pull the trigger + okay
48.		um + one and two that that was looking like it was on down there
49.		so the slip's definitely there to make use of now
50.		but again role clarity and pull the fucking trigger + okay
51.		um + on theirs we've just got to get a bit more aggressive also
52.		let's fucking (.) Seb is getting in there and getting a couple of fucking in the baskets and getting his hand in there
53.		but (unclear) (smash the glass)
54.	Player ?:	mm
55.	Greg:	fucking get across and fucking start giving them shit ball
56.		prob- probably same- same feeling around scrums the same feeling around lineouts we're just a bit nice==
57.		==we're just happy to let them play away
58.		just fucking get in + alright

Extract 6: [match-day data] half-time team talk with the forwards subgroup

Throughout this extract, Greg, the assistant coach, is delivering **pejorative statements** of the forward's playing performance (see, for example, lines 3, 5, 15 and 26). These arguably function as critical assessments of aspects of the team's performance that the coach has noticed and is not happy with in his viewing of the match. We also see a number of directives being issued in this sequence of talk which, in this performance evaluation interactional context, arguably function as solutions to the problems identified by the coach. However, the use of strongly worded directives shapes these solutions as impositions or obligatory actions required by the coaches on the players.

Through this behaviour, we have further evidence of the coach claiming exclusive rights to control the players, in this case by controlling sequences of talk where performances are evaluated (or interpreted) and solutions are designed. Through this control, it is the coach's assessments, their view of events, their understanding of the issues players are experiencing or creating, their intel and data-collecting processes that are being drawn on to shape the interactions between coaches and players, in what is an important problem-identification and problem-solving sequence of talk in this professional context.

As well as dominating these performance evaluation sequences, coaches also restricted and/or narrowed the contributions of players in these sequences. Unlike in previous extracts, where the players were not invited to contribute to the ongoing sequences of talk or did not take the floor from the coach, in this extract, in line 9, we see the coach directly hand over the floor to the players to comment on the line out (another set play in rugby). In this case, some players **self-select** themselves to speak and offer what can be read as their own pejorative assessments of their performance with this set play. However, again, while there are more speakers selecting themselves to speak and contributing to the ongoing interaction in this extract, the coach is still exercising a considerable amount of control over the interaction at hand. For one, the coach has handed the floor over to the players to perform a very specific task and talk about a very specific topic, likely one that he himself wants to talk about and discuss. This is especially the case if we assess what follows in lines 14 to 27 where the coach provides a criticism of aspects of the team's play in the line out. Players were, therefore, handed the floor in a controlled fashion, one that imposed upon them a particular topic to discuss (i.e. one not of their own choosing) and, arguably, encouraging them to take and offer a negative assessment of it.

The players also **relinquish the floor** rather quickly after offering their pejorative assessments, handing back control to the coach for more extensive turns at talk. This pressure to relinquish the floor is not necessarily encoded in the question syntax, and the coach may very well have accepted longer more critical accounts from a player. Instead, what might be being signalled here is a cultural understanding by the players that these half-time talks belong to the coaches and that any invitation the players are offered to speak is primarily designed to briefly supplement coach assessments or to display compliance, comprehension or alignment with the coach's remarks. In this instance, after two players offer very brief, general remarks on the lineout, the coach then **reclaims the floor** and launches into another long sequence of evaluative commentary, again offering directives for how to address the problems he has identified.

In Extract 7, a continuation of the half-time team talk in Extract 6, we see further evidence that the players view these interactional spaces, and the tasks performed within them, as belonging to the coaches. In this extract, there are a number of what are referred to as **transition-relevance places** (Clayman, 2012), where players could, technically speaking, take the floor due to a gap in the interaction being left by the current speaker (in our case, the assistant/forwards coach, Greg). Transition-relevance places (TRP) are moments in an interaction where a current speaker signals that they are coming to or have come to the end of their turn and the floor is available to be claimed by another speaker. Other speakers usually look out for and predict these TRPs to help them time their entry into the interaction so as to minimize potential interruption of the current speaker. In Extract 6, we see a number of question tags (*okay*, *alright*) and a period of **silence** (line 40) that are, technically speaking, opportunities for other speakers to enter the interaction. However, as can be seen, these opportunities are not taken up by the players.

28.	Greg:	and that adds to where we need to get to with um anything around
29.		this bloody breakdown mess + we're just accepting shit to happen there now + okay
30.		when we present we fucking hold onto the ball until it's gone and or we can get the pop
31.		we don't want these guys kicking it
32.		and we need to get into some (unclear)
33.		just fucking start bursting them a little bit + alright
34.		and we're going to bring a policy in which we should've or what we've trained let's make sure that we're getting into that space
35.		the soldier's gotta fucking keep working forward
36.		and if we can we set early on our tens we'll fold in and fucking counter it
37.		put three through there + alright
38.		it's just too it's just too easy ++ okay
39.		we don't wanna be that we wanna be a contestable team
40.		{3.0}
41.		okay?
42.		and just when they get us you see their policy coming out the back and they're holding us
43.		we've gotta fight to fucking free ourselves + alright
44.		so the whole lot the key message in everything we're talking about is fucking lift up the aggression
45.		let's get a bit more fucking angry and and do a bit of fight on them

With specific reference to the question tags, the fact that players do not take the floor at these moments in the interaction suggests that they are not interpreted by the players as transition relevance places, perhaps reflecting a broader understanding that the floor during half-time team talks belongs to the coach. Rather, they appear to be interpreted by the players as pauses in a monologue (in the case of silences) or confirmation checkers or even compliance markers (in the case of question tags following a directive). Through the latter of these practices the coach seeks an acknowledgement the players are following his (long and uninterrupted) evaluative remarks.

Such a pattern suggests that players view the coach as having the right or the authority to dominate and direct these performance evaluation sequences, and they respect that authority by constructing or playing the subservient role that is simultaneously being constructed for them by the coach. The silence in line 40 is also particularly telling in this regard. After holding the floor for a significant period of time, in line 39, the coach concludes his evaluative commentary and there is a period of three seconds of silence – a long silence in what is a fast-paced and time-restricted interactional event. Even at this more obvious and potentially legitimate transition relevance place, players do not take up the opportunity to self-select themselves to take the floor and join in with the performance evaluation.

These interactional practices are perhaps further evidence of how the coaches control the interactional spaces of the team and foreground, in this specific case, themselves as primary problem identifier and problem solver. Not taking up these opportunities to take the floor could, of course, mean that players do not have anything to add on the particular issue being discussed. Or, it could reflect more of the cultural understanding that diagnosing issues, in the team-wide interactional activities, is within the purview of the coach. In any case, these dynamics of a dominant coach and subservient players do construct a less dynamic floor and in the process a less dynamic approach to diagnosing problems and identifying solutions the team are experiencing.

Wrapping up: Interactional mechanisms of control: How coaches construct asymmetrical power relations with their players

In this chapter we have begun our mission to shine a light on the interactional practices of our professional New Zealand rugby team and use these to identify relational dynamics that are being constructed, negotiated and managed in and through these interactional dynamics. In this chapter, we began our analysis of a significant role-relationship in professional sports teams – the coach–player relationship – by looking at interactional practices evident across a range of interactions between coaches and players in our team.

From this survey of key recurring interactional practices in our data, we have illustrated how coaches regularly claimed control and/or were afforded control by players of the interactional floor. Coaches dominated the interactions, controlling when they would take place and how they would progress from start to finish. In the process of interacting with players, we also saw evidence of coaches issuing non-negotiable and largely unidirectional agendas, instructions, assessments of performance and strategy decisions for the team to follow. In such instances, coaches would position players as recipients of these agendas, instructions and assessments and not as parties capable of jointly shaping them. They also controlled the degree, topic and nature of any input from the players to interactions that did involve player voices and exercised control over who contributed, sanctioning those who were able to contribute to overall team governance activities.

These practices or **mechanisms of control** by coaches arguably reflect what is a familiar and often-cited relational dynamic between coaches and players in high-performance sports teams – asymmetrical power by coaches over players. By establishing control over the shared interactions of the group and the interactional tasks within, coaches establish or talk their power over the players into being. However, players also play an important role in this process, actively performing a subservient or subordinate role in these interactions, by affording the coach the space to perform these tasks, accepting the agenda, instructions and performance assessments outlined or issued to them by the coaches, and adding their voice to the interaction as and when it was required or requested. These practices by the players help to perform a subordinate role that aligns with, accepts and ultimately co-constructs a shared understanding of the asymmetrical power relations between themselves and the coaches.

Making the claim that coaches are establishing an asymmetrical power relationship over players in our team is certainly not groundbreaking, nor was it intended to be the central purpose of this chapter. This asymmetrical power relationship is a familiar, recognizable and well-cited characteristic of social structures in sports teams (REFS). Rather, in line with the goals of this book, we hope readers walk away from this chapter with a greater awareness of *how* this asymmetrical relationship can be performed, enacted and co-constructed through very taken-for-granted and deeply ingrained interactional practices. The extracts presented above illustrate where coaches exercise control over players (i.e. in what settings and interactional tasks) and how this control is established through a range of specific interactional dynamics and practices in the team's shared interactional spaces. There are undoubtedly other situations in which coaches exercise control and other interactional mechanisms through which that control is performed or enacted, several of which we introduce and discuss in subsequent chapters. However, in this first findings chapter, in a book dedicated to unpacking interactional practices, we have provided readers with an insight into core, recurring practices we identified in our data set and ones they will encounter in subsequent chapters of this book as we delve deeper into the interactional and relational dynamics of our team.

The findings presented above, in this first foray into the data, also hopefully provide a useful indication for what readers can expect in the chapters to come. However, it is important to reiterate that what we are presenting here is and should not be read as criticism or critical in nature. Our primary goal is to reveal practices and interpret their social implications and significance – *not* to criticize them. Having said that, there is research and increasing amounts of reflection from practitioners that suggest sharp asymmetrical power relations between coaches and players, of the kind illustrated above, may not be fit for purpose in a high-performance sporting context (Balaguer et al., 2012; Duda, 2013; Hodge et al., 2014; Lee et al., 2013; Schofield, 2017). This debate around power and empowerment of players is in its infancy and is in need of greater theoretical and empirical attention. However, we hope that the interactional practices we have shone a light on in this chapter, and the asymmetrical power relations they construct, can help to inform and guide these debates and discussions going forward. In particular we hope the practices we have drawn attention to can help practitioners design the power dynamics in more aware ways, by pointing to concrete practices that can be targeted should consolidation or change to asymmetrical coach–athlete power dynamics be desired.

In the next chapter we continue to look at the coach–player relationship, this time looking closely at an interactional resource that has been identified as central to the task of coaching – **questions**. In the following chapter, as we have done so here, we unpack interactional dynamics in **question–answer sequences** between coaches and players in a range of performance evaluation settings, using the findings to further assess the relational dynamics of coach–player relations in our team. As we will see, the theme of control is again evident with questioning styles, patterns and practices help to further reinforce coach control over players.

4

Exercising power through questioning

How coaches *use* their questions

Introduction

In this chapter, we continue to shine a light on the way the coach–player relationship worked in our team, this time by focusing closely on the way **questions** were used in coach–player interactions. Questions and the answering patterns they elicit from players are a useful interactional resource to focus on when attempting to understand how institutional role-relationships work. Other researchers have shown how the authentic questioning patterns exhibited by individuals in a workplace context can encode all manner of information about the organizational relations (J. Holmes & Chiles, 2010). In our institutional context of high-performance sport, questions have also been cited as a key feature of the register of coaching (Heath & Langman, 1994; O'Connor et al., 2021) and were frequently used by coaches in their interactions with players, making them a relevant interactional resource to further unpack insights about how the coach–player relationship is working in our team.

In this chapter, we explore how question and answer patterns played out in a series of activities where they were frequently and variably deployed – **performance evaluation settings** like match evaluation meetings and half-time team talks. In particular, we present analysis of the functions coach questions appeared to be performing in these performance-evaluation sequences of talk and use these functions to speculate further on the coach–player relationship being constructed in the process.

In the previous chapter, we provided evidence of how an asymmetrical power relationship was being constructed between coaches and players in our team, in and across a range of interactional settings and in and through a range of interactional practices. The findings from our analysis of question functions (and the player's answering patterns) in this chapter provide a further illustration of that asymmetrical power dynamic and how questions are being deployed to construct asymmetrical power relations.

However, in presenting and explaining the findings of this analysis, we will also consider the various dimensions of the coaching role that certain questioning practices signal. These dimensions could be seen as sub-roles of the coach–player role-relationship each of which sees the coaches adopt a sub-role that in turn positions them as more powerful than the players. In this chapter, we present four dimensions or sub-roles that coaches appeared to enact or perform in and through questioning practices. These sub-roles – coach as educator, coach as chief problem-solver, coach as sheriff and coach as motivator – allow us to develop a finer-grained understanding of the ways in which coaches were enacting power over their players in these important performance evaluation interactions by drawing attention to the privileged positions (or roles) they adopted in the governance structure of the team.

Coach as educator: Using designedly incomplete questions to establish shared knowledge

One of the more typical functions of coach questions in the performance evaluation settings was to elicit (and verbally) establish shared knowledge using **display questions** (Boyd & Rubin, 2006) or **designedly incomplete utterances** (Koshik, 2002) (defined further below). Extract 1, from a half-time team talk, provides a useful illustration of this interactional practice. In this extract, we see the head coach (Tane), in line 1 (and again in line 3), using a question to check or ask players to *display* their knowledge of a technical aspect of play.

1. **Tane**: [**QUESTION**] just the last thing what's the key for the choke tackle?
2. {3.0}
3. [**QUESTION**] so how do we know if it's gonna if it's a choke tackle or not?
4. **Leaf**: [**RESPONSE**] comms
5. **Maz**: [**RESPONSE**] yeah comms + call it

6.	**Tane**:	[**EVALUATION**] yeah [**ELABORATION**] gotta blimmin get the ref to buy into it + okay
7.		as soon as he says choke then we're in it for the long haul
8.		that's when we go down and we don't let go of that ball
9.		okay but get the get the ref to buy into that too

Extract 1: [match day data] talk from the end of a half-time team talk

In line 1, the question put to the players requires one of them to provide a piece of missing information regarding a technical play (the choke tackle, holding an opposition player up off the ground in order to gain a turnover of the ball) in order to satisfy the coach that this knowledge is understood, at least by someone in the playing group. In this instance, the coach tries more than once to get the players to display this knowledge, arguably putting on record his expectation that this knowledge should be shared or understood by the group. When no one answers after his first attempt, and there is a period of silence, instead of giving the answer himself, the coach reformulates the question in line 3. This might be a further indication that he expects the playing group to know this information and be able to recite it when cued. In lines 4 and 5, two players provide the right **response**, which, in line 6, is confirmed or positively **evaluated** by the coach. The coach then goes on to **elaborate**, providing additional details and directives to the players regarding what to do when they need to execute this particular play.

In Extract 2, this time from a match review session where performance evaluation was also a key activity, a similar pattern can be seen.

1.	**Tane**:	okay so if we have a look here ++ you know that's +++ that's
2.		just one step in and moving
3.		so that's almost gonna be a + that's almost going to be a voluntary tackle
4.		so if that happens ++ and I've got no problem with this + got
5.		no problem with this
6.		[**QUESTION**] but ++ if it happens where where should the penetration come from
7.	**Salu**:	[**RESPONSE**] the tip support
8.	**Tane**:	[**EVALUATION**] yeah ++ [**ELABORATION**] so these guys
9.		should be you know if this guy's standing still then these guys need to be penetrating and getting the tips on out there

10.	okay + cos if you have a look ++ being there + you know these
11.	guys are all in
12.	here's a little bit of a gap that we can get into ++ okay

Extract 2: [team meeting data] talk during a match evaluation meeting (of previous match)

In lines 1 to 3, we see the head coach speaking to a video clip, providing a running commentary, pausing and replaying footage and adding a series of evaluative messages. In lines 4 to 6, based on the commentary and footage, he directs a **question** to the players that again requires them to demonstrate the extent of the knowledge in the group concerning another technical aspect of play. In line 7, a player provides a **response** which, in line 8, is then confirmed or positively **evaluated** by the coach as the right answer. After a short silence, the coach then reclaims the floor and **elaborates**, offering additional technical explanation (lines 8 to 12) and checking comprehension and compliance along the way through question tags like 'okay' (lines 10 and 12).

Questioning sequences of this kind were littered throughout our data and might show the coach performing an aspect of their role that is concerned with educating the players based on shortcomings he has identified in the playing performance. This label of educator may be appropriate based on the fact that this sequence of **question–response–evaluation–elaboration** has been identified in other educational settings (Candela, 1998; Sinclair & Coulthard, 1992; Wells, 1993). Questions of this kind have also been variably labelled by researchers as exam questions (Puchta & Potter, 1999), display questions (Boyd & Rubin, 2006), known information questions, or **designedly incomplete questions** (Koshik, 2002). Using the latter of these labels, we view the coach's questions as deliberately, strategically or purposefully designed to test the degree of shared knowledge usually regarding a piece of technical information. For the interaction to proceed, the addressees need to provide the correct piece of information and illustrate for all involved (both coaches and players) that the group shares (or now shares) this piece of information or knowledge. In the process, it is perhaps the assumption that those who did not know the answer will now know it and that everyone, including those that did know the answer, will now be aware of the importance the coach attaches to idea conveyed in the questioning sequence.

Puchta and Potter (1999) contrast these types of question to 'real' questions which in contrast are seen as genuine attempts by the question-asker to seek information that is unknown to them. In the above cases, the coach is not seeking new information he does not have. Rather he is seeking confirmation that the players have this important information. The agreement token, *yeah*, uttered by the coach in line 6 in Extract 1 and line 8 in Extract 2, is particularly telling for understanding that these questions are not genuine or 'real' information seekers. His response indicates that he knew the piece of information he was seeking and was primarily testing the players also knew it. In both cases, a player provides the right answer, satisfying the interactional requirements of these sequences, allowing the coach to go on and build up additional knowledge around the idea or issue that has been highlighted in the question.

Such a practice arguably constructs an educational dimension to the coach's role, whereby through his use of these designedly incomplete questions the coach is raising awareness or reminding the group of important and relevant aspects of the shared technical knowledge that he perhaps feels are not on display or that the group need to be more conscious of. In the process of adopting this educational role, the coach is claiming, constructing and performing a greater degree of epistemic authority or technical knowledge than his players.

However, the actual use of questions as a linguistic device to drive these performance evaluation sequences is also important to reflect on here. The coach could, arguably, shape these performance evaluation sequences quite differently, perhaps by simply using direct acts of criticism. Why is it, then, that coaches, particularly the head coach, draw on question-fronted sequences in our team? It may be that by using questions, coaches can more explicitly orient to the educational dimension of his role, perhaps by drawing on associations of these practices in other educational settings. Alternatively, it may be that questions help coaches to indirectly perform feedback of a critical nature (a point we will pick up further in the next section). Critical feedback like '*you are not providing the support at the tip*' may be more palatable and less face-threatening as an act of feedback when it is dressed up and performed indirectly in question–answer sequences. For a team that is newly assembled, this may be an important relationship management resource.

However, what is clear is that these questioning patterns further foreground the coach's powerful role in the team, indexing or pointing specifically to power associated with the culturally recognizable sub role of teacher or educator. As controllers of these designedly incomplete questions, coaches are able to dictate what is discussed and exercise control over the role and contribution of the players in the ongoing interaction. In the process, the coaches elevate their own status as experts, prominently position their vantage point and expertise for addressing the issues of the team, identify solutions for the players to problems they as coaches have noticed (primarily in elaboration slots) and exercise control over the players future actions in these performance evaluation sequences. As an interactional resource, then, these questions–answer patterns and the educational role-relationship they construct between the coach and the players are a further mechanism in the establishment of asymmetrical relations of power.

Coach as chief problem-solver: Using questions to direct attention to problems

An interlinked feature of the use of coach questions is that they nearly always seemed to pre-empt or anticipate talk about problems or issues. We saw this in the two examples above, where in each of the extracts there was a clear orientation in the talk to identifying and addressing a problem the coach had noticed. By being the custodian of the questions in these problem-solving sequences, the coach not only constructs himself as educator but also as the team's **chief problem solver** in the process. This dominance of evaluation and assessment of performances was also mentioned in Chapter 3.

Players also illustrated an understanding that questions asked by the coach, regardless of whether they appeared neutral in their form, should be interpreted as the beginning of a sequence of problem solving or critical reflection. In Extract 3, from a half-time team talk between the head coach (Tane) and the backs subgroup, we see an example of the coach and players using and orienting to questions as invitations to critique aspects of performance targeted by the question.

1.		*{Players come into the changing room and are discussing the first half amongst themselves. The coach enters the group and the players draw their interaction to a close}*
2.	**Tane**:	sooo ++ everyone had a chat
3.		[**QUESTION**] what do reckon of our skills
4.	**Maz**:	[**RESPONSE**] poor
5.	**Tane**:	[**EVALUATION**] pretty poor
6.	**Leaf**:	no execution
7.	**Tane**:	[**QUESTION**] yep + why do you think
8.	**Leaf**:	[**RESPONSE**] oh they're bringing line speed so we're just under pressure
9.	**Tane**:	[**EVALUATION**] yep
10.	**Player ?**:	yeah
11.	**Maz**:	we talked about that
12.	**Tane**:	[**ELABORATION**] even even with line speed if we get our fucking catch pass fucking accurate which + we should still be able to + get on the outside of them + okay
13.		make sure that + off the lineouts + it's no use + and you need to tell the forwards +

14.	it's no use them going to the front of the lineout and then you're fucking digging and giving us shit ball
15.	if it's going to the front of the lineout we need to go tank + okay

Extract 3: [match day data] talk from the beginning of a half-time team talk

In this extract, as in Extracts 1 and 2, the coach again uses questions to direct the players towards the aspect of play he wishes to raise for critical assessment. In line 2, after asking the players to close their conversations with one another the coach asks the players what they think of the team's general skill level in the first half. This question is, grammatically at least, quite neutral in its design, one that, on the surface, does not encourage or lean addressees towards a positive or negative response. However, in line 4, a critical assessment (*poor*) is provided by an experienced player in the team (Maz), perhaps reconstructing the broader understanding that the coach would not have raised the topic if he did not have an issue with it.

The head coach then picks this term *poor* up and mirrors it with the **modifier** *pretty*. In this case, *pretty* arguably functions in a New Zealand English sense as *really* or *very* poor. At this point, another player (Leaf) extends the assessment of their skills, suggesting, more specifically, that the team are not *executing* their core skills. This then prompts a second question to the players asking why they think their execution rates are poor. The same experienced player (Leaf) provides an explanation that the opposition's line speed is fast and is putting pressure on them. The coach again indicates that this (in his view) is an accurate assessment, this time using *yeah* tokens. Another player jumps in and agrees with this assessment, before Maz again takes the floor and indicates that as a playing group they have already discussed this. However, at this point, rather than asking the player to elaborate on their discussions as a group, the coach (perhaps ritually/routinely) reclaims the floor and launches into a characteristic, long-turn elaboration where he counters the explanation given to the players, suggesting that it is not only down to the opposition's line speed but is something they can exercise more accurately themselves. He also issues several directives to the assembled group about how to address this problem in his elaboration slot.

These moves illustrate that coach–player interactions in performance evaluation settings are predicated on the understanding that the participants are engaged in the process of identifying and solving problems and that it is the coach who initiates and therefore decides what problems are to be addressed or what aspects of performance are deemed to be problematic. The use of question–answer sequences in these problem-solving episodes of talk makes problem solving a jointly accomplished activity. However, because it is the coach who initiates the sequences and encodes a topic for discussion in the question, they claim the role of, and are positioned as, the chief problem solver in the team. Not only does the coach control the questions and, by extension, the topics for discussion, he also controls the elaboration sequences where he takes on further rights (or responsibility) for providing explanations of the issues and directives to the playing group for addressing them. Through these elaboration sequences, the coach takes long, uninterrupted turns that are never challenged, interrupted or extended by the players.

Extract 4 is interesting in that it perhaps illustrates what happens when this particular interactional routine breaks down and the players do not provide the coach with the response he needs to progress the routine towards the evaluation and elaboration stages. In this extract, again from a halftime team talk, we see the same type of questioning pattern from the above extracts only this time the players do not give a critical evaluation in response, leading the coach to continue probing for one.

1. **Tane**: [**QUESTION**] so um + what do we think about our decision making
2. from our set pieces at the moment?
3. **Players**: [**RESPONSE**] {nodding} good
4. **Tane**: [**QUESTION**] we getting in the right place?
5. **Players**: [**RESPONSE**] yep
6. **Tane**: [**QUESTION**] yep +++ from our set piece strikes?
7. **Leaf**: [**RESPONSE**] yep our scrum's working well eh {looking around at the
8. players} the shooter um==
9. **Tane**: ==yep + yep so just on that on that scrum…

Extract 4: [match day data] talk during a half-time team talk

In this extract, we again see the head coach and a group of players (the Backs) engage in a series of these question–answer exchanges that concern the backs' positioning decisions at the set piece (a name for a range of recurring match actions in the game of rugby, i.e. the scrum and lineout). In line 1, the coach launches a sequence of performance evaluation talk by asking the players for their thoughts about decision making at set pieces. However, in this sequence, the routine progresses differently. Instead of providing a critical evaluation, the players respond by *nodding* and one or two indicate that the decision making was *good*. At this point, the coach asks another question, this time one that is more specific and targets the back's positioning during set pieces (*are we getting in the right place*). Again, the players provide a positive affirmation of the performance, nodding and one provides a yes answer to the coaches **yes/no interrogative** about whether they are getting in the right place.

In line 6, the coach tries again. He offers an acknowledgement of the player's positive evaluation but again asks the group a question, this time asking them about an even finer-grained aspect of decision making at set-pieces (the *strikes*). At this point, Player 2 takes the floor, offers a positive assessment of this aspect of play and starts to give a more extensive assessment of the performance of the team. However, at this point, in line 9, the coach **interrupts** the player and launches into more of a critical assessment of the backs' performance in this area. He refocuses the group's attention on a set-piece decision-making issue the backs have made at the scrum and launches into the elaboration component of this episode, offering a detailed explanation of an issue he has observed.

One interpretation of this specific sequence above is that the coach is asking the players questions about aspects of the performance that he has found positive and is raising these for positive reinforcement purposes. The players provide positive evaluations of these aspects of play from their perspective, and it isn't until the issue of the scrum is directly raised that the coach has something critical to say. However, another interpretation of this prolonged sequence of questions and answers is that the players have not provided the appropriate pejorative assessment required in this ritual interactional routine that will allow the coach to perform this role as chief problem solver. By offering positive assessments in response to the coach's questions, the players make it harder for the coach to provide critical interpretation of the aspects of play because to do so in a subsequent turn would dis-align with the players. To work smoothly, as we have seen in Extracts 1 to 3, players need to interpret the coach's questions as pre-empting talk about problems and allowing him to provide critical feedback.

The use of *yep* by the coach throughout this exchange might suggest that the coach agrees with the positive evaluations being offered by the players. However, these tokens in the interaction are arguably not functioning to show complete agreement or alignment with these player assessments. Rather, and with reference also to the tentative way they are phonologically encoded, these *yep* response turns primarily function to acknowledge that the player's assessments have been received by the coach but also indicate to the players that he is looking for something else or something more.

On the evidence presented in Extract 4, it would also appear to be the case that these coach–player performance evaluations run in a very unidirectional fashion. The player's role is to acknowledge there is an issue with an aspect (or topic) of play raised in the questions and give the coach the mandate to provide more detailed and critical remarks about an aspect of play. They do not appear to bring their own issues to the coach for discussion in these speech events, nor are they asked to raise these issues by the coach. Instead, the coach positions himself as the chief problem solver, claiming the primary right and responsibility to identify problems, provide in-depth critical accounts and design solutions. This practice again highlights the coach as an expert and illustrates how their expertise is constructed and mobilized through questions that also establish a subordinate role for players in the evaluation of performances.

Coach as sheriff: Using questions to hold players accountable

A third dimension of the coach's role that could be deduced from a deeper look at their questioning practices might best be summed up as the coach as sheriff. Through the use of questions in these performance evaluation sequences of talk, the coach could pose and elicit quite face-threatening admissions of fault from players, and, in doing so, position himself as the law of the team, holding others accountable and requiring them to publicly acknowledge their shortcomings.

In Extract 5, from a half-time team talk, we again see the head coach (Tane) using questions to draw attention to problems in performance, this time during a passage of play in which the opposition scored a try against them. In the early stages of this interaction, we also see some of the same practices we have reviewed above. However, the questions in line 13 and 21 vary somewhat in form and function. They still elicit a response from the players, one that the coach arguably knows the answer to. However, encoded in these questions is an assumption that the individual or individuals being addressed are personally at fault and are being asked to acknowledge this.

1. **Tane**: um {2.0} talk me through what happened through our um through our kick chase from our exit
2. {2.0}
3. how did they find space to the right
4. {2.0}
5. **Leaf**: when was that
6. **Tane**: where they scored
7. **Leaf**: oh yeah
8. oh I think we + we sort of had it and just
9. **Tane**: yeah
10. **Leaf**: I don't know
11. **Timmy**: yeah I was up I was up in the line

12.	**Tane**:	yep so + that's one
13.		*where were you* Lagi {pointing at Lagi}
14.	**Lagi**:	I was on the on the
15.	**Maz**:	he took he took the left
16.		nah we only had we only had two at the back
17.		the eight the eight didn't hold
18.		so I sh- I should've /been\
19.	**Tane**:	/so what is\ so what is our policy off that play +++ off our kick strategy
20.	**Leaf**:	(unclear) holds aye
21.	**Tane**:	*who should be who should be holding the blind and who should be /on the\ on the open*
22.	**Maz**:	/ten\ ten on the + on the blind
23.	**Tane**:	kicker should hold there and the fifteen should've been over there so +
24.		we made it harder for ourselves because [name of the 10] kicked +
25.		both of you are on that side now you- now [name of the 10] has gotta work over that way +
26.		as opposed to [name of the 10] can kick and hold there
27.		and you should've already been + been over there okay
28.		so let's just get that (right)

Extract 5: [match day data] talk from a half-time team talk

In both of these questions, but particularly the instance in line 13, a specific individual or individuals are being asked to out themselves as culpable for the opposition's score. The extract starts like many of the others we have unpacked earlier, with the coach using a question to direct player's attention to a particular issue he wants to focus on. However, in line 13, by pointing directly to Lagi and asking him *where were you* in the middle of an episode of talk designed to identify issues, the coach implicates Lagi as guilty and at fault in a more direct way than we have seen in previous extracts. This direct question puts the player in a very face-threatening position where he needs to either defend his actions against someone who likely thinks he is at fault or admit his part in letting the opposition score.

In this particular case, Lagi starts to defend himself in line 14, implying he is not at fault because he had taken up one of the other necessary positions in the defensive structure. Lagi is interrupted as he tries to speak by Maz (in line 15) who appears to offer an explanation that implicates himself, noting that he should have seen that another player (the number eight, who is not present in the interaction) did not hold (the line) and left a gap open for the opposition to exploit. With the perspective that Maz has in his position, to see these gaps in the defensive line and act to fill them, he admits that he should have seen this gap and filled the hole in the defensive line to reduce the threat of letting the opposition through.

Technical details aside, the above extract illustrates how coaches can use questions in more direct and more face-threatening ways in these performance evaluation settings to elicit ownership and admissions of fault directly from players. Such questions still function to help perform the broader task of evaluating performances, but they illustrate the coach's rights to hold individuals directly accountable for errors on the pitch. Admittedly, such questioning strategies were rare in our data. Yet, their use does suggest that they are part of the coach's armoury and perhaps signal a right the coach claims to play sheriff and threaten player faces in cases where he deems admissions of fault necessary for the effective evaluation of performance.

From this extract, then, we can argue that the coach can and does claim the right to impose upon players the need to go on record and admit fault in front of their peers and the coach(es) when things have gone wrong. Questions help coaches to perform this interactional routine as through a question like *where were you* in an episode of performance evaluation, the coach can encode a particular fault (i.e. a positioning mistake) and require an individual to take ownership for the mistake by putting their explanation or admission of fault on record. Whether this more face-threatening and direct strategy is appropriate in the eyes of the players is an interesting question, but it does not change the fact that from a power perspective, through such questioning practices, the coach can exercise the right to perform a sheriff-type role that holds players directly accountable for their mistakes. Player's questions to one another did not index or encode this role.

Coach as motivator: Using questions to get a rise out of players

One final dimension of the coach's role to highlight here, that was signalled in their use of questions in performance evaluation settings, was the role of motivator. The skilled use of questions in sequences of performance evaluation talk could help coaches to perform motivational functions by requiring players to respond in an engaged and committed way to questions that were sometimes designed to provoke the players. In Extract 6, which comes from the end of a half-time team talk to the entire group, the assistant/backs coach, Terry, offers some final remarks about the team's alignment when on defence. As he gets to the end of his address, he adds a message on increasing tackling intensity (lines 12 to 13) and then links a question to

EXERCISING POWER THROUGH QUESTIONING

the players in lines 14 to 15 asking whether the group have *got some more to give physicality wise*.

1.	**Terry**:	(just to reiterate) they got one fucking good try from a lineout
2.		special that was it aye
3.		it just tells the forwards + to get our alignment we wanna spend
4.		more time on bodies==
5.		==small time ball long time bodies
6.		make sure you get your alignment (unclear words)
7.		because you're doing too much ruck watching
8.		so we're fucking ruck watching and then oh fuck I want him but
9.		he's over here
10.		just get the bodies on bodies okay
11.		and then you can bring your line speed
12.		and when it's your turn to put in a tackle drop the fucking
13.		shoulder into these cunts
14.		<u>out of ten our physicality do you think we've got some more to</u>
15.		<u>give physically wise?</u>
16.	**Players**:	YO
17.	**Terry**:	well fucking get into these white redneck cunts
18.		alright so (when) it's your turn to drop the shoulder fucking
19.		drop the shoulder into one of
20.		them fucking make sure you do + alright + up the physicality

Extract 6: provoking players through questions

This question again differs to others we have viewed above, not so much in form but rather in function in the ongoing interaction. Instead of trying to walk players towards a realization, draw out a piece of shared knowledge, highlight a problem for attention or hold an individual accountable, this question arguably functions to provoke a response out of the players which is duly provided in line 15. By shouting a loud, resounding *YO*, the players indicate that this is how they interpreted the question, as some kind of rallying device designed to provoke them or pump them up before they head back out onto the field.

To use questions in this endeavour is particularly powerful because it is directed at the whole group and creates the need for the players to involve themselves in the motivational sequence at hand. In providing their answer to this question, the players resoundingly satisfy the coach's inquiry and as a collective group engage in a show of solidarity amongst one another at the same time. The question itself, in this instance, is also arguably provoking the players to accept a challenge embedded within it that as a playing group need to, want to and can give more effort and do better. Being physical is a value of professional sport, particularly one like rugby, as is giving the greatest effort and commitment to the team's cause. Therefore, questioning whether the players can give more on a physicality front can be seen as a direct and provocative assay of their commitment to taken-for-granted values of their game. Finally, at a purely interactional level, this questioning practice or routine also creates favourable conditions for a successful exchange between coaches and players. By asking players a question that they can and will only likely agree with, the coach and the players accomplish a solidarity with one another in the process.

We pick up on themes of solidarity again in the later chapters of this book. However, in summing up what we have seen here, questions provide a flexible resource for performing a number of interactive duties in these performance evaluation sequences, including rallying and motivating the troops. In the final section of this chapter, we bring these findings together and consider what they tell us about the dynamics of the coach–player relationship.

Wrapping up: Exercising expert power through questions

In this chapter, we have homed in on questions in coach–player interaction, specifically in performance evaluation settings like half-time team talks and match review sessions. Questions are often cited as a key coaching tool and therefore are a relevant one to study as we try to locate patterns in coach–player relations. By understanding how questions work in these coach–player interactions, we can, by extension, provide further evidence as to how coach–player relationships are working in our team.

In the sections above, we located and illustrated a range of functions that coach's questions were performing in performance evaluation talk and through this analysis presented further evidence as to how coaches exercise power over players. Coaches used questions to probe whether a piece of knowledge or a particular attitude was known and/or shared across the group; they used questions to signal, initiate and coordinate problem talk and problem-solving episodes on particular topics they deemed worthy of attention; they used questions to hold players accountable requiring sometimes face-threatening admissions of fault; and they used questions to rally or challenge players by presenting them with provocative ideas embedded in questions that they needed to positively (and sometimes robustly) react or respond to.

In the process of interpreting these functions of the questions, we were notably drawn to the notion of power again. However, in order to refine this understanding of how power works, we considered specific dimensions of the coaching role that coaches were enacting (or claiming) in and through these questioning practices. By using questions to elicit displays of knowledge from the players, coaches are performing an **educator** aspect of their role; by using questions to initiate and control episodes of talk about issues, the coach is acting as the team's **chief problem-solver**; by using questions to elicit face-threatening admissions of guilt, the coach is performing a role tantamount to that of **sheriff**, and by using questions to provoke or elicit a robust response to implied accusations they are not giving it their all (for example), coaches are performing a **motivator** role.

Each of these roles provides a finer-grained understanding of the way coaching is working in these performance evaluation settings. However, from a coach–player relationship perspective, in adopting and performing each and all of these roles – the coach as educator, coach as chief problem solver, coach as sheriff and the coach as motivator – the coaches are positioning themselves as more powerful vis-à-vis the players. For example, by being an educator, the coach positions himself as having greater epistemic claims to knowledge and positions the players in the institutionally subordinate role as students; by being chief problem solver, the coach positions his perspective on the performance and his expertise as the most significant for solving problems, by positioning himself as sheriff, he positions the players as accountable to him, and by positioning himself as motivator, he positions the players as needing to be motivated.

Questions play a significant role in the interactional accomplishment of these roles and therefore directly help shape asymmetrical power relations between coach and player. Interactionally they put pressure on an addressee and, in doing so, allow the coach to perform an array of institutionally powerful dimensions of their coaching role. This may, in part, reflect why questions are seen and frequently referenced as an important coaching resource in the armoury of a coach, because they allow the coach to maintain a significant amount of control over the interaction and the players and adopt and enact powerful (sub)roles in the overall governance of the team in the process. Questions, in this regard, are going to present themselves as a useful and relevant tool that can be deployed strategically by the coach to reinforce their authority over the players.

The questioning patterns presented in this chapter, then, can be seen to reinforce cultural beliefs, understandings or 'realities' of the coach's status in sports teams, in terms of both their institutional authority and claims to greater degrees of technical expertise. Culturally, coaches are endowed with institutional authority in sports teams in much the same way that teachers are in classrooms and doctors are in medical settings. Previous research has illustrated how questions are and can be a particularly evident marker of these taken-for-granted power structures (A. Freed & Ehrlich, 2010; J. Holmes & Chiles, 2010; Rubin, 2016; Wang, 2006), many of which are, in professional settings at least, understood or founded on the basis and belief that those with institutional authority *know* best.

Coaches in our data, as a reflection and reconstruction of this institutional authority bestowed upon them, claimed near-exclusive access to questions and, by extension, near-exclusive rights to the expertise needed to right the ship (in these performance evaluation settings). Players did use questions but did so rarely. The primary function of player questions we identified in our data was, particularly in these performance evaluation sequences, to seek clarification of confirmation of issues being raised by the coaches, a move which, in itself, positions the player in an institutionally subordinate position as expertise seeker. Players certainly did not use questions to educate one another, initiate, coordinate and control episodes of problem talk or hold one another accountable. Such unequal access to questions in these institutional contexts reflects and reconstructs the authority and dominance by a particular individual rather than equality and solidarity between individuals (Bubel, 2006, p. 243).

However, these practices do raise interesting questions about the role of players and the status of their on-field experiences, issues and observations in the overall analysis of performance in these problem-solving, performance evaluation settings. The role of the players in these performance evaluation tasks, as it was being constructed in these interactions, appears to be restricted to largely following the orders and direction of the coach and satisfying the coaches' will. While there does appear to be more involvement in the interaction by the players, courtesy of the speaking role they are afforded in a question–answer sequences, that involvement is heavily constrained and any influence the players can exercise through this involvement is illusory. These practices interactionally restrict player's ability to drive and contribute meaningfully to the governance of the team and, in the process, reinforce player identities as subordinate and reinforce relations between the coach and the players as of the superior–subordinate kind. Whether this is a model fit for purpose in a high-performance sports team is a question worthy of reflection by practitioners, and question–answer sequences appear to be ripe for reflection should this model need critical attention.

The data presented and discussed in this chapter, then, continue to tell a story about how coach–player relations work. The findings presented above build on those in Chapter 3, providing further evidence of both the establishment of an asymmetrical power relationship between coaches and players and illustrate specific practices that establish this relational dynamic. The linguistic mechanism we focused on in this chapter was questions, specifically the array of question–answer dynamics we saw in performance evaluation settings. These practices leave little doubt as to the power, particularly expert power, that coaches wield over players in our team's social structure. In the next chapter we continue looking at power but introduce another role with notional claims to power into the overall picture – the captain. In particular, we ask whether and, if so, how coaches share power with others by concentrating on the interactions involving coaches, captains and players in our data.

5

How does power sharing work?

The interactional distribution of power between coach and captain

Introduction

In the previous two chapters we have focused on the coach–player relationship in our team and how it appears to be working in the back-and-forth interactions involving coaches and players. In these chapters, we have presented evidence of a quite sharply stratified, asymmetrical distribution of power being constructed between coaches and players, in which coaches establish themselves as the authority of the team and players co-construct the coaches' authoritative position. However, there is another individual with claims to institutional power in a sports team structure who has so far in our analysis been lumped together with the players. That individual is the captain (Sebastian or Seb), and, in this chapter, we focus on a collection of texts from our data in which the captain spoke that will allow us an opportunity to look more closely at how the coach–captain(–player) relationship is working, in practice, in our team.

Some previous research has found that coaches perceive the captain to be an extension of their authority (Cotterill et al., 2019), particularly in situations where the coach is not present. Such findings raise the potential of a power-sharing model being culturally relevant within sports team contexts. However, little evidence has been presented to date as to the dynamic realization of a power-sharing relationship between coaches and the captain. For example, how does this power sharing between coaches and the captain work in practice, if at all? How is power claimed, distributed or negotiated by both coaches and captains in their everyday interactions? As we have seen in previous chapters, coaches dominate and exercise significant control over a great number of the interactions of the team. So, how might power sharing work in our context and what practices might we interpret and view as attempts to share power?

In this chapter, we put a collection of texts involving the captain under the microscope to see how the captain performed his role in the everyday interactional tasks of the team, particularly vis-à-vis the coaches. Doing so provided an opportunity to explore power sharing between our coaches and captain in action, homing in on how power is claimed, distributed and managed between these two individuals in their interactions with the team.

As we will demonstrate, power sharing between coaches and the captain appears to be a complex accomplishment, one that does not simply involve the simple allocation of authority to the different spaces or domains that the coaches and captain 'own'. We also see evidence of both individuals respecting one another's overall claims to power and influence when they are co-present with one another. However, at the same time, there is also clear evidence that while the captain is offered some power, he is not free of the confines of the coach and there are subtle clues to suggest that power sharing, in our context, is not the wholly democratic practice that the label may uncritically suggest. Rather, power is dispersed to the captain, temporarily and conditionally, and even in settings where the coach is not present, coaches can still exert influence through other communicative means and measures. In the extracts presented below, we pin down and illustrate the way power can be seen to be working in coach–captain(–player) interactions and use the interactional practices to put forward empirical evidence of the complex accomplishment of power sharing in our team.

Making space for the captain: Inviting the captain to contribute to team addresses

In this first section, we look at one of the more obvious moves by the coach to share power with the captain – **inviting** the captain to address the group. In previous chapters, we have seen that much of the coach's power is enacted through their almost exclusive claims to the interactional floor across contexts and settings that involve the team as a whole group. In inviting another person to address the group, the coach is effectively handing over power, temporarily, to enact/perform team governance tasks on or with the group.

Extract 1, already encountered in Chapter 3, is the best illustration in our data of the captain being offered the floor by a coach (in this case, Tane, the head coach) and actually taking up the invitation to address the group. In other cases, the captain was often invited to take the floor but would decline the opportunity to speak. In this instance, we see the head coach, having finished his address, invite the captain to speak to the group (in line 10) and the captain accept this invitation, taking the opportunity to address poor professional standards and behaviour he has witnessed from the players during the training session.

10.	**Tane**:	um + anything from Seb [**the captain**]
11.		nah?
12.	**Seb**:	oh just when ah + like we know tonight's about learning + obviously getting to know each other and shit
13.		but ah when we're doing the changeovers and stuff let's just get there you know
14.		straight change over run to- get to where we need to be so we just get straight into it get to the what we need to do and go home aye right?
15.		not this walk around change over bibs walk over alright?
16.		let's get into good habits aye
17.		we're into a professional environment now
18.		so changeover get there + rest there + and go again
19.	**Tane**:	very good point
20.		so when you're standing on the sideline boys you're actually learning and watching what's happening
21.		you're not there just having a break
22.		{2.0}
23.		that's us
24.		well done
25.	**Players**:	shot boys
26.	**Seb**:	hey hey
27.	**Players**:	ho

Extract 1: [training session data] closing a team training session

Of particular interest for our discussions in this chapter is the design of this invitation, and others in our data that were directed at the captain. The choice to offer the floor to the captain for *anything* the captain wants *to add* is handing over the floor with no specific conditions attached. In other words, he gives the captain freedom to choose what topics he wants to raise or what actions he wants to perform, should he decide to take up the invitation from the coach. In previous chapters, we saw other players who were directly handed the floor by the coach were given it with specific conditions attached that restricted or controlled the contribution the speaker could make. In many of these cases, particularly those illustrated in Chapter 4, the players invited to speak were not necessarily individually selected and were more often than not asked to merely confirm they knew the missing piece of technical information or offer a short critical assessment of an element of performance introduced for discussion by the coach.

The fact that the coach does not encode preconditions into his invitation to take the floor could be seen as a reflection of the notionally powerful role the captain has in the team's social structure. It may reflect an understanding that the captain has rights and expertise enough to be able to identify relevant topics he considers to be important and/or issue directives to the group that help with overall team governance tasks. In providing these opportunities, the coach sanctions and provides space for the captain to exercise power over the group and to construct himself in a leader–follower relationship with the players.

However, there were also cues within these invitation sequences that construct the coach and captain as being on an unequal footing in their claims to power and authority over the group. One of these cues concerns the positioning or timing of these invitations. Such invitations, as outlined in Chapter 3, were often given towards the end of an interaction once any talk by the coaches was finalized and wrapped up. This could on one level encode meanings that these invitations were somewhat token in nature and offered after all of the significant or official business of the team has been covered and managed by the coach. There might also be an implication in the design of this invitation that anything the captain says should *add* to the coach's remarks, and, by implication, not conflict with them. The use of *anything* (instead of constructions like *something* as in *something to add Seb*) has been shown to pre-empt *no* responses by the addressee (Heritage & Robinson, 2011). The design of this invitation, then, may imply and create pressure on the addressee (in this case the captain) to decline the invitation to address the team, so everyone can go home.

However, what is perhaps the most obvious and taken-for-granted indication of the coach's over-arching authority over the captain is that these opportunities to address the team were *given* to the captain by the coach. In other words, the coach authorizes the captain, like he does for any other player, to contribute to the interaction. The captain, in our data, like other players, also waited for these invitations before speaking, particularly in these training-session debriefs and in team meetings.

Such moves are a clear indication of power distance being constructed between the coach and the captain. Despite being invited to address the group, the invitation is at the behest of the coaches and therefore dependent upon when they saw it as necessary. So, while these moves by the coach can be interpreted as power sharing, and as a public acknowledgement of the leadership status of the captain, they also subtly encode power sharing as being layered and ultimately subject to overarching control by the coach. In taking up his opportunity and delivering directives to the playing group, the captain does claim and enact an institutional leadership role and, in the process, distinguishes himself from the wider group of players. However, his contributions and messages to the team are subject to sanction by the coach, who, as we have illustrated in Chapters 3 and 4, is ultimately pulling the strings.

Claiming rights to share the floor with the coach on match days

There was, however, one situation in our data where the captain would take the floor from the coach uninvited, and that was during half-time team talks, particularly when the captain and the assistant/forwards coach (Greg) were together in their smaller unit or group of forwards (of which, the captain is a member). Extracts 2 and 3, from the same half-time team talk, illustrate the captain (Seb) taking turns to talk, in the company of the assistant/forwards coach (Greg) and without being invited to by the coach. Through such moves, the captain is arguably claiming the rights or authority (the power) in this situation to address the group and perform important team governance, in this case various first-half performance evaluation tasks.

1. {*players coming into the changing shed at the completion of the first half*}
2. **Greg**: forwards this side
3. {20.0}
4. {*inaudible conversations happening*}
5. {*loud speaker announcer coming through the changing rooms*}
6. **Seb**: their scrum can be dominated aye
7. fuck we can push them over aye
8. we're being too nice aye
9. (unclear) we're getting our ball we can get there's as we showed in that last
10. ah that second to last scrum before the half
11. we can fucking push over (right)
12. {to the front row} (unclear) let us know if you guys wanna push over

13.		everyone stays on aye even loosies + and we go for it aye
14.		dig in tight eight + and we'll fucking push them over
15.	**Greg**:	okay well said
16.		so the call's gun alright that's fucking all over this we gun it
17.		{longer address given by the coach}

Extract 2: [match day data] initiating a half-time team talk

1.	**Greg**:	[…]
2.		let's get a bit more fucking angry and and do a bit of fight on them
3.		okay let's put a job in at set piece {1.0} and around the field + alright
4.		let's shift this part of the game right now for ten minutes and see how it
5.		(unclear (explodes on them) – because someone coughed) + alright + okay
6.	**Seb**:	their forwards have got nothing aye boys
7.		the backs are running the game for them
8.		(you know) their forwards are just fucking carrying it one by one
9.		(you know fuck) let's fucking belt them and take the line to them aye + alright
10.		don't let them come ah don't let them come to us boys
11.		we take it to them boys ah second half
12.		attack set piece delivery + as (asst coach name) says alright
13.		fucking let's just take ownership of that ball when we get it
14.		score the tries alright fucking buys time for our cleaners to get in there + alright
15.		it's a bit of a shit fight at the moment + okay
16.		getting ah (half back name) we're putting him under pressure + alright
17.	**Greg**:	just /shift your\ personality up
18.	**Seb**:	/inaudible)\
19.	**Greg**:	just shift- a little bit more personal in our tackle and our aggression + okay
20.		we'll lift that up and fucking things will start coming
21.		it's all too nice
22.	**Seb**:	the guys that are coming around fuck on on on their D fuck guys in the ruck
23.		grab them and ice them in boys
24.		(inaudible)

25.	if you're in the rucks grab them + alright
26.	be a nuisance boys + okay
27.	these new laws we can't turn over so fuck do something else + okay
28.	disrupt their ball
29.	fucking get in there

Extract 3: [match day data] continuing a half-time team talk

In both of these extracts, we see the captain **self-selecting** and freely taking turns at talk in this half-time team talk without any official invitation from a coach. In Extract 2, we see the captain actually also initiate the discussion amongst the forwards group as they are coming in and sitting down as a group. In line 6, the captain self-selects himself to address the group, taking a long turn to outline an opportunity the team have to take advantage of (what he perceives to be the opposition's weak scrum and a chance to push it over). In line 15, the coach then takes the floor, acknowledges and positively evaluates the captain's remarks and supplies the players with a specific code word, *gun*, that a member of the forwards can utter to help coordinate the efforts for pushing over the opposition's scrum.

In Extract 3, we see even more back-and-forth sharing of the floor between the assistant coach and the captain as they both continue to claim equal rights to perform performance evaluation tasks in this team address. In line 6, the captain **times his entry** to the discussion after what has been a long address by the coach and takes a long turn at talk for himself. Upon taking his turn, the captain also **introduces a new topic for focus**, albeit one that is linked to his earlier discussion in this half-time team talk about the poor quality of the opposition forward pack. However, in essence, the captain **shifts the topic**, a move that we could associate, in this context, with claims to authority and power. Shifting the topic of discussion implies that the previous topic can now be concluded and that nothing further needs to be added on that topic.

As his turn develops, the captain issues several pejorative **assessments** of the opposition's forwards and then issues a number of **directives** to the group to *take it to them* and *attack* the opposition's *set piece delivery*. He also issues directives to protect the ball better and give the halfback better quality ball so he is not under as much pressure. In line 17, the assistant coach reclaims the floor and issues related messages to *lift their aggression* and *stop being nice* to the opposition. The captain, then, takes the floor again and builds on this message by issuing specific situations where that greater aggression can be exercised, *around the ruck*, by grabbing opposition players and dragging them in, so as to disrupt their play.

Through this behaviour in this setting, we see the captain claiming and enacting power over the players and in coordination with the (assistant) coach. The actions taken by the captain in these addresses, particularly the assessments (which can be quite critical) and the directives to the group, are similar to the actions taken by the coach that we illustrated in Chapters 3 and 4. In self-selecting himself to speak in these half-time addresses, and not waiting for the assistant coach to invite him, the captain is also claiming, at least interactionally, to be on an equal footing with the coach in this particular activity, claiming and exercising the same degree of authority, right or responsibility to address the team and perform important team governance tasks. Stylistically, within their turns, both speakers also perform these team governance actions in similar ways, drawing on grammatical forms to encode their assessments and directives in very direct ways, that impose upon players the view being instilled by the speaker (in the instances of assessment) and the need to perform particular actions in the second half (in the instances of directives). Both also use swear words and other aggressive language forms to add intensity to their assessments and directives, further heightening any directive force behind these messages.

Taken together, the turn-taking and turn design actions of both the captain and the assistant coach in these extracts above mirror one another on a number of levels and, to some extent, reflect an equal distribution of linguistic rights and labour between both the captain and the coach in these half-time interactions. The fact that the captain is taking turns freely, is coordinating his own entry into the interaction, is performing important team governance tasks in conjunction with the assistant coach, is taking long turns and is using his turns to issue directives to the assembled group all construct the captain as powerful. The patterns in the above extract at least raise the potential that in some situations, perhaps settings like the half-time team talk, both the captain and coaches have (or are culturally expected to have) equal claims to the authority to address the group and equal rights and responsibilities to deal with issues, comment on performance and coordinate the group's actions going forward in the next half.

However, there are several aspects of these interactions to bear in mind when we interpret the freer claims to the floor demonstrated by the captain in these extracts, particularly in comparison to Extract 1. First, the interactions in Extracts 2 and 3 involve the assistant coach and not the head coach, who is, at the very same time, running the same interactional sequence with the backs. The greater freedoms taken by the captain may reflect the fact that both or multiple coaches are not present and that the absence of the head coach may provide more of an opportunity (or responsibility) for the captain to perform leadership. The freer contributions by the captain in a situation without the head coach may also point to how much respect the position of head coach garners in our team. We might tentatively put forward the idea that in situations where the head coach is present, the captain may need to wait to be invited to speak; whereas, in situations where the assistant coaches are present, such a norm may be less pertinent to observe.

The captain may also be exercising greater claims to the floor in this particular interactional context because the group assembled are discussing concerns specific to the forwards, of which the captain is a (ranking) member and has expertise and experience with. Put another way, the variation we see between Extract 1 and Extracts 2 and 3 may in part reflect the fact that the latter extracts are taking place in a smaller unit and do not concern the whole team. Being a forward himself and being able to comment on things he has experienced in his first half play as a forward may provide greater comfort for the captain that he has something relevant to contribute based on the technical and experiential information he can lay claim to.

However, again, despite the evidence of some shared rights and responsibilities, we also see some marking by the assistant coach of his higher status. For example, in Extract 2, we again see the assistant coach evaluating the captain's messages as being *well said* in line 15. Such moves imply a greater ability or right by the coaches to be able to evaluate the content of messages by other speakers and sanction it. This was not an action that was reciprocal, and the captain (or players for the matter) did not issue such evaluations after a coach's remarks in any interactional setting. Additionally, while the captain did initiate the talk in Extract 2, he did so while the group were coming in and settling for the half-time team talk. Some players were walking around, others were getting water and some were engaged in their own smaller conversations with others. Arguably, this stage of the half-time team talk is less structured and may actually signal that the official talk itself has not actually started yet. Perhaps the captain has eyed this space as a culturally appropriate opportunity for him to get some messages in before the official half-time team talk starts, in a way that also allows him to show respect for the assistant coach's primary rights to the interactional floor.

Finally, while we do see, on the whole, careful timing and entry to the interaction by both the coach and the captain, there is an instance of interruption in Extract 3 in line 17. Interruption (and the way interruptions play out) has been shown to be a particularly useful resource for probing relational meanings that are being constructed or oriented to (Goldberg, 1990). As a simple example, those who give way in cases where there is overlapping or interruption may be deferring to the other and their greater claims to the floor, perhaps based on their institutional role or interactional rights. In lines 17 and 18, the coach and captain overlap. The coach has identified what he thought was a gap in the captain's long turn address and seeks to reclaim the floor. However, at the same time, the captain looks to extend his turn at talk, perhaps after regathering his breath and seeks to continue, or perhaps wrap up. At this point, both overlap, but it is the captain who gives way to the coach, and he waits until the coach signals that he has finished his new turn before reclaiming the floor and continuing (or restarting) his message to the forwards group.

So, while we do see greater rights being claimed in Extracts 2 and 3 by the captain to contribute to the interactional floor, there are some caveats in the context of this particular interaction, namely the absence of the head coach, that might explain the patterns we see. There are also subtle cues of greater authority being claimed by the coach and oriented to by the captain, as well as markers of respect being shown to the coach by the captain that again co-construct the coach as a higher status individual in the team set-up.

Leading in the coaches' absence

However, while on the field, and with the coaches far away from the action in the coach's box, the captain was, at least in principle, the ranking member of the team. In these situations, we observed the captain claim greater power to lead the group, by taking up and exercising greater rights in and over the team's on-field interactional activities.

Extract 4 comes from an on-field huddle from the first half of a match. This huddle is taking place immediately after our team have scored a try against the opposition. As they wait for their kicker to complete the conversion, the remainder of the team assemble around the water bottles in their own half that the researcher and other members of the team's support staff have brought onto the field. Timmy, an experienced player, initiates conversation in the huddle, by offering a general criticism to the assembled group of an aspect of performance. However, it is the captain (Seb) who performs the more significant team governance duties, as we will discuss below.

1. **Timmy**: we're just getting a bit lazy um setting that [strategy name] early
2. **Player ?**: yeah
3. **Timmy**: and it's not dragging them wide and we're just slow to (move them there)
4. **Seb**: that's cos we're watching the ball go boys
5. we're watching the outside
6. soon as your job's done
7. get back and do your second job
8. the ball's gonna come back
9. alright

10.	let's get excited to carry the ball boys
11.	so fucking work back there
	[...]

Extract 4: [match day data] talk on the field during a stoppage in play

After Timmy's critical assessments in lines 1 and 3, the captain claims the floor and performs more direct team leadership actions that extend beyond just providing evaluative remarks to the group. In extending Timmy's topic of their lazy execution of a strategy, the captain offers an **explanation** for why the team are not able to *drag* the opposition *wide*, adopting and performing an expert identity that is signalled by explaining and identifying technical reasons for problems the team are experiencing. After elaborating and providing this explanation for the issue Timmy has identified, in lines 6 to 11, the captain issues a series of **directives** to the group. These directives require the players to *get back*, *do your job*, *get excited to carry the ball* and *work* and are arguably attempts by the captain to coordinate the team's actions so they can address the problem they are experiencing.

Both of these actions (**explaining** and **directing**) are predicated on and reconstruct claims by the captain that he possesses the power, both in terms of the relevant expertise needed to be able to diagnose the issues the group are experiencing and the rights to control the group by directing or coordinating the actions of the group so they can solve the issues at hand. We will not discuss these huddles in too much detail here as in the next chapter we make this collection of on-field problem-solving texts the central focus of analysis. However, what we have seen here is that in the absence of the coach, the captain can and does claim the responsibility to lead the diagnosis of issues and the issuing of instructions for addressing these problems. Through these actions, the captain is claiming the right to control the group and establishes a powerful identity which, in our data at least, was unchallenged by the players.

Animating directives from the coach during the match

Yet, despite being spatially distant, the coaches were still able to perform acts of authority over the players and, by extension, the captain during the match, while sitting in a coach's box away from the action. During live matches, coaches could and did communicate with players through an intricate system of runners, water carriers, physios and doctors, who were all connected with the coaches via a radio-intercom transmission system. These runners would pass on messages from the coach, particularly directives to the team at times when there was a stoppage in the match, for an injury, during a substitution, after a try was scored or to just allow the players a chance to catch their breath before a scrum or lineout.

Because of these affordances of radio communication systems used by the team, the captain was arguably never completely free of the coaches and needed to attend to and factor in the potential for coach influence during these huddles. In Extract 5, we see how this influence was accomplished and managed in of on-field stoppage talk: a runner grabs the attention of the captain, delivers a message privately to him that the captain then relays to the rest of the team (see lines 5 to 11).

1.		*{players congregate around the drink bottles. As they congregate they are*
2.		*having their own inaudible conversations in smaller units}*
3.	**Topper**:	that was my bad Seb + (was) a a bit slow off the mark
4.		*{the physio has a conversation with the captain relaying messages from the coaching staff while the players take on water}*
5.	**Seb**:	just ah forwards pack
6.		alright just a relay from the outside
7.		we need to get into shape earlier eh
8.		so (from now) forwards if you don't wanna carry put yourself out to the half + alright
9.		if you don't wanna go A everybody else get around him + okay==
10.	**Leaf**:	==yeah==
11.	**Seb**:	==A gets a their first and we get momentum from that eh you are A
12.	**Leaf**:	I think we are a bit messy eh
13.		so if we're that we might just go tank for a bit
14.	**Kingy**:	yeah
15.	**Leaf**:	then if we get to the sideline go back to the shape
16.		sweet?
17.		just when it's a bit messy
18.		*{players disband from the loose huddle and move into position}*

Extract 5: [match day data] talk on the field during a stoppage in play

In this extract, the team are assembling around the water carriers and water bottles at the halfway point after conceding a try to the opposition. As the players are coming in and taking on water, Topper, an experienced player, initiates interaction in the huddle by making an admission, perhaps taking on some of the blame for the try the opposition have just scored. At the same time that this admission is being delivered, the physio, positioned directly behind the captain, is passing on a message that is barely audible to the researcher and not picked up by the recorder. This in itself is an interesting feature of the communication patterns here, as the physio is trying to reduce the audience size (or participation framework) to himself and the captain and make himself largely inaudible to the rest of the team.

In line 5, the captain then begins to pass on or animate (Goffman, 1979) the coach's message to the team, explicitly marking it as being a *relay from the outside* perhaps to distinguish it from his own words and maybe to give the message the added authority of being from the coach. The message, as it is designed by the captain for the team, is a directive to *get into their defensive shape earlier* and to provide support for ball carriers, if they choose not to carry the ball themselves. After he has finished this message in line 12, Leaf, another experienced player in the team, takes the floor and provides further assessments and directives to the group.

In this interaction, then, the captain does not deliver his own messages but provides space for the coach's remarks. With respect to power sharing in the coach–captain relationship, through these particular interactional practices, we see the coach attempting to exercise some power over proceedings and trying to do so *through* the captain. The captain, in choosing to relay the message being passed on from the coaches, respects and co-constructs the coach's right and authority to provide guidance and directives at this time during matches. In marking the message as coming from the coaches (*from the outside*) and not as a message of his own, the captain actually creates space for the coaches' voices in these on-field, captain (and player)-led huddles, and helps the coaches to achieve their goal of providing guidance and exerting influence over the playing group, in a situation where they might not ordinarily be able to do so.

The power sharing in these settings is intricate. The captain is arguably sharing *his* space, where he, by virtue of his notional role as captain and the absence of the coaches, has greater rights and responsibilities to coordinate the actions of the group. However, at the same time, in making space for the coaches' directives, the captain could be simultaneously undermining his own claims to authority over the playing group on the field. At the same time, the coach is simultaneously constructing the captain as directly connected with the coach and, by extension, as having the authority to deliver the coaches' messages or act as their mouthpiece. The coach may also be taking strategic advantage of the captain's authority by designing these interactional message-transfer encounters in this way. By getting the captain to voice these messages and directives, the coach is likely to be drawing on understanding that it is the captain who usually runs these on-field encounters, or, as we have seen above, plays a significant role in the performance of team governance tasks in these on-field huddles. He may also be borrowing the proxy leadership status of the captain for the added effect this might have. Because the coaches' messages to the players at this time are typically directives, they may be more effective if they are voiced or animated by someone with leadership status. In other words, the captain's status is likely to lend the messages greater authority than if they were merely delivered by a water carrier directly to the group.

These particular settings provide a very interesting test for the coach–captain power-sharing relationship. In what might otherwise be a clear demarcation of principal authority and rights by domain (coach off the field – captain on the field), the communication affordances of this set up again complicate this more simple allocation of power by creating the need for powerful individuals to actively manage each other's rights to govern the team and, for the captain at least, to stamp his authority on the team as more than just a conduit between the players and the coaches.

Dividing the labour: Allocating interactional responsibilities to the captain

In the final section of this chapter, we discuss two situations where we saw evidence of the captain claiming greater rights and authority over a particular interaction or interactional task. The first of these concerned the delivery of the pre-match motivational team talks, or the *hoo-ha* as it was referred to by one of the coaches. These pre-match huddles were player-led interactions that took place as the last interaction immediately before the team went out into battle. The coaches were either not present when they took place or were in the process of taking their leave from the changing room, having delivered their own final messages immediately prior. In these huddles, the captain took charge, initiating the beginning of the huddle, controlling the floor as he delivered this final briefing and deciding when it should be closed with one of the team's chants. We dedicate Chapter 7 of this book to unpacking these pre-match talks and so we will not provide an illustration here, other than to say that the responsibility for these huddles was delegated to and/or claimed by the captain.

Another of the responsibilities the captain appeared to claim was the responsibility for upholding the professional standards of the team. In Extract 1 in this chapter, we saw an example of this. When invited to speak by the coach towards the end of a training session, the captain used his turn at talk to make players aware of the expectation on them to behave in accordance with *professional standards* by showing the appropriate degree of effort and not wasting time or leisurely moving between training drills.

Extract 6 is another illustration of this practice, although one that comes from a different context. This extract comes from the Captain's Run, the last training session before a match, where the captain is also afforded the responsibility of leading the players through practice of some of the final match preparation drills. The coaches were not involved in this stage of the training session and so the captain is, much like he is on the field, the ranking member of the leadership group.

In the lead-up to this huddle, the team's starting line-up for the upcoming match has just completed their version of the training drill and it is now the turn for the reserves to come and do the drill. As we will see, this huddle in Extract 6 appears to be called by the captain to debrief the starting line-up and check if there are any issues, and to prepare the reserve unit for their turn at the drills. However, the captain also takes the opportunity to remind players of expected professional standards, particularly the need to demonstrate energy and personal responsibility.

1. **Seb**: bring it in boys
2. {*players begin assembling*}
3. {*shouts something to other players not involved in the drill*}
4. {*players run over*}
5. alright changes on boys eh
6. anything that anyone doesn't understand?
7. that pack there that just started?
8. boys this is where we just you know sort of do a walk through
9. so we know what our roles are
10. but doesn't mean that we + you know that we stay quiet huh
11. still get our execution right and get our comms go- comms going like a normal game
12. this is our rehearsal for tomorrow
13. alright (but) its a bit flat
14. okay
15. need some energy levels
16. it doesn't come from me it comes from everyone
17. alright so next pack + okay
18. let's get into it eh
19. /unclear\

20. **Maz**: /nice job boys eh\
21. {*players start organizing themselves into groups for the next training drill*}

Extract 6: [training session data] talk in between drills during a training session

In line 1, the captain calls the group together (*bring it in boys*). Importantly for understanding the behaviour in this extract, some of the players appear to be slower to join than others and are hurried along by the captain in lines 2 to 4. The captain then performs a number of functions associated with the more transactional task at hand. Firstly, he indicates that there is to be a changeover between the playing group and the reserves (line 5). He then asks the group that recently completed the drill (*that pack there that just started*) whether there is anything they did not understand (lines 6 to 7).

However, the captain dedicates the bulk of this huddle to outlining the expectations of these training drills in the final session before a match and the wider attitude he expects the players to take or demonstrate towards these drills. As this extract progresses, it becomes clear that the captain is unhappy with the concentration and attention of the reserves group who have been talking on the side-line and have not responded quickly to the call for a changeover. In lines 8 to 9, the captain introduces the purpose of the captain's run to the group before launching into a more critical account of what he perceives to be an unprofessional attitude being displayed. He implies that the team may not be treating these exercises with the same intensity as a match day experience, which is the level of intensity that the captain clearly expects to see. He evaluates the performance as *a bit flat* and in need of *some energy*. In line 16, he goes on to claim that demonstrating this level of energy is something that individuals should take responsibility for themselves and that it is not the responsibility of the captain to rally these energy levels in the group. In line 18 he indicates that the next group should ready themselves to perform the drill and then directs everyone to *get into it*.

As we will demonstrate in future chapters, upholding professional standards was not a task that was exclusively performed by the captain; coaches would also discuss and seek to address dips in professional standards through their talk. However, based on the evidence presented in Extracts 1 and 6 above, it is apparent that the captain does see this task as being within his remit, and, in initiating and leading these interactional tasks, he claims the power to be able to hold players accountable for professional (or unprofessional) displays of their attitude.

Wrapping up: How does power sharing work in the coach–captain relationship?

In this chapter, we have carried out an exploratory look at how the coach–captain relationship works in our team by studying cues of power sharing in interactions in the team, particularly those where both the coach and captain are co-present. In looking closely at these patterns, we attempted to locate evidence of how power was working or how power sharing was working between these two individuals both of whom have institutional claims to power within a high-performance sporting culture.

The data suggest that power sharing between the captain and the coaches is not a simple democratic allocation of all rights to all members who have institutional claims to power, but rather a complex accomplishment, and one that arguably reflects the continued, overarching influence of the coach over everyone – including the captain. Not only do the coaches largely control the captain's entry into the team's interactions, particularly when captains should address the team, they also evaluate or sanction the captain's directives or contributions to discussions and continue to enact influence in interactional spaces where the captain might more obviously be viewed as the leader of the group (i.e. on the field). There were also subtle cues within the captain's utterances that encoded his respect for the overarching authority of the coaching staff. For example, by giving way when there is noticeable or accidental competition for the floor from the coach, the captain orients to the coaches' authority over him and, in the process, positions himself as unequal in status to the coach.

The practices exhibited by both the coaches and the captain in these interactions illustrate an understanding that the captain is a member of the leadership group, and perhaps needs to be if the team are to avoid a vacuum in leadership in situations where the coaches are not physically present. However, these practices simultaneously and implicitly position the captain as subordinate to the coaches, as subject to the overarching control of the coach and as someone that is also responsible for performing the coaches' will in the course of team interactions (especially when the coaches are not physically co-present). Coaches do take steps that could be read as attempts to prop up and legitimize the captain's authority to control the group and enact certain responsibilities in their absence. The invitation to share the floor when both the coaches and captain are co-present is one potential strategy that may help to establish understandings of the captain's leadership status. Allocating or delegating certain responsibilities to them, perhaps ones that are deemed better suited to being performed by a member of the playing group, is also another way the coach can and may be attempting to instil in the team culture the genuine view that the captain has authority in the group.

However, ultimately, through these practices and actions, we could argue that coaches are again constructing themselves as the team's primary authority and by respecting the coaches' overarching rights to most of the team's interactional spaces, the captain also co-constructs this authority. While there appear to be some greater rights and responsibilities attached to and exercised by the captain in team interactions, the version of power sharing being constructed in our data is not one that reflects a broader ideology of equality between these different members of the leadership group. In other words, wholly democratic notions of power sharing that propose the exercising of equal rights and the equal distribution of responsibilities between members of the leadership group are not evidenced here. Instead, the practices we have located in this chapter provide evidence to suggest that underlying the relationship between coaches and the captain is what underlies all relationships in our team – the overarching acceptance of the higher power status of the coach. Coaches and captains do share claims to power, but they enter into a hierarchical relationship, one that again sees greater interactional rights and responsibilities claimed by and distributed to the coaches.

Such findings help to provide some empirical evidence of the coach–captain relationship working in practice and locate several interactional practices that establish the complex power-sharing dynamic we see being enacted in our team. They also raise further questions about how power works or suggest ideological views about how power is seen to need to work in professional sports teams. Perceptions that modern leadership dynamics in sports teams may benefit from being more inclusive and shared are starting to emerge, with notions such as leadership groups now commonplace and a push for the broader distribution of rights across teams being seen in the mission statements of teams (Jones, 2019; Schofield, 2017). However, such notions are grossly undertheorized and there is a lack of empirical evidence regarding how leadership groups operate and how power is ultimately distributed in these groups.

On the basis of the taken-for-granted practices we have reviewed here, particularly those wielded by coaches, we might claim that models of shared leadership can be watered down significantly by practices that continue to reflect and construct a need for coaches to exercise greater amounts of control over the governance of the team. Arguably, the practices evident in coach–captain interactions reflect what are sharply stratified power structures that might point to a wider reluctance to invite discussion and greater involvement from the captain (and the wider group of players) in the real and consequential processes of team governance. If such practices persist in a particular context, then genuine shared leadership models, where coaches and players share rights and responsibilities equally, are unlikely to be developed.

Ultimately, though, the bigger question is whether shared power is desirable in a high-performance sporting team, particularly this hypothetical, open and democratic distribution of rights across the leadership group. Such a model of power sharing may present as a challenge for individuals in a high-performance sporting culture that simultaneously values such things as team discipline, chain of command and respect for authority. With respect to these cultural values, ideas of shared power may undermine attempts to establish these values by opening up the floor to multiple perspectives. Ultimately, decisions and actions need to be taken, and whether power-sharing models facilitate this or can be designed and enacted in ways that facilitate or strengthen these decision-making processes is an open question. On the basis of the evidence we have seen in this chapter, it would appear that power sharing and the nature of power-sharing models in sports teams may themselves be subject to deeper, underlying values that support and encourage the clear demarcation of power into hierarchical orders and structures.

In the next chapter we take one last look at power, this time looking at how power works in player–player interactions when the coach is absent. To do this we studied a collection of texts where the coach is not physically present and the players are left to their own devices. On-field huddles during stoppages in the match fit this description, and we unpack the interactional dynamics of these texts in the next chapter to shine a light on how relations of power work within playing groups.

6

Power dynamics amongst players

Establishing flatter social structures in on-field problem-solving talk

Introduction

In this chapter, we put player–player relations in our team under the microscope looking for evidence of how power worked within the playing group. To do this, we look at one of the only situations where players were, by and large, free of the physical presence of the coaches and left to their own devices: **on-field huddles**.

As we noted in the previous chapter, these on-field huddles occurred during stoppages in a match and served as a useful opportunity for the players to come together to diagnose problems and to identify and convey solutions. We also presented some evidence in that chapter of the captain claiming the right and responsibility to lead these on-field huddles in the coach's absence and as the remaining member of the leadership group.

However, as we will demonstrate in this chapter, we also saw a lot more talk by other players as they interacted together as a playing group to work through the unfolding circumstances of the match. In this chapter, we shine a light on patterns and practices in these player–player interactions to help probe evidence of the way relations of power are being constructed and/or enacted amongst the players in what is, theoretically at least, a less hierarchically stratified group of individuals.

The patterns in the player–player interactions support this general conclusion about hierarchy. On the evidence presented in this chapter, on-field huddles are more open interactional spaces, where multiple individuals, regardless of their notional status, respectfully negotiate their entry into the interaction, establish their identities as experts and/or attempt to influence the behaviour of the playing group. These practices, we will argue, establish a flatter hierarchical structure that shows players constructing values of equality and respect for one another's rights to contribute actively towards the governance of the team. However, again, while individuals did contribute more freely, there were subtle cues that suggest players do respond to forms of status within the playing group that distinguish certain players. We draw attention to some of these features as we unpack the interactional behaviour of players in their on-field talk.

Multiparty interactions: Constructing a collaborative floor

While we did see captains speak a lot in these on-field huddles, one of the more observable features of these on-field interactions was the larger number of contributors to the talk. Not only that, but we also found there were a larger number of individuals, without notional power roles, claiming the right to issue directives and direct the team.

We see these patterns in Extract 1 which comes from an on-field huddle during a stoppage in the first half of a match. This stoppage was prompted by the opposition team scoring a try against our team. This event in the match, while not positive for our team, has given them an opportunity to regroup and gather behind the try line while the opposition performed the conversion attempt. As is evident in the interaction, we see evidence of the talk in these huddles being geared towards identifying and addressing problems the team are experiencing. However, perhaps more significant for our purposes in this chapter, we see a **multiparty interactional floor** being constructed, with a number of speakers negotiating entry and contributing freely to the interaction at hand.

1.	Topper:	back your systems aye
2.	Maz:	oi boys ++ and I know it's because we're getting puffed aye
3.		cos a lot of these penalties we're giving away are just laziness penalties
4.		there's fucking five minutes seven minutes to go
5.		let's fucking just dig it in man
6.	Nikau:	still get our connection too aye ++
7.		too many times you're shooting up in

8.		/ones\ and twos
9.		get our connection then move our line up
10.	Lima:	/oi\
11.	Player ?:	yeah
12.	Lima:	on that lineout too if you- if we're doing a man out +
13.		need to be a bit tighter on me and just cos that ten's just getting that sneaky gap
14.		and he's making those extra metres==
15.	Kingy:	==/boys that first tackle\ + that first tackle fucking make it easier for
16.		us and make it dominant aye
17.	Nix:	==/good talk Lima good talk\
18.	Player ?:	yeah
19.	Kingy:	so it's not fucking quick quick all the time fucking get them back
20.		{players start disbanding from the huddle, start walking to the line to await
21.		the conversion}
22.	Jez:	same call aye we've got this tackle (unclear) metre aye
23.	Player ?:	tackler roll away we'll get that metre
24.	Player ?:	back up there aye straight away
25.	Topper:	get a chaser on this guy aye

Extract 1: [match day data] on-field huddle problem solving after opposition try

Even a cursory glance at this extract shows individuals, several of whom we have not seen or heard from in previous chapters, **claiming the floor** and contributing to the problem-solving work that is being undertaken. Players **negotiate their own entry** to the ongoing interaction and do not wait to be invited by a more powerful other. Instead, they look for a space in the interaction to contribute their thoughts or observations and self-select themselves to address the group. Another interesting feature of Extract 1 is that it is not the captain that initiates it. In fact, the captain, who is present, does not actually speak at all in this extract. This was rare but does show that these huddles can potentially be run by individuals without notional claims to institutionally powerful roles.

Looking more closely within the interaction and at the actions people perform in this extract, we see a number of speakers without notionally powerful roles performing quite powerful actions through their talk, including claiming rights to direct the team. In Extract 1, six different players give directions to the team (or particular members of it). Using imperative syntax, these players ask others to **dig** it in, **get** their connections sorted, **get** tighter *in defence* and **make** *tackles more dominant.* One particular example that is worth highlighting here is the instance of Lima's directive in lines 12–14. Lima is a young and inexperienced player who is new to the team and is in his debut professional season. Anecdotal evidence suggests that such players are often shy or feel the need to remain quiet and not talk in group settings, let alone claim the rights to be able direct others (Knowler, 2017). However, in this extract, Lima self-selects himself to speak, indirectly evaluates an aspect of performance by others and issues a directive to the group designed to improve performance in the area he has identified.

This marked and perhaps brave action by a young player may help explain why Nix provides supportive remarks in line 17, something he does not do for the other speakers. Nix may be acknowledging that the remarks and directives are directed at him as one of those players needing to *get tighter in defence* against the opposing number 10. Or he may be trying to offer supportive feedback to the young player for speaking up and claiming rights to address the group, evaluate performance and issue a directive to help address issues he sees as needing to be addressed. In either case, both of these potential explanations or accounts point to a collaborative floor in these player–player interactions, where any player appears to be free to actively hold one another accountable, and an appreciation for players taking up these opportunities to help identify and share issues and consolidate team performance.

In Extract 2, from an on-field stoppage in a different match, we see similar actions being performed by multiple individuals, this time in conjunction with the captain. This extract comes from an on-field huddle early in the match after our team have scored a try. Our team are running back to the halfway line where the water carriers and physios have assembled. In line 2, with the bulk of the squad loosely assembled, the captain directs the group to *bring it in*, and initiates an address in which he issues what might be considered critical feedback, including some gently directed at an individual player (line 4), and provides a series of directives to the group *hit the [strategy name] flatter*, *hit flat off the ten* and to *bring the line speed up*. However, again, we see another young and inexperienced player, in line 11, providing a directive to the rest of the group designed to effect change to the group's lineout preparation process.

1. {players walking towards the drink bottles}
2. Seb: (attack) bring it in ++ bring it in boys
3. Jase: {speaking to researcher as I hand a water bottle over} cheers mate
4. Seb: Jez you're on ah ++ you're standing a bit too +++ ah- cos we're setting off too and we're standing another (sort of) five metres deep

5.	Jez:	yep
6.	Seb:	let's just try and hit those [strategy name]'s /flatter\
7.	Player ?:	/yep\
8.	Seb:	+ so we're playing on top of them aye + alright but giving them the extra two metres to + bring that line speed up aye
9.	Player ?:	yep
10.	Seb:	/just\ one (hit it) flat off ten
11.	Ashton:	/just one-\ one thing too um on that [strategy name] we'll just come together first and then we'll walk in and walk in /and\ go up + so they don't know our calls
12.	Jez:	/yep\
13.	Jase:	yeah sweet bro
14.		{players start walking away from huddle}
15.		{trainer and water carrier begin to run off}
16.	Player ?:	off his heels aye off the ten's heels if we have to (see) eyes up ++ watching

Extract 2: [match day data] on-field huddle problem solving after scoring a try

In this extract, we do see the captain claiming greater rights to lead the interaction than he did in Extract 1. As well as directing everyone to come together (in line 6), he also provides critical feedback to Jez in line 8 and issues directives, in line 10, albeit modified ones, realized (or encoded) using *let's* to mitigate the strength of the directive being issued. All of these moves, as we have seen in the previous chapter, can be explained as evidence that in absence of the coach, the captain claims or is perhaps expected to claim rights and responsibilities to direct the group and address problems and issues in line with responsibilities associated with his position as a member of the leadership team.

However, the action performed by Aston, another younger and more inexperienced player, in line 11, is further evidence that rights to speak in these huddles are more equally distributed and claimed by those present in the interactional context. In this instance, Ashton exercises the right to perform directives and evaluative acts aimed at increasing the coordination or effectiveness of the team, and the other members of the team acknowledge his rights to do so (see lines 12 and 13 in particular).

There are some linguistic features within Ashton's turn at talk that are worth reflecting on further as we unpack power dynamics within the playing group. One of the key features is the indirectness of his directive to the group to *come together* before deciding the lineout call. Instead of using imperative syntax (i.e. *guys, come together*), he shapes his directive using declarative syntax (*we'll just come together*) which perhaps reflects an uncomfortableness on Ashton's behalf with performing strong, direct and assertive acts of power. In other words, in shaping directives indirectly, Ashton may be delicately balancing his need (as the lineout caller) to tell others what to do so he can do his job more effectively with an awareness of his lower and less experienced social status in the group, particularly in comparison to the bulk of the individuals present who are older and more experienced than him. He also waits until the captain has finished before claiming the floor, a move that can be interpreted as showing respect for the current speaker, and he is quite tentative in his entry to the interaction, using *just* to initiate his entry, a move that may reflect a desire to ensure any imposition read from his remarks is minimized or as minimal as possible. Such actions might suggest that younger, more inexperienced players may need (or feel the need) to carefully navigate their status as juniors in the squad when asking others to do things. Patterns of this kind – the more indirect linguistic design of social actions like directives – illustrate how subtle hierarchies within the playing group might be realized and (re)constructed.

However, as far as floor management and the performance of team governance go, the patterns presented in the above two extracts differ significantly from those presented in previous chapters. The patterns in our data suggest that when players are left to their own devices and are free from the physical presence of a coach, rights to the floor and, by extension, rights to team governance can be more evenly claimed and/or distributed. This more collaborative, multiparty floor is a pervasive feature we will see across the extracts presented in this chapter and raises important and interesting questions about the different ways in which power works in playing groups, including why we see a more even distribution of power in this interactional setting.

Respectful management of each other's rights to the floor

As well as being more interactive spaces that multiple individuals could freely contribute to, there was also evidence that the players sought to respectfully manage the interactional floor with one another, respecting one another's rights to speak and the significance or value of the messages they shared with the group. We have seen some supportive moves in earlier extracts in this chapter, which suggest this underlying value. However, there were other patterns in the interactions that point to this more respectful acknowledgement of one another's rights to the floor.

For one, from a turn-taking perspective, we see very little overlapping talk, little interruption and no obvious forceful commandeering of the floor by a specific individual. Rather, we see players waiting for others to complete their turn before attempting to take the floor, an interactional move that arguably shows the players paying respect for one another's rights to speak and address the team. In cases where we did see overlapping talk, these overlaps appeared to be mistimed entries to the interaction and not attempts to commandeer the floor or challenge the speaking rights of the current speaker. In our data, these entries to the interaction were abandoned by the speaker who mistimed their entry resulting in the overlap. We see an example of this in Extract 1, line 10 above where Lima misreads the ending of Nikau's turn and begins his own. Upon realizing Nikau has not finished, he stops and releases the floor back to him, allowing him to complete his turn. In other cases, overlaps appeared to be performing largely supportive functions, such as offering a positive acknowledgement of the current speaker's remarks *while* they were delivering them (as seen in Extract 1, line 17 above).

Such floor entry and multiparty communicative actions construct what could be seen as respect for one another's rights as contributors to the team's ongoing governance in these on-field interactions. In the example in line 10 above, Lima could have continued and aggressively competed for the floor, a move that, if frequently deployed, would characterize the interactional floor of this group in quite different, more competitive ways (Edelsky, 1981; French & Local, 1983). However, in respecting the rights of the current floor holder, and in choosing to release the floor back to Nikau, Lima shows respect for the player's contribution and waits his turn. Additionally, by the time Lima speaks in line 12, his earlier mistimed start has pre-signalled to the group that he wants to contribute next, and the others may have ceded control of the floor to Lima as a result of this pre-signalling of intent to contribute. This may be more tenuous to claim, however, based on the fact that other speakers do contribute to the interaction, and do so after Lima has taken his turn, we could argue that his pre-signalling moves have contributed to other speakers holding back their turns until Lima has got his chance to share his message with the team.

Another feature that arguably reflects and performs functions of respect in these player–player interactions is the players' use of the **adverb** *too*, particularly when negotiating entry into a huddle. In Extract 1 above, Nikau and Lima, in lines 6 and 12 respectively, use the additive adverb *too* when they shape their entry to the ongoing interaction. Ashton in line 15 of Extract 2 also uses *too* when negotiating his entry to the interaction. Players in other interactions we will see later in this chapter use other similar variants of *too* to perform this function (such as *as well*). While this linguistic feature may seem relatively insignificant, it arguably does a lot of important interpersonal work in these fast-paced, multiparty interactions where multiple messages are being delivered. At an information level, the use of *too* in the design of another message to the huddle indicates that the current speaker is adding to the ongoing diagnosis of issues and the provision of solutions. However, at the same time, interpersonally, the use of *too* by a speaker who is entering the interaction also arguably denotes respect for the previous speaker, indicating agreement with these previously uttered messages and explicitly marking that the current speaker's own turn, ideas or messages should be read as 'in addition to' and not 'in contrast to' the previous speaker's turn.

In this regard, the use of *too* may be a way that speakers can manage time pressure constraints in this interactional context; namely, managing the need to raise new topics in what is a time-constrained interaction while at the same time ensuring the significance of prior topics is not undermined in the quick transition between multiple topics. As we have seen, at times there are multiple issues to raise and bring to the attention of the group, and sometimes there is less than a minute to do so. Abruptly changing the topic of the interaction might indirectly send a range of signals to those gathered that the current speaker feels the topic is finished or perhaps even less important than their own. The use of *too* may help speakers to directly navigate that threat, by achieving the aim of shifting the topic onto something that is also important and that they want to bring to the attention of the group, while at the same time showing respecting the previous speaker and positively orienting to their contribution.

Proposing strategic action: Multiparty contributions to strategic decision making on the pitch

As well as more equal rights to directing the team, there was also evidence that decision making was a multiparty activity in player–player interaction on the field. In Extract 3, we see another instance of these multiparty on-field interactions, this time involving multiple individuals feeding into and contributing to the making of a strategic decision. The extract comes from an on-field stoppage that has been called by the referee to allow an opposition player with an injury to receive treatment from their team's physio. The players have already assembled in a huddle as the researcher and other water carriers arrive with the water bottles. While we again see the captain leading talk in the huddle, there are a number of contributors in lines 11 to 17, where a strategic decision is made to attack the opposition's scrum.

1.	Captain:	[...] we'll take it up and then that gives us time to set up the {strategy name}
2.		again + or whatever the game drivers are calling
3.	Player ?:	{someone speaks to the half back} come round
4.	Player D:	yeah yeah come round
5.	Captain:	we need to tidy up that clean up area aye
6.		(we're) standing a bit too deep and it's getting messy
7.		ah [half back's name] is having to scramble for the ball (that's how) (unclear)
8.		let's fucking make sure that we clean up that ball
9.		all good
10.		fuck we're not tired bro we're good
11.	Tamati:	(we're all good at the scrum) their scrum's (a bit) (shit)
12.	Captain:	and ah oh yeah their scrum's weak
13.	Beef:	let's have a go at the scrum boys
14.	Captain:	we can contest it at both sides (unclear)
15.		if you guys want it fuck we'll stay in and we'll push
16.		alright?
17.	Jay:	yeah yeah
18.		{1.5}
19.		all good
20.	Player ?:	yeah
21.	Captain:	pack on three
22.		hey hey ho ho HEY HEY
23.	Players:	HO
24.	Captain:	nice boys
25.	Player D:	let's go big scrum here boys

Extract 3: [match day data] on-field huddle during an injury stoppage

Early in the huddle, we see the captain, as was fairly typical, delivering several assessments of the forward's play and issuing directives that aim to clean up the areas of concern he has observed. In line 10, he ends his turn at talk by claiming the group is *not tired*, a move which is arguably functioning to motivate the group and demand more effort from them despite being so late in the game. However, at line 11 we also see another player, Tamati, initiate another topic of discussion – the opposition's scrum. In raising this topic, he negatively evaluates it as *a bit shit* which the captain agrees with. At this point, another player, Beef, in line 13, joins in and offers a suggestion to the assembled forwards group to *have a go at their scrum* and compete against them by pushing the opposition scrum backwards in order to regain possession of the ball.

This is an interesting move here as it arguably amounts to a strategic proposition being put forward by Beef, an individual with no recognizable, institutionally powerful role in the team's official structure. Whether Beef intended to make a proposition to the group or to just indicate generally that the opposition scrum is there to be dominated is beside the point. The captain takes it and interprets (or accepts) it as an attempt to direct the forward's scrum strategy and offers the help of the back row of the scrum, who need to be told by Beef and the front row whether to push and attack or not, should the team decide to *have a go*. The reason this is directed more at Tamati, Beef and Jay is because it is those three individuals who are part of the front row that connect directly to the opposition scrum. Because of this position they play, they are likely to be best placed to determine whether such a strategy can be accomplished (based on their feel for the opposition's readiness and ability to repel it). Therefore, not only does the captain sanction and support Tamati's suggestion, he also positions Tamati and his front row colleagues as having the rights and control to decide whether and when to enact the strategy.

More broadly, these actions by the captain indicate that a more multiparty approach to making strategic decisions is possible in these player–player interactions on the field and may suggest that decision-making power in playing groups can be distributed across the group. In this particular instance, the captain, through his supporting actions, empowers the front row to make the decision as to whether and when to put pressure on the opposition scrum, and hands over authority to others to guide and coordinate the group's actions and playing activity. This may reflect a degree of trust in other individuals based on the expertise different individuals can bring to the team's governance based on their particular positional knowledge and expertise. We pick up on this point in the next section.

Claiming (and being afforded) expert power to direct the team

In our last extract for this chapter, we provide a final illustration of the dynamics of multiparty interaction in these on-field player–player interactions. This particular extract was particularly interesting as the language use and key features of the context (specifically, who the speakers were and what they were speaking about) provided a useful example to help unpack and explain why we might get these more collaborative and multiparty exchanges in on-field interactions between players.

Extract 4 comes from another on-field interaction after our team have scored a try. During this stoppage, the forwards group have assembled at

POWER DYNAMICS AMONGST PLAYERS

the halfway line while the kicker takes the conversion. Of particular interest here are the contributions underlined in lines 17 to 21 and 29 to 34. In these two sequences, we see the two players who speak diagnosing issues and giving directives to the group regarding aspects of play that are central to their own areas of responsibility within the team. In other words, they claim responsibility for these aspects of play and for ensuring the rest of the group are aware of issues that need addressing.

1.	Seb:	come in boys come here
2.		{3.0}
3.	Player ?:	keep going aye boys keep going
4.	Player ?:	yeah
5.	Player ?:	good structure
6.		{players form into a huddle, grabbing drink bottles}
7.	Player ?:	let's go {name}
8.		awesome aye boys
9.	Player ?:	yeah
10.	Player ?:	good platform aye lads
11.	Player ?:	nice aye
12.	Player ?:	good scrum boys good scrums good set piece aye
13.	Seb:	we've gotta get that set D on the inside aye
14.	Player ?:	yeah
15.	Seb:	fucking keep loading on
16.		because as soon as we're scratching they're getting the edge /and an extra\ push
17.	**Jase:**	**/we could probably go\ a bit more hydro**
18.		**cos on the bind I feel like I'm coming back**
19.	**Player ?:**	**yep**
20.	**Jase:**	**so we get a bit more weight going through hopefully I can stay there**
21.		**and then hit and (unclear) {speech tails off}==**
22.	Player 2:	the kick's pretty good aye
23.		we just need to get our chase line to come out a bit further
24.	Player ?:	yep
25.	Player 2:	cos they might look to go wide
26.		so just really get that line
27.		but otherwise (unclear) is doing good
28.	Player ?:	sweet
29.	**Azza:**	**boys just on that scrum as well aye**
30.		**when we're coming down we're just moving a bit**
31.	**Player ?:**	**yep yeah**

32.	Azza:	**we've just gotta stay square aye /stay\ straight**
33.	Player ?:	**/yep**
34.	Azza:	**we can't afford to {shakes hand side to side to show an unstable scrum}**
35.	Player 2:	(nice boys aye)
36.	Player ?:	way to chase wingers + good stuff {claps hands}
37.	Player ?:	yeah good stuff boys
38.	Seb:	HEY HEY
39.	All:	HO

Extract 4: [match day data] on-field huddle after our team have scored a try

The extract features a number of patterns we have outlined in our analysis in this chapter already. It begins with a number of different players providing supportive and positive remarks about passages of play (lines 1 to 12), including those that have led to the try they have just scored. In lines 13 to 16, the captain claims the floor and initiates a sequence that outlines a defensive problem he has identified. However, again, he is not the only speaker and not the only person to issue evaluative remarks of directives to the group. In line 17, Jase, a prop in the front row of the scrum, and, incidentally, another inexperienced young player in his debut season, raises the issue of force on one side of the scrum. As a prop in the scrum, this issue is specifically within his playing sphere, as he relies on the coordination of others behind him in order to be able to get stability and the upper hand over the opposition (at the 'hit'). In lines 17 and 20, he issues what could be read as mitigated directives to the group to provide more force. This is acknowledged and positively responded to by one of the players in line 19. In lines 29 to 34, we see another player perform similar actions concerning his specific sphere of activity, also the front row of the scrum. Azza, who is a hooker, is in the front row together with the props. In his turn at talk, he also offers a directive to the group, in his case to try and maintain stability during the scrum so that the group can coordinate and push more effectively as a unit.

Both of these players who speak in this extract are discussing issues within their specific spheres of playing activity in the front row. As members of the front row, and as the players that bind directly to the opposition in the scrum, both of these players are likely to be the ones that most acutely feel the pressure from the opposition and the dominance their own team is getting over the opposition in the scrum. Their talk, then, can be seen as an attempt to take responsibility for the coordination of the group in their specific sphere of play and, ultimately, improve the team's chances of gaining an advantage over the opposition. In earlier extracts in this chapter, Lima in Extract 1, Ashton in Extract 2 and Tamati in Extract 3 all perform actions that can be recognized as directives to the other players, and upon closer examination, these instances can be connected to problems or potential opportunities linked to their specific spheres of play. In Extract 1 above, Lima spoke about the need to be tighter in the line defence to make it more difficult for a dangerous opposition player that he is predominantly responsible for guarding from taking advantage. Ashton, in Extract 2, also speaks about lineout calls which directly concern him (as a lock), noting that if the opposition can hear the team's strategic lineout calls it will make it harder for him to exercise his role and secure the ball from the lineout.

Based on this evidence, the multiparty nature of these on-field interactions might be explained by a shared understanding of the need for teams to rely on multiple individuals to raise and address issues they are experiencing in the various spheres of activity in which the game is being played. Addressing the various aspects and passages of play is important if the team are to achieve their united goal of improving playing cohesion or fluidity so they can dominate the opposition in and across all aspects of the match. A more open and multiparty interactional space, one that supports individual's rights to raise issues and share issues from their own spheres of expertise and experience, is likely to be a significant contributor to a team's ability to coordinate their physical activity and win sports matches. We pick up this point further when we wrap up these findings together in the discussion section of this chapter. However, before we look more broadly at the evidence presented in this chapter, we want to draw specific attention to some of the more nuanced ways in which power and hierarchy in the playing group were realized linguistically.

Indirect directive design: How subtle cues to hierarchy are encoded in player directives

The above extracts have painted a picture of relations between players being more equal, certainly when compared to the dynamics we saw being constructed between the coaches and players. However, there were subtle cues in the message design that reveal aspects of structure being constructed in playing groups, even as members claimed more equal rights to the interactional floor. We've already picked up on this in our discussion of Extract 2 above, where we identified the indirectness of the directives issued by the young, inexperienced player doing the directing. However, there is a further example of this subtly in Extract 4 above where we see some interesting variation in the degree of (in)directness in the design of directives (or proposals) by the three players who take significant turns in the huddle (the captain Seb, Azza and Jase). For ease of retrieval, each of these player's directives is reproduced below:

- **Seb (the captain)**: *fucking keep loading on because as soon as we're scratching they're getting the edge and an extra push*
- **Azza**: *we've just gotta stay square aye stay straight + we can't afford to {have an unstable scrum}*
- **Jase**: *we could probably go a bit more hydro*

The captain's proposal is the most direct of the three, designed using imperative syntax, which is the most unmarked and direct way to shape a directive or instruction. The captain's directive is also further strengthened through the use of *fucking* which is arguably functioning here as an **intensifier**, adding further force to the directive being imposed on the playing group. The effect of shaping of directives in this direct and unmitigated way is that it makes clear to the addressees that the speaker is imposing upon them and is simultaneously making claims to having the right to be able to make such bald and direct impositions on others in the group.

Jase and Azza, on the other hand, draw on different linguistic strategies to design their directives that shape them as more indirect and mitigated attempts to impose on the players. Azza's directive to the group is still quite strong and is strengthened by the modal verb 'got to' (*gotta*) and *just*, the latter of which is not functioning here to mitigate the strength of the directive but to emphasize the need to *stay straight*. However, while the message does clearly function to influence a change in the playing group's actions, it is not realized directly through imperative syntax. Rather, it is shaped using declarative syntax which shapes it more as a statement. In other words, Azza does not draw on imperative syntax to directly impose this on the playing group; instead, he hopes that the players will pick up this meaning. In drawing on linguistic practices to realize his directives in more indirect ways, Azza may be trying to balance the goal of issuing a directive to the playing group while at the same time protecting himself from accusations by others that he is unjustly claiming the rights and power to directly impose his will on the group. Such a strategy may reflect and reconstruct an understanding that he does not have an institutional role that gives him the right to impose on others and therefore must negotiate his lower status when delivering directives to the group.

Jase's directive is even more indirect and may not even meet the (linguistic) test for being a directive. Instead, based on the way it is shaped, it may be seen more as a **suggestion** or a proposal. However, even so, Jase is still arguably attempting to influence the behaviour of others in the group, in his case to engage in a particular approach to pushing at the scrum (*hydro*). Like Azza, he makes a statement (using declarative syntax) which can be read as an indirect attempt to influence the behaviour of players, but one that does not commit the addressees to the action being suggested. He also uses the modal verb *could* which arguably encodes his directive more as a suggestion and really weakens any requirement on the players to accept it. He also uses the modifier *probably* which further reduces any commitment the speaker wishes to convey to those assembled. Taken together, these design moves shape the directive as particularly indirect, especially in comparison to the captain's and even Azza's directives.

Mapping these different strategies onto contextual information we have about the three individuals, we see differences in the **institutional roles** and the **degree of experience** each of these players have had that might explain the differences in message design, particularly between Azza and Jase. The captain's apparent rights to shape proposals in direct ways, encoding proposals with imperative syntax to issue unmitigated directives or instructions, may reflect and reconstruct rights culturally associated with his institutional role as captain. His behaviour may reflect his understanding that in his role he has the unquestioned authority to oblige others and impose his will on the team. However, Azza does not have a specific institutional role in the team, but he is an experienced player for the region and has some higher-level honours playing at professional levels above the current team context. Jase, as we have discussed earlier in this chapter, is a very inexperienced player and is in his debut professional season. This pre-season fixture is, in fact, his first game for the team.

These patterns potentially highlight how power difference in player–player relations, while not being as sharply stratified as they are in coach–player relations, can be subtly oriented to and constructed in player–player interactions through the careful selection of linguistic features. On the basis of evidence presented in this chapter, player experience levels may be one way that players (subtly) organize themselves structurally while performing acts of team governance in these on-field huddles. The use of **indirect strategies for realizing directives** helps the players to navigate this need or expectation on them to raise issues and search for ways to take advantage of the opposition while at the same time not claiming or exercising rights to commit others to their directives or directly impose their will on the playing group. Through such action, these players perform their identity as active members of the team, seeking to perform their role well in order to help the team achieve the result, and make sure they are attending to their relations with players, positioning themselves within the informal hierarchy of the playing group. More directness might be found in players that have greater experience levels while the evidently direct acts that impose and commit individuals to a future action appear to be more comfortably performed by those with an institutional role. Such findings show that while player–player relations are more equal than those we have seen being performed in coach–player interactions, there is an orientation to hierarchy that may reconstruct the understanding that playing experience (and higher honours) gives individuals cultural capital that they can draw on to establish themselves as leaders in the group.

Wrapping up: Levelling the playing field: Power in player–player relationships

In this chapter we have shone our linguistic lens on player–player relations, looking for evidence within patterns of player–player interaction as to how power works in the playing group. In this chapter, we analysed how on-field huddles worked and considered the way players behaved as they engaged in these problem-solving interactions. Together with the analysis presented in Chapter 5 on the captain, the findings presented in this chapter have helped to provide a fuller and more nuanced look at power and social structure in our playing group.

Through our analyses, we presented illustrations that suggest player–player relations operate on more of a level playing field, particularly in comparison to the way coach–player relations work. The primary piece of evidence presented to support this claim was the more interactive, open and multiparty nature of these on-field team interactions. We saw individuals without official institutional roles (like captain) claiming the floor and, in the process, claiming rights to perform important team governance actions through talk. This included players of all ages and all experience levels, including young and largely inexperienced players in our team. As for the actions these individuals performed, these included the rights to direct the wider group, contribute actively to the decision-making process, propose strategic directions the group might take and issuing acts that expressed (albeit indirectly) a critical view of the group's performance.

However, while players did appear to be freer to contribute, there were subtle indications of an informal or less visible (i.e. not institutionally stated) hierarchy being constructed by speakers in their talk when addressing the group. This hierarchy was visible when we homed in on the way directives, assessments and propositions were performed by different speakers in the team. In short, those with greater degrees of playing experience were more direct in the shaping of directives, propositions and assessments delivered to the team. These patterns point to playing experience being a potentially significant factor in the organization of player–player relations and arguably as a key factor underlying player–player relationships in this particular professional culture. While all individuals are apparently free to perform team governance in these on-field huddles, those with less experience show deference when doing so by shaping their contributions to this governance in more indirect ways. Inexperienced players that did contribute also seemed to stay in their lane, offering remarks in relation to their specific spheres of playing activity. More general criticism and wider directives to the whole group, particularly to not be lazy or lift the performance, were more likely to be performed by the captain or more experienced players.

Taken together, the findings presented in this chapter suggest, on the one hand, that social structures in playing groups are flatter than those constructed between coaches and players and show how that flatter hierarchy is being constructed – particularly in on-field talk. We see more players contributing to the interactions, players selecting themselves to speak, and players performing an array of speech actions that have been identified in other settings (and presented in earlier chapters) as being largely afforded or distributed to those in notionally powerful roles (particularly the coach and captain).

In trying to explain the variation we see in practices and power dynamics in coach–player and in player–player interaction, we could argue that they reflect and reconstruct an ideology that for teams to function as cohesive and coordinated units they need to invite their members to contribute to team governance, particularly when in the heat of battle (i.e. on the field). The more fluid and open interactional floors we have seen in the data presented in this chapter reflect and reconstruct an understanding that for teams to function as coordinated and cohesive units, they need to welcome the analyses, observations and experiences of multiple individuals who may see issues in and through their unique positional play during a match. Such a practice is arguably more favourable to the accomplishment of teamwork and team coordination. In this regard, through these power dynamics in player–player relationships, the team may be better placed to support and accomplish teamwork, by creating and instilling in players the understanding that their contributions to the ongoing coordination and management of the team are valued and expected. Team structures that do not allow for or foster a flatter social structure in these moments may find the accomplishment of team cohesion hindered.

Additionally, upon evidence presented in this and previous chapters, it is perhaps fair to claim that players only take the lead on the field. While they clearly demonstrate a capability to take the lead and engage in team governance, the diagnosis of issues, the evaluation of performance and the design of strategic action, their input and their rights to govern are largely restricted to on-field interactions. This does raise interesting questions about why players do not take or are not afforded greater rights to involvement in coach–player settings, and what teams might stand to gain (or lose) from less sharply stratified social structures between coaching staff and players.

In the next chapter, we shift our focus from power to solidarity, aiming to contribute sociolinguistic insights that can help us to better understand how relations of solidarity are being performed (or not performed) in and through interaction. We begin by exploring the way solidarity or, more specifically, belonging is attempted and accomplished amongst members of the playing group in a specific interaction, one widely known for fostering solidarity amongst members of a team – the pre-match team address.

7

Bonding before battle

How the captain fosters togetherness and belonging in *pre-match team-talk* rituals

Introduction

In this chapter, we begin exploring how **solidarity** worked – or how it was attempted or accomplished through language or interaction rituals – in our team. We do this by locating interactional practices and language use patterns in pre-match huddles that can be seen as recognizable attempts by speakers (and addressees) to foster bonds of belonging and togetherness amongst one another. While solidarity might be most simply understood as an affective bond of attachment that is produced and reinforced through intense collective emotions, our goal is to locate linguistic practices that help to foster this 'affective attunement' or awareness of solidarity between individuals in our team in and through their interaction rituals (Salmela, 2015, p. 55).

The pre-match huddle is a useful interaction to study for our initial look at solidarity dynamics, as these interactions appeared to function primarily as resources for fostering solidarity. As we will demonstrate, a great deal of the interactional work, by speakers and addressees in these pre-match talks, appeared to be geared towards accomplishing or heightening feelings of togetherness and belonging amongst those members assembled. Our primary goals in this chapter are to illustrate the ways in which this solidarity was being attempted and/or accomplished in and through ritual and by and large mundane linguistic practices in pre-match huddles and use these insights to discuss underlying cultural understandings about how relations of solidarity worked in our team.

These pre-match huddles were one of the interactions the coach delegated to the captain to lead (see discussion in Chapter 5). Therefore, much of what we discuss in this chapter will draw attention to the ways the captain used language to rally solidarity amongst the players in the moments immediately before battle. However, we will also draw attention to the important role the addressees (i.e. the playing group) played in the joint performance and co-construction of solidarity in pre-match huddles. As these huddles involve the captains and the players, the findings offer us an opportunity to unpack the way solidarity is working within the playing group and contribute these observations to our overall understanding of how solidarity is working in our team.

Non-linguistic markers of belonging and togetherness in pre-match huddles

Before we turn to the linguistic and interactional practices of these pre-match huddles, we dedicate some specific attention to important elements of the context of the pre-match huddle and non-linguistic behaviour we observed in these interactions. We feel it is important, in this chapter particularly, to highlight these features of the context and the non-linguistic behaviour we observed during these huddles, as much of it contributed to our understanding of the linguistic actions of speakers as being geared towards performing functions like fostering togetherness and belonging. Many of the features we highlight here are taken-for-granted aspects of the pre-match huddle context but are important contributors to the meanings of solidarity speakers (and groups) are generating.

One of the most obvious features, in this regard, is that when these pre-match huddles take place, all members of the playing group are **physically co-present** or in the same place. By being in and sharing the same space, the assembled individuals are connected in a specific moment in time and in a specific place in the world. They cannot escape one another, they can all see each other, they maintain close contact with one another and are able to read cues from each other's behaviour that help them to understand how others are feeling. As well as sharing the same physical space, at the time of the pre-match huddle, the playing group are likely to share similar feelings about the prospect of playing a game of professional rugby against another physical team and in front of a crowd. They all know that the match is about to begin and that this is their last few moments that they will be together before they go out onto the field to perform their job. This **shared knowledge of what is to follow** and the understanding of the significance of the event they are all about to take part in (as the biggest moment of their week) is likely to serve as a strong binding agent for the group.

The setting itself, the team's changing room, can be seen to contribute significantly to meanings of solidarity in these pre-match huddles. The changing room is an exclusive site solely for the group and their support staff that is guarded and that only those possessing the right credentials (or official badges) can enter. As **an exclusive or restricted space**, members are bound by their status as official members of an exclusive group. People cannot just join this group if they want to and need to earn their status and be ratified as a member of this unit. Such exclusivity arguably constructs meanings of inclusivity for those who have made it and are part of the changing room – an exclusive form of inclusivity.

Additionally, in this setting, all members of the group wear clothing that is the same colour and design and has the team's badge on it. The players, as a subgroup, all **wear the same playing uniform**, another contextual and non-linguistic manifestation of unity and togetherness. That kit also has a history that connects the players to previous generations of players. The players have also colonized the setting with their own gear and other artefacts that function to establish the space as belonging to them. For example, during home fixtures, their changing shed has their logos and messages attached to the walls of the room.

However, perhaps the most obvious non-linguistic contributor to feelings of solidarity in these speech events is **the configuration of the speakers and addressees** during these events. They are all interlocked together in a circle or huddle in what is clearly a physical manifestation of solidarity between members of the group. On a physical level, by coming together and locking arms, players create closeness to other members of the team, have visual access to everyone in the group and create an exclusive membership by enclosing themselves and keeping others who do not belong out at the same time. Such a configuration, especially in contrast to other settings where players are not locked in huddles, arguably heightens feelings of togetherness and belonging at this important time in the week of a professional sports team. These feelings were felt by the researcher when he was invited into the huddle, an action that was interpreted as being afforded status as a member of a wider group.

This configuration of contextual features is important to highlight here in this chapter on solidarity as together they contribute, on a broader level, to the performance and accomplishment of solidarity in these pre-match huddles. However, to be able to illustrate how solidarity works in these huddles, we also need to pay attention to the language being used at the same time, as this mode of communication, as we will demonstrate, allows some of these physical manifestations of solidarity to be heightened further and offers another mode (or set of mechanisms and tools) that assembled members of the group (but particularly the captain) can use to perform or choreograph the performance of belonging in these ritual interactions. In the next section, we begin to illustrate how several mundane linguistic and interactional practices of speakers and addressees helped to perform these important functions in pre-match huddles.

Establishing a shared purpose and shared emotional pulse through directives

One of the most evident linguistic practices in these pre-match huddles was the issuing of directives by the captain to the group, which, in this particular interactional context, could be seen to perform important solidarity functions. Extract 1 comes from the last match that we observed during our time with the Rhinos. After assembling the group together (lines 1 to 14), we see the captain begin what is a typical pre-match address in line 15, a significant portion of which is made up of directives to the group (see underlined utterances).

1.	Seb:	**let's** go **boys**
2.		**let's** pull up
3.		{10.0}
4.		**everyone** in
5.		{players continue their own conversations}
6.	Player ?:	**let's** go aye **we**'re in
7.	Player ?:	**let's** go **boys**
8.	Player ?:	work 'em over **boys**
9.	Hopper:	come on *eh* basics
10.	Guz:	{clapping}
11.		{8.0}
12.	Seb:	**let's** go **boys**
13.	Player ?:	(unclear question to the captain)
14.	Seb:	ah **we**'re seven going up
15.		alright **boys** another day at the office
16.		fuck **no one's** new to this team now **we**'ve had three- this is
17.		**our** third game third preseason
18.		so fuck <u>own that jersey</u> now *huh*
19.		fuck another opportunity to put your hand up **boys** + okay
20.		<u>don't get fucking complacent</u> alright

21.		and <u>fucking challenge **yourselves** boys</u>
22.		(and) <u>fucking work as a **team**</u> now alright **we**'re all **brothers** as a **unit**
23.		**we** fucking <u>go out there and smoke these cunts</u> *huh*
24.		<u>don't think it's gonna be a walk in the park</u> like the last two games **boys** *alright*
25.		it's gonna be a physical game so fucking take it to them *huh*
26.		<u>don't let them come to</u> **us**
27.		**we** set the tone of the game and control it *huh alright*
28.		that's **everyone**
29.		<u>forward pack set the platform backs you finish</u> **us** <u>off</u> *huh*
30.	Players:	{murmurs of agreement, nodding}
31.	Seb:	**let's** fucking hiss **boys** *huh*
32.		<u>bring it in</u>
33.	Players:	{inaudible, noisy} LET'S GO YEAH
34.	Seb:	first touch huh first touch of the ball first carry
35.		RHINOS ON THREE ONE TWO THREE
36.	Players:	RHINOS
37.	Seb:	that's **us brothers**
38.		first touch **boys** first tackle
39.		make sure **everyone's** got their mouthguards

Extract 1: [match day data] pre-match team address

In Extract 1, the sheer number of directives issued by the captain illustrates how pre-match addresses were, in our team at least, stitched together by a series of instructions and demands issued by the captain to the assembled group of players. In this particular address, the captain, amongst other demands, directs the team to *own the jersey* (take responsibility), *challenge themselves*, *work as a team* and *smoke* (or punish) the opposition. He also issues a series of directives that could perhaps function partially as warnings for the team to be alert to, including to *not get complacent*, not to be too confident and think that the match to be *a walk in the park* and not to let the opposition dictate the game (*don't let them come to us*).

Directives are not the most obvious feature to focus on in at the beginning of a chapter on solidarity. As we have seen in previous chapters, directives, particularly those that are not mitigated, are more of a reflection of power difference, heightening distance between the person uttering the directive and the addressees being required to do something. In these addresses, the captain's power is certainly on show in ways that clearly distinguish him from the other players. The baldness or lack of mitigation of these directives also encodes the captain's authority and right to impose directly and unapologetically on the members of the playing group.

However, while they do index the captain's authority over the players, directives in this specific interactional context can be seen to function simultaneously as attempts to foster a **shared** or **coordinated** purpose, reaction or approach amongst the group to the ensuing match. At a message level, in directing the group to *challenge themselves*, *own the jersey*, *not get complacent*, the captain can be seen to establish (albeit rather forcibly) a shared attitude, purpose and/or a shared sense of responsibility for all assembled and addressed members of the team for the upcoming match. Other researchers have claimed that pre-match addresses or team talks are sites where a shared purpose is established and directives may be one of the practices speakers draw on to try and foster or remind the group of that shared purpose in a direct and unambiguous fashion.

This interpretation of directives as attempts to foster solidarity along shared purpose lines can be supported when we consider the **participation framework**, particularly the joint role of the captain. As a leader in the team, it appears to be the captain's responsibility to rally individuals under a shared purpose or attitude. However, at the same time, because he is also going out onto the field together with the players, he is arguably committing himself to the messages and performance contract he is outlining to the players. This participation dynamic could shape the meaning of directives from the captain in these pre-match addresses in different ways to those issued by the coach, who is not going onto the field, as they are orders for all players who are about to play, the captain included.

There are also other more subtle cues within the design of the captain's directives that hint at meanings of solidarity being attempted. For example, some of them take on quite conventionalized forms (i.e. *own the jersey* and *put your hand up*) which arguably draw from a shared register of rugby (or professional sports) language. In such cases, these conventionalized directives mean something more in this context than what the collective words represent, and the speaker is expecting the addressees to be able to retrieve those meanings because they share membership to the cultural group. By drawing on the shared register, the speaker is further establishing the shared cultural boundaries of the group by drawing on cultural indices. However, more specifically, in both of these cases, there are meanings of belonging and togetherness encoded in the phrases. Both *own the jersey* and *put your hand up* implore individuals to show others that they belong to the group.

In issuing directives in these interactions, the captain may, of course, be performing other interpersonal functions, independently or simultaneously. Motivating or inspiring, for example, have been cited as being one of the key functions of the pre-match huddle in sporting contexts (Smith et al., 2018) and the rather direct and sometimes abrasive nature of directives may facilitate motivational aims. Directness, of the kind evident in the directives being issued by the captain in these huddles, is, and can be, attention-grabbing, demanding and confronting, requiring individuals to acknowledge demands and orders being presented to them. By drawing on directives the captain may be attempting to grab the attention of the players and add to or lend from the intensity of the moment immediately before the battle.

Finally, and as a brief aside, lines 1 to 14, while not technically part of the huddle, are important to briefly reflect on here as well. In these lines, there is a significant amount of time, in what is a time-constrained speech event, dedicated to getting the group together and ensuring their involvement in the pre-match huddle. In this instance, most of the group has assembled but several players were still finalizing their preparations. The captain and the other players urge those still finalizing preparations to hurry and join the group. These players do noticeably speed up their preparations, and it isn't until everyone has joined the huddle that the captain begins his team address. From the action taken in lines 1 to 14 and in other huddles, being assembled as a complete group of players was an important precondition for these pre-match addresses to start.

The directives in these pre-match huddles can be interpreted as direct attempts by the captain to align the group's commitment and attitude at an important time, immediately before the impending match. In issuing directives, he encourages, at least in part, the convergence of attitude and approach, albeit in a top-down fashion. Yet, the perlocutionary effect of these directives is arguably some form or feeling of coordination, alignment or togetherness. In this regard, directives can be seen as an important resource for helping to foster solidarity immediately before battle.

Encoding togetherness: Frequency of collective pronouns and familiarizers

As we have alluded to above, the use of directives might not be seen as an obvious marker of relations of solidarity. However, the frequent use and the choice of **collective pronouns** and **familiarizers (familiar terms of address)** in messages by the captain in these huddles certainly are. As we outlined earlier in the book, the pronouns and terms of address people use in their interactions with one another can be particularly revealing as to the nature of the interpersonal relationships they are signalling, constructing and negotiating with one another (Bull & Fetzer, 2006). It is frequently through pronouns that people position themselves and their relations to others in an ongoing interaction. Even out of context, the difference between **you** *do this* and **we** *will do this*, for example, signals quite a different relationship, perhaps along responsibility and authority lines.

The captain frequently used personal pronouns in these pre-match huddles and from the choices he made we can see he is construing himself, the players and their relations with one another as collective or *together*. In Extract 1 above, the collective pronouns, other collective reference markers and collective terms of address have all been bolded. In nearly every utterance by the captain, we see a collective personal pronoun or collective term of address, including *we*, *us* (as in *let's*), *no one* and *everyone*. There are also other lexical items that assign meanings of togetherness to the group, like *unit* and *team*. Across the different types of interaction in our team, the pre-match team address was the speech event where the use of these collective personal pronouns was most evident.

Equally telling is the lack of personal pronouns I and you in the pre-match huddle data to set apart, speak about or speak to specific individuals. While there are some uses of pronouns you, your and yourself, these arguably do not refer to a specific individual and rather function as a collective pronoun. The pronoun *you* in English can function to mark a specific individual, but in the cases above, it is arguably functioning to refer to the entire group as the captain implores with all individuals in the group to challenge *yourselves* and put *your* hand up. The use of the familiarizer *boys* after many of these uses also perhaps encourages a more collective reading of the use of *you* in these directives (see lines 19 and 21 in Extract 1 above).

Some of the other collective **terms of address** and **familiarizers** in these huddles encode similar senses of togetherness, but through different linguistic means. One of those is by drawing on the reference of family (and meanings of solidarity that are entwined with family) in and through the use of familial reference terms like *brothers* (see lines 22 and 37). *Brothers* is also used frequently in other pre-match speech extracts and team huddles as part of the team's chant repertoire (discussed further below). Wilson (2010) has argued in other data from rugby teams that choosing terms like *brothers* may be an attempt to construct or establish closer-knit relations between members. While family is a collective institution that is arguably important to everyone, in the context we are analysing here, where there are a large number of Maori and Polynesian team members, notions of family are hugely central to the identity of the people (Metge & Laing, 1984; O'Connor & Macfarlane, 2002). The captain also has Polynesian roots, and so the use of this term may reflect and reconstruct the speaker's own cultural beliefs about the importance of family and may be being strategically drawn on here to encourage a view of the group as close.

As well as construing the group as together, the use of these personal pronouns in these addresses can also be seen to function (interactionally) as an **involvement** marker – a further dimension of solidarity – by drawing the audience into the ongoing pre-match address and the performance of solidarity being orchestrated by the captain. Underlying this are principles of attention; when we hear our name or we hear ourselves referenced in an interaction, we pay attention. Personal pronouns, in this regard, are a key engagement or involvement resource and may be particularly important in what are largely captain-led addresses, as they draw the gathered audience into the discourse and force them to consider themselves as the target for the messages, directives and information being conveyed by the captain. From a solidarity perspective, these collective pronouns may play an important role in encouraging outcomes of solidarity in what is by and large a monologue address. They allow the main speaker to perform the important task of encouraging shared purposes and attitudes while also encouraging the audience to see their collective selves as the subject of these talks and directives.

We pick up on the notion of involvement again later in the chapter. However, through the practice of littering and exclusively using collective personal pronouns (and other similarly functioning lexical resources) in these pre-match huddles, the captain can be seen to be constructing the group (as the direct and sole addressees for the talk) as united and together, emphasizing their sameness and collective identity. The prevalence of these resources in this specific speech event suggests that minimizing difference and building bonds before battle is a key function of the pre-match address. Captains may be trying to take advantage of the moments immediately before the match to ensure the players go out onto the field prepared for the joint activity, effort and responsibility of the impending match.

Reducing potential divisions in the membership

As a further message-level attempt to establish togetherness, the captain also designed messages that specifically identified potentially peripheral subgroups of individuals in the team and worked to directly (and verbally) integrate them into the membership. Extract 2, from another pre-match huddle, provides an illustration of this.

1. Seb: right game time now aye boys let's just start flicking on our switches now + *okay*
2. prepare for our warm up *aye*
3. so let's just start hissing up and take it out onto the field

4.		alright fucking **big game for everyone** *okay*
5.		some of us might be ah anxious and what not and little bit of nerves
6.		but fuck that's a good thing *eh*
7.		and **those boys trialling for spots + alright + it's all up for grabs** *eh*
8.		it's up to you um do your role right on the field and the rest will take care
9.		of itself + *okay*
10.		**we're all here for a reason (now) we can show the coaches why alright**
11.		that's us aw
12.		bring it in
13.		{3.0} {group come closer together} {some clap}
14.		RHINOS ON THREE ONE TWO THREE
15.	Players:	RHINOS
16.	Trainer:	EIGHT MINUTES INDIVIDUAL FELLAS
17.		EIGHT

Extract 2: [match day data] pre-match team address

In the above huddle, we see many of the features we saw in Extract 1. However, there are a series of more specific messages that are directed at a subgroup (*those trialling for spots*). In line 4, the captain exclaims that it is a *big game for everyone* but also acknowledges that there are some (unspecified individuals) that may be anxious or nervous. In line 7, the captain isolates *those trialling for a spot*, in essence temporarily separating them from the remainder of the group, for specific attention in the address. In shaping a specific message for this group, the captain issues them a directive to *do their role right on the field*.

In our pre-match huddle data, apart from messages for *the forwards* or *the backs*, this is the only occasion that another subgroup of the team was isolated as the subject of the talk and directly addressed in these pre-match addresses. By assigning them a status as trialling player which will be understood by those around them as not equating with full membership to the team, the captain may be (inadvertently) establishing an outgroup identity for those players – a practice that arguably runs counter to functions of solidarity we have discussed above. However, in line 10, the captain, perhaps upon realizing this, verbally returns the subgroup of trialling players to the wider membership by indicating that they are *all here for a reason now*. In line 10, the captain is arguably encouraging the subgroup of trialling players (along with the other players in the team) to see themselves as part of the collective pronoun *we* in the messages here and, by extension, as part of the collective.

An alternative reading of the move in line 10 could be that the captain is actually assigning the status of trialling player to all members of the team, indicating that showing the coaches *why they belong* is the responsibility of all individuals in the team, regardless of their contract status. In either reading, though, the captain, through the action in line 10, can be seen to legitimize those trialling for a spot as members of the team and encourage those listening, perhaps who might think of themselves or think of the trialists as temporary members of the team, to (now) consider themselves as part of the collective.

Encouraging togetherness through involvement: Interactional tag particles *eh* and *huh*

In the section on pronouns above, we noted that the frequently used collective personal pronouns functioned in part as **involvement markers** in these huddles, grabbing the attention of those assembled and encouraging them to see themselves as being directly addressed and therefore involved in the unfolding interaction. However, this involvement is created quite passively. The players, in listening to the talk, are encouraged to see themselves as both the target for the messages and the subject of the talk, and to reflect on the relevance to the messages privately and quietly. Perhaps to create more *active* involvement from the addressees, we did see the captain use resources that required the playing group to actually partake in the ongoing pre-match address.

One of these practices was the use of the tag particles, such as *eh*, *alright*, *okay* and *huh* by the captain when delivering these pre-match addresses. As a practice, these actions arguably invite the addressees to actively involve themselves in the joint demonstration or performance of solidarity in these huddles, by requiring them to verbally or non-verbally acknowledge the messages being delivered. Extracts 1 and 2 contain a number of these tags (marked in italics) as does the pre-match huddle presented in Extract 3.

10. Seb: alright boys let's not slip back on our Wednesday's performance *huh*
11. fuck this is another opportunity to go out there fucking put your hand up you know *alright*
12. you guys who are first time putting on the jersey boys fucking make it count *eh*

13.		this is your shot + opportunity so fucking take it (you've) (unclear)
14.		*alright* boys +
15.		leave nothing to chance today boys *huh*
16.		take everything
17.		I don't care how shit the field is (up in here) fuck we play *huh*
18.		we play we fucking keep working
19.		alright you're chosen for a reason so fucking work ++ *alright*
20.		empty the tank
21.		we've got plenty of (legs) to come on
22.		so fucking go out there and play your game *alright*
23.		enjoy it as well *eh* boys
24.		come on let's have some fun boys *huh*
25.		nothing better to do on a Sunday but play some footy *huh*
26.		you all good?
27.	Players:	YEP YO
28.	Seb:	let's go boys

Extract 3: [match day data] pre-match team address

Like the use of collective pronouns, these tag particles were littered throughout these pre-match addresses. At an interactional level, these particles invite those listening to involve themselves more dynamically in the joint performance of solidarity, in what is by and large a monologue address. The players play their role as well by responding to these tags which, in essence, allows them to support or co-construct the joint accomplishment of solidarity being orchestrated by the captain.

As the extracts above illustrate, that involvement is rarely performed verbally and rather is marked through a series of non-verbal acknowledgements of the captain's messages in his address not evident in the transcripts. In the above extract, we do not see any verbal responses from players until they are directly asked to engage in a unified team chant in lines 27 to 28 (we discuss these chants further below). However, the video recording shows nodding as a form of positive non-verbal feedback being enacted by members of the group, as well as player's gaze being directed at the speaker. The huddle also tightened at particular moments during these addresses, as some members squeezed tighter and closer together as the talk unfolded.

We have seen a similar linguistic practice used by the coaches in an earlier chapter, where these tag particles function differently as comprehension checkers. This may also be an intended function of the captain's use of these resources in this context. However, researchers have identified these resources as functioning to seek reassurance from those listening that they are paying attention or to acknowledge that they share the ideas, attitudes, experiences or knowledge being expressed in the messages of the speaker (Bell & Johnson, 1997, p. 6). The specific tag *eh*, as seen in lines 12 and 23 of Extract 3 above, has a history of use in New Zealand English as a solidarity marker. It has been identified as an addressee-oriented resource that is frequently deployed by speakers to establish common ground with their communicative partners (Meyerhoff, 1994). It is also identified as a tag form that is commonly used by working class and Maori speakers. As our team are predominantly of Maori and Pacific Island heritage, the choice of such tags in these pre-match huddles may simultaneously function to indicate and encode solidarity along ethnicity lines.

By involving the players in the ongoing address, even if it is rather minimally, the captain is creating some opportunity for the joint performance (and accomplishment) of solidarity by the assembled group. In positively responding to and acknowledging the captain's messages, the players indicate their acceptance and understanding of those messages, a move that arguably establishes togetherness – or talks it into being – in the process. Also, in putting their acknowledgement on record (through nods), they are showing not only the captain that they are on board, but also other players in the team. With multiple members of the group engaging in this practice and also seeing it being widely engaged in by others in the team, these particle tags and the widespread, non-verbal responses they elicit from players are an important resource in the joint performance of solidarity.

Performing shows of togetherness: Team chants

However, perhaps one of the most obvious joint displays of solidarity amongst the group was the use of the team's chant. In our data, chants were frequently used in the closing stages of huddles, in part functioning to indicate a close to the official business of the huddle. However, they also perform a solidarity function by uniting the group in a very public display of togetherness. In Extract 4, which comes from the end of the huddle in Extract 1, we see the team's chant being deployed at the end of a pre-match team address.

1. Seb: let's fucking hiss boys huh
2. bring it in
3. Players: {inaudible, noisy} LET'S GO YEAH
4. Seb: first touch huh

5.		first touch of the ball first carry
6.		**RHINOS ON THREE ONE TWO THREE**
7.	Players:	**RHINOS**
8.	Seb:	that's us brothers
9.		first touch boys
10.		first tackle
11.		make sure everyone's got their mouthguards

Extract 4: [match day data] pre-match team address, team chant segment

The chant sequence involves the captain shouting the team's motif (in line 6) and counting the players in so they can recite it together and in unison, which they do in line 7. We see other instances of this chant being enacted in previous extracts in this chapter.

Rituals like team or in-group chants have been identified as key solidarity resources and the linguistic and interactive features evident in these chants show how they work as solidarity resources in our context. For one, the words the team are encouraged to shout in many of the team chants were collective terms like the team name (in the above extract), the team's animal or icon, the city name that the team represent or terms denoting a family bond like *brothers*. Which of these options is chosen appears to be the captain's decision to make.

Additionally, these chants, as they are in our data, are typically simple and by being simple, new members of the group are able to learn them easily and can therefore quickly find ways to contribute to the collective practices of the group and indicate their belonging. In-group rituals are said to help members cope with 'potentially problematic situations' (Kádár & Bax, 2013). One of those problems may be generating a sense of belonging and togetherness, particularly in a new team. By being simple, they provide a quick and easy way for all individuals, but particularly those who are new to the team and working out how to fit in, to learn how they can explicitly express their membership and assert their identity as a member of the team.

As with many of the features we have highlighted in this book, the count (*one, two, three*), while it may seem mundane, insignificant, or arbitrary, is an important feature in these chants as it increases the chances of a coordinated response. These chants are likely to be considered successful as solidarity resources if the members are coordinated in their verbal response and that response is loud and stirring enough to signal to those assembled that they have a strong and unified group. The counting acts as a cue that gives the players a clear indication of the time they all need to join in and helps to ensure the greatest chance for cohesion and success in these public displays of togetherness.

As with the tag particles, these chants provide an opportunity for the playing group to explicitly involve themselves in these solidarity rituals by adding their voice to the chant and showing their belonging in the process. In joining in the team chant, individuals respond to the captain's call for membership. They verbally claim that membership to the collective by joining in with the chant, and, in doing so, perform and illustrate, to all of those co-present, their claim to belong. And, by performing their role in these chants, the individuals assert a group identity and make clear to others around them, to whom they are in the process of bonding, that they are a part of the group. To not engage in these chants might, in some cases, raise questions about an individual's commitment or belonging to the team.

Performing supportive talk before and after the huddle formalities

In this last section we focus more directly on other ways the assembled players contributed to these largely captain-led solidarity rituals. Above, we have shown how the captain seeks their involvement, but there are other practices that are worth highlighting here before we round off this discussion of how togetherness is fostered in these pre-match huddles.

One of the patterns we observed in our data was for players to do the bulk of their talking immediately before the huddle began and after the captain had brought the huddle to a close. Their talk in these stages of the huddle contributed further to the desired outcome of solidarity. As we saw in Extract 1 above, **before** the huddle began, multiple players spoke in an effort to ensure everyone was assembled or aware that they needed to assemble together. They would hurry each other along and tell those who were slow to join the huddle to hurry up. **After** the huddle, the players would exclaim messages that contributed to efforts to foster togetherness. Extract 5 below, which shows the end of another pre-match huddle, illustrates several players issuing supportive remarks to each other, but to no one in particular.

		{…pre-match huddle coming to a close…}
1.	Seb:	cool
2.		let's bring it in
3.	Player ?:	let's go brothers
4.	Player ?:	shot boys
5.	Nix:	let's work brothers let's work
6.	Team manager:	FORTY-FIVE SECONDS
7.	Seb:	BROTHERS ON THREE ONE TWO THREE

8.	All:	BROTHERS
9.		{14.0}
10.	Team manager:	THIRTY SECONDS
11.		{14.0}
12.	Jay:	let's go [name]
13.		let's go [name]
14.		{12.0}
15.	Team manager:	TIME TO GO GENTLEMEN
16.		{1.0}
17.	Fletch:	let's go boys
18.	Player ?:	come on let's go let's go
19.	Tee:	let's go starters
20.	Kingy:	let's go boys
21.	Jay:	go hard boys
22.	Nix:	shot boys let's go aye {claps} let's work
23.	Tee:	let's go boys
24.		work hard

Extract 5: [match day data] pre-match team address, closing sequence

In lines 1 to 8, we see the captain finishing his pre-match address and preparing to engage the group in the team's chant. As the group are getting physically closer to one another (and raise their hands in unison), a number of players issue their own acts of encouragement to the group (*let's go*) or directives to the group to *work hard*. The captain then claims the floor again and initiates the chant which brings the formal address component of the huddle to a close. At this stage, in lines 12 to 24, we see a number of the assembled players, many of whom are part of the reserves and non-starters, addressing the wider group with further messages of support, motivation (*come on*) and directives to *work hard*.

These rapid and often overlapping turns at talk are taken by multiple players at a stage in the interaction when the formalities of the huddle have been brought to a close. At this stage, there does not appear to be the same restrictions on turn-taking or the orderly allocation of turns. Instead, players find their voice, claim the space and create an energy through their rapid building of turns, supportive overlaps in their talk and increased volume. These practices by the assembled players can, on the one hand, be seen to contribute to the solidarity goals of these huddles through the offering of **words of encouragement** to one another. However, interactionally, the **repetition** and **mirroring** of one another's contributions, as players build a space full of encouragement, also helps. Mirroring another speaker's acts and repeating similar actions can also be seen as a further linguistic manifestation of solidarity between the members of the interaction, as they simultaneously sanction and reinforce each other's messages and actions.

The speakers in these stages appeared in our data to be predominantly the reserves of the team, and their encouragement moves are directed at the playing group (the starters) as the ones who are about to enter the field of battle. In line 19, one of the players does acknowledge this group explicitly as the target for his words of encouragement. By adding their voices at this stage, together with others, the reserves appear to be in large part responsible for providing a cacophony of supportive messages for the starting group before they begin the match at hand.

So, despite being offered limited opportunity to take the floor in the formal stages of these pre-match huddles, players find opportunities to contribute to the overall performance of solidarity and togetherness in more informal and unstructured stages of these talks. We now consider what these patterns in this particular interactional context tell us about how the dynamics of solidarity work in our team.

Wrapping up: Performing solidarity in pre-match team talks

In this chapter, we have begun to look for evidence of how solidarity works or how it is being attempted and accomplished in the interactional practices of our team. In particular, we have illustrated how ritual language use and interactional practices in pre-match huddles are employed and deployed to help accomplish the interpersonal goal of solidarity – or feelings of togetherness and belonging – amongst the membership of the team immediately before battle. We have, in a sense, presented evidence of how bonds of attachment within the playing group are, in Salmela's (2015) terms, attended to, produced and reinforced in and through non-linguistic and linguistic practices in these pre-match interaction rituals.

Of those practices that can be seen as attempts to foster solidarity in these pre-match huddles, non-linguistic practices such as the huddling into a single unit, maintaining close physical contact, adopting both a shared and an exclusive space, and maintaining eye contact are some of the taken-for-granted ways in which solidarity is encouraged and performed in these huddles. The closeness individuals maintain to one another in these huddles, the actual physical bonding or connecting of the group as a unit, the shared uniform and the visual access they have to one another in these huddles all contribute to the construction of unity and camaraderie amongst the assembled group of individuals in this context.

However, it is the taken-for-granted linguistic practices that perform solidarity in these huddles that we have really tried to draw attention to in this chapter. We have suggested that the frequent use of directives by the captain can be interpreted on one level as an attempt to solidify a shared attitude and purpose amongst the assembled group, as can the frequent use of personal collective pronouns, familiarizers and ethnic in-group markers littered throughout the captain's messages of these pre-match addresses. The collective pronouns functioned to construct the addressees not as individuals but as a unit, emphasizing their sameness, either in sporting terms (i.e., as a *team*) or by construing their bonds along familial lines (i.e., through use of the term *brothers*). We also saw direct efforts by the captain to design messages in ways that sought to reduce any potential divisions within the membership that may be indirectly signalled in the process of issuing directives and motivational messages to members of the assembled group.

There were also attempts by the captain to actually draw the addressees into the performance of these solidarity rituals, encouraging them to contribute to the ongoing performance of group solidarity at hand. This included the frequent use of tag particles, such as *eh*, *alright* and *okay*, that provided an opportunity for players to acknowledge the captain's messages, a move that interactionally, at least, establishes togetherness. The use of team chants, which required players to join in unison with one another, was also a feature of these pre-match huddles and is perhaps the most evident and explicit way in which solidarity was jointly constructed by the team in these huddles.

The analysis presented in this chapter has provided an illustration of how mundane, everyday linguistic mechanisms in these pre-match huddles help perform solidarity functions at an important time for the unity of the team. The last question we need to ask in closing this chapter is what these patterns suggest more broadly about how solidarity works in our professional New Zealand rugby team. One point that is clear is that some of the speech events in our team appear to function more exclusively as solidarity resources and, by extension, are perhaps deployed at times in which fostering solidarity is seen as being particularly important. The prominence and collection of a range of non-linguistic and linguistic practices that appear to perform predominantly relational functions establish these pre-match events as important solidarity devices, and their deployment immediately before battle suggests that this is an important moment when bonds of togetherness need to be heightened and explicitly marked. This point about explicitly marking these bonds of solidarity also suggests that our team prefer to perform this solidarity rather than assume it exists. In other words, the team do not leave solidarity to chance; rather, they ritually require the joint performance and celebration of unity and togetherness, a function these huddles perform.

Secondly, we cannot escape the significant role the captain plays in the performance of these solidarity rituals. One of the more pervasive features of these huddles is that they are led, controlled and dominated by the captain, a point we alluded to in Chapter 5 when outlining the responsibilities afforded to and claimed by the captain. On the evidence presented in this chapter, it is clear that the captain in our team claims and enacts this responsibility to rally the players and to perform important functions to establish bonds of togetherness before battle. This potentially directly connects the captain (and their degree of comfort with such responsibilities) to a team's ability to engage in these joint displays of solidarity and foster togetherness and belonging.

It is important to address the position of power the captain constructs over the players as he leads these pre-match rituals, directing and imposing on players with directives and the requirement to join in with the unfolding pre-match talk. Such a powerful display by the captain does threaten to distinguish or even isolate himself from the players along asymmetrical power lines in much the same way the coaches did in and through their dominant displays in other team interactions. Such practices theoretically undermine attempts to build solidarity with the players, if we consider the potential for asymmetrical power to create distance between individuals. However, one key difference between the coaches and the captain is that the captain is simultaneously a member of the leadership group and a member of the playing group. In other words, he has what Wilson referred to as a foot in both camps. He has the power and authority to impose, while at the same time, the status as an immediate member of the playing group. It is arguably his position as a member of the team that helps to shape interpretation of the captain's interactional practices in these huddles more along solidarity lines. This may in part explain why the coach leaves the hoo-ha to the captain, acknowledging that meanings of solidarity are perhaps less likely to be picked up from the same tokens or actions if delivered by the coach, who is not going onto the field with the players.

In sum, despite dominating these addresses and performing at times quite imposing actions in and through his talk, the captain's position as a member of the team arguably helps to shape his actions more as aides for fostering solidarity than instructions he is imposing upon the players. Solidarity, then, can work *through* the captain who claims the responsibility to lead the group in these ritual solidarity performances, but simultaneously relies on the interpretation, by the addressees, of his membership to the playing group if his messages are to be read as performing solidarity functions. Without this, the captain and his actions may just be interpreted as a leader exercising his power over the players.

In this chapter, we have begun to look for evidence of how solidarity is being performed in and through ritual and routine interactional practices of our team. In particular, we have looked at how togetherness and belonging are attempted and accomplished in and through the linguistic practices of our team's captain and his addressees (to the playing group) in pre-match huddles – an interactional setting where solidarity appears to be a key goal. Based on who is involved in these pre-match huddles, this analysis has also naturally led us to discussion about how solidarity works in the playing group and the role the captain plays in the process. In the next chapter we look at coach–player interactions again, looking for evidence to inform an understanding of how solidarity works between coaches and players in our team context.

8

Maintaining professional distance in interaction

The nature of solidarity between coaches and players

Introduction

In this chapter, we continue to highlight everyday linguistic practices that can help illustrate how solidarity works in the different relational dyads of our team. In this chapter, we return to focus on the coach–player relational dynamic and examine (or re-examine) some of the typical coach–player interactions in our data for evidence of how solidarity worked between coaches and players. In this specific case, we concentrate on practices that shine a light on the degree of social or professional distance coaches manage or maintain, if any, between themselves and their players.

This notion of social distance – i.e. the closeness-distance scale (see Holmes, 2013, p. 9) – is an interesting dimension of solidarity to focus on in the coach–player relationship. Players have been quoted in the media talking positively about friendship-type relations they have with their coaches (Walsh, 2018). However, at the same time, competing evidence suggests that by being friends with players, coaches risk losing authority over players deemed necessary in order to make tough decisions that might not necessarily please the players (Bergmann Drewe, 2002). In this chapter, we contribute indirectly to this debate or discussion by sharing empirical insights from coach–player interactions that help to us put coach–player solidarity, specifically social distance (i.e. closeness), under the microscope.

In what follows, we report on a range of the more pervasive linguistic features that we saw in the coach–player interactional data that encoded clues as to the way solidarity worked in coach–player relations in our team. In particular, we present evidence of interactional practices of **informality** or the use of informal language, situations where **directives** were mitigated, **humour and joking**, and the use of **expressives** (i.e. very revealing and sometimes emotional revelations by the coach) that ultimately provided players with a clear indication of how coaches felt about certain matters and topics.

As we will demonstrate in this chapter, these four linguistic or communicative systems provide a good basis to inform discussions about coach–player solidarity. What the patterns ultimately reveal is that while solidarity between coaches and players is important and it is something coaches orient to in the interactional practices, the resources they draw on to perform solidarity functions, and the way they deploy them, reflect an attempt to maintain social or, perhaps in our specific case, professional distance with the players. We discuss why this relation dynamic might be evident in a professional sporting context in the concluding section of this chapter.

Informal language and leadership: Making oneself approachable

One of the more pervasive practices by coaches that can be seen to function as a solidarity device was the frequent use of informal language features by coaches when delivering team addresses. In addresses during training sessions and on match days, we identified a tendency for coaches to encode their messages with a range of informal lexical items or choices frequently seen in more informal or casual conversation settings, where there is typically a higher degree of solidarity (Eggins & Slade, 1997). Extracts 1 and 2, from training sessions, show one of the assistant coaches in the team (Greg) delivering instructions for a training drill. As can be seen, each extract contains a number of informal language features (several of which have been underlined).

1. **Greg**: <u>**hey boys**</u> we<u>**'re gonna**</u> go straight to those two drills
2. we just <u>**gonna**</u> maybe modify <u>**a couple of**</u> little things
3. this one over here we<u>**'re gonna**</u> do standard as we did the other day but we<u>**'re gonna**</u> play out of that phase <u>**for the bob**</u>
4. okay
5. so first one is <u>**the bill**</u> which would obviously be their forward runners

6.		second one is that first set of hands and will be **the bob**
7.		okay
8.		so we**'re just gonna play out of it**
9.		only want to **hit it** for four minutes
10.		so it's functional roles understanding the soldier goes in tackler out to twenty
11.		yeah? **let's get a little vibe around it** and then **move on over** to the other one
12.		let's go {walks away with purpose}

Extract 1: [training session data] outlining a training drill

1.	**Greg**:	well done **eh**
2.		so **I think** the biggest thing we've got to get to is just **a little bit of** sharing
3.		so we've got oh **fuck** he's higher or lower
4.		let's just **feel a bit of love out fucking talk each other through**
5.		it's not **gonna** be perfect
6.		we've just got to share with each other
7.		the key to it is the biggest thing out of what we got the other day was our tension had **too much daylight** ++ too much movement + okay
8.		so if we can get that tension round up from below through our binds and across our backs elbow in it's **gonna** help us a lot
9.		and it will keep our power lines going + directly down the field
10.		yeah and then we just **fucking** fight
11.		okay? **sweet**?
12.		well done {claps and starts walking away}
13.		**good morning's work**

Extract 2: [training session data] closing a training drill

The linguistic features underlined above are littered throughout coach addresses in our data and show coaches drawing on linguistic choices associated with informal contexts. These features include expletives, like *fuck*, which have been noted elsewhere as a feature more likely to appear unmarked in informal settings (Biber, 1999; Eggins, 2004; Love, 2021; McEnery, 2006). We also see hedges like *a bit* and *a little bit* and vague language features like *a couple* that are also more common in conversations. Their use in other more formal workplace settings can perhaps be seen as attempts by speakers to index or construct a more informal situation between participants. The same principle is in action with the phrase *let's get a little vibe around it* which is an informal way of expressing his desire to see the team perhaps *put effort in* or *become familiar with* the actions being practised in the drill. This assistant coach also favoured phrases like *piss about with* (as in we'll *piss about with* this drill for a bit) instead of more unmarked verb phrases like *do*. There are also examples of a range of effort-saving features frequent in face-to-face spoken interaction in less formal settings, like situational ellipsis, grammatical contraction (i.e. *we're gonna* versus *we are going to*) as well as informal variants of question tags such as *eh* and *sweet* (versus *isn't it*). Such features are much more likely to occur in less formal communicative settings (J. Holmes et al., 2012; Marra et al., 2008; Meyerhoff, 1994).

Technical vocabulary is also an interesting case to reflect on here. While large amounts of technical vocabulary can signal more formal contexts, such as workplace environments, the shaping of technical concepts in the extracts above is in some cases achieved using more informal variants, for example in the use of phrases like *the bob* and *the bill* to refer to more technical roles in a particular training drill. The phrases *power lines* and *too much daylight* are other examples where technical concepts are construed in more informal ways. *Too much daylight*, in Extract 2 above, refers to a weak bind by the forwards (the lack of tight coordination) with the metaphor of letting light in being used to highlight the team's inability to tightly connect with one another (to block out the light). More informal lexical choices and phrases like *hit it* (instead of *push against* the scrum machine) also construe technical activities in more informal ways.

The choice to draw on these informal features in delivering team addresses might reflect many aspects of the context of these interactions. The fact that these extracts are episodes of unplanned spoken speech is one explanation. In line with the constraints of spoken interaction, particularly with respect to the economy of online speech processing, features like ellipsis and grammatical contraction are going to be prominent. The coach may also be attempting to reduce the technical knowledge burden on new players by encoding technical insights with more approachable lexical items.

However, there are also more interpersonally or relationally oriented explanations, one being that these choices and an informal tenor more generally is a way coaches might attempt to build solidarity with players. The persistent drawing on of informal features may be functioning to establish a less formal speech event and a more informal coach (identity). Formality creates distance while informality between speakers suggests lower degrees of social distance. By drawing on informal linguistic features to shape the messages and actions in these formal tasks and activities, the coach may be trying to reduce the formality of the situation and, in the process, obfuscate some of the formal power and authority they have and ritually enact over the players. Another way of putting this is that coaches are actively drawing on informal features to strategically rebalance or reduce the social distance between themselves and their players – a social distance that is simultaneously being created in and through their extensive claims to rights to the interactional floor. The reasons for such a strategic rebalancing may be multiple but may include attempts to construct a more approachable coach. At the very least, the use of these features may help to (re)construct the 'implicit ideological belief (fantasy) that we interact with others as equals' (Eggins, 2004, p. 139).

Another solidarity-related explanation for a specific informal feature used by coaches may lie in the New Zealand cultural context from which the data comes. The question tag *sweet*, for example, is a frequently deployed New Zealand English form and may index the New Zealand identities the speakers share and are publicly claiming and presenting to one another. In this regard, these markers may be functioning as solidarity resources by constructing themselves and the assembled group as together and united along important cultural lines.

Hiding and mitigating directives

Another feature of interest when exploring coach–player solidarity was the degree of mitigation applied to directives issued by the coach to the players, particularly in training sessions. In Chapter 3, we outlined how directives helped coaches to exercise control over the players and were a key resource in establishing themselves as powerful. While this is a pervasive feature of coach–player interaction and coach directives can and were often shaped in very direct ways, in training session data, there was evidence to suggest that coaches could and would draw on linguistic features to design their directives in more mitigated and less direct ways.

Extract 3, from a training session, provides a good illustration of one of the assistant coaches mitigating their directives to players. In this extract we see the coach walking the players through a lineout training drill. The drill is designed to help coordinate the movement of the players (particularly the props and locks) in the lineout and the directives are functioning to indicate to players where they need to position themselves. Of particular interest in this extract is the way the coach performs these directives (see underlined) to the players that indicate where they need to go and what they need to do in the drill in order to coordinate the lineout movements as a group.

1.	Jase:	you want the prop to go in and the lock to just go straight
2.	Po:	yes please
3.	Players:	{players discuss and organize themselves}
4.	Po:	okay **we'll just take a half a metre on each side** + just take another
5.		half a metre off the line + good
6.		okay NAME **when you're ready**
7.	Ashton:	ONE THREE FIVE ONE
8.		{players execute drill}
9.	Po:	good
10.		okay **we'll go with the second movement okay**==
11.		==everyone happy with the number one
12.		{players nod}
13.		okay good
14.		number two **we've got two bailouts** + okay
15.		so the prop bailout
16.		yeah **we'll just walk through guys**
17.		come forward NAME bail out
18.		right to the front on the five + okay==
19.		==only two calls

Extract 3: [training session data] outlining a training drill

Each of the underlined actions above is arguably functioning to tell players what to do and where to be as they coordinate the strategies being practised in the line out training drill. However, instead of taking the typical form of imperative syntax (we do see two examples of this being used in line 17 of this extract – *come forward* and *bail out*), the bulk of these directives are shaped using declarative syntax, where the coach is delivering his directives more indirectly by making statements to the players. These directives are shaped in a form of what Bellinger and Gleason (1982) refer to as **implied directives**. The use of the ritualized phrase *when you're ready* is also arguably performing a directive function here to indicate to the line out caller when they should start the drill; however, this is also not performed using imperative syntax and therefore can be seen, at least on the surface, as an indirect realization of directives to players.

Other linguistic choices used in conjunction with these implied directives also contribute to a more mitigated performance of power in training sessions. Mitigators like *just*, politeness markers like *please* (Vine, 2004, pp. 98–9) and familiarizers like *guys* are design features that perhaps shape the social interactions between powerful and less-powerful members of this professional team in a more collegial, informal manner.

By using declaratives instead of imperatives to shape directives, the coach can also use collective personal pronouns when shaping his messages, where they would otherwise not be able to. Imperatives in English do not typically (i.e. syntactically) allow any pronoun other than (the presumed) *you* to be encoded in the structure (i.e. '(you) do it'), whereas declarative syntax does. The preference for declaratives when issuing directives, then, may allow the coach the opportunity to use these more inclusive pronouns when shaping his messages in ways that further hide or obfuscate the coach's authority and rights to direct the players. The use of *we* in such sequences is arguably **pseudo inclusive** in nature as the coach is not directly including himself when he says *we'll have a go*, as the coach cannot play and is not going to get involved in the training drill. However, in using statements to direct, the coach is able to also use collective pronouns when shaping his directives in ways that may further signal some connection, solidarity or approachability with the players, perhaps at a strategic level.

In this regard, these implied directives signal or symbolically construct, at least in part, a less sharply stratified relationship and therefore may function in a similar way to the frequent use of informal language – to reduce or disguise the power difference that is evident between the coaches and the players. By choosing to perform actions like directives indirectly, particularly in situations where a person has an institutional right to be direct, the speaker can be seen to be orienting more towards their addressees (rather than their own power rights), perhaps in an effort to make their directives more palatable, construct themselves as more approachable and/or to construct a dynamic where power distance is not as pronounced. The use of this feature in training sessions perhaps points to the importance of a more approachable coach at this time, when the goals appear to be more educational and instructional. The fact that this extract comes from the very first training session of the group may also suggest that getting such bonds and an air of approachability set up from an early stage may be viewed as important.

Levity and humour in coach–player exchanges: Unpacking episodes of teasing

One of the more obvious linguistic features that, at least theoretically, signals solidarity and reduced social distance is the sharing of a joke between individuals. Humour is a multifunctional interactional resource, with one of the most widely understood functions being the establishment (or attempts at the establishment) of solidarity between speaker and addressee of a humour attempt.

However, while this is generally considered to be true, researchers have found that it is much more complex than this and certain types of humour may in fact heighten or increase social distance between individuals (Boxer & Cortés-Conde, 1997; Schnurr, 2009). Teasing, for example, establishes quite a different relational dynamic to other forms of humour exchange shared between individuals. Therefore, it is important to locate how the humour is functioning if we are to better understand the particular relational dynamic being reflected and/or constructed by the speakers. In this section, we assess and unpack two extracts that show humour working in the interactions between the coach and the players.

The first point to note from our data was that it was those with powerful institutional roles (i.e. the coaches) that were the only ones to initiate joke-telling sequences in the wider team interactions. This finding perhaps makes sense when we consider that it is coaches that control and dominate team interactions in any case (as discussed in Chapters 3 and 4). However, with specific respect to humour, at a broader level, the apparent right that coaches have to decide when to initiate a humour sequence means that it is down to the coaches to decide when humour is appropriate and perhaps, by extension, when it is time to lighten the mood in and through humour.

However, with respect to the nature of the humour, we noticed that coaches did use humour attempts to tease players. Extract 4 comes from a match evaluation session where the players and coaches are looking at video footage of the team from a recently completed game. The assistant coach (Greg) is leading this segment of the meeting and is focusing player's attention on a clip that shows a defensive issue that led to the opposition scoring a try against our team. This critique focuses on a mistake made by Maz who was playing out of position in fullback but prefers to play at first five. As the segment unfolds, we see a humour attempt by the head coach (Tane) in line 13 that refers to this positional preference of Maz's, insinuating that the player deliberately made the mistake so he would be put back in his favoured position.

1.	**Greg**:	so this one here + we've gotta look up and get these comms in
2.		so clearly on this we needed a flag
3.		ripping out==
4.	**Maz**:	==nah nah that that that was me
5.		I should've been up on him
6.	**Tane**:	mmhm
7.	**Maz**:	up on him early
8.	**Greg**:	back here
9.	**Maz**:	yeah every- everyone was going on

10.	**Tane**:	yeah that's it that's where
11.	**Maz**:	and that should be me there
12.	**Greg**:	okay
13.	**Tane**:	are you doing that so I don't have to put you back at fullback
14.	**All**:	{scattered laughter}
15.	**Maz**:	hhhe eh +++ harsh
16.	**All**:	/{louder laughter}\
17.	**Greg**:	/ah something that arose\
18.		something that arose out of here was...

Extract 4: [team meeting data] talk from a match evaluation/review session

This extract begins with the assistant coach (Greg) assessing the issue in the clip that is being played on the screen indicating what was needed during this sequence of play to avoid letting the opposition score. Interestingly, in lines 4 and 5, we see Maz volunteer himself as the guilty party, interpreting the events that led to the opposition scoring a try as the direct result of his decision to not enter the defensive line. After some back and forth, in which the assistant coach (Greg), Maz and the head coach (Tane) try to confirm what the issue is and whether it contributed to the opposition try (lines 6 to 12), Tane then initiates what can and was interpreted as a humorous assessment of Maz's mistake, implying that it was deliberate and that he intentionally made mistakes in the fullback position so he would be shifted to his favoured position at first five.

At this point, there is scattered laughter from the group who have clearly interpreted the remarks of the coach as functioning as humour. This interpretation is perhaps built on an underlying sociocultural belief in a high-performance sporting context that no one would deliberately sabotage the success of the team in order to get moved into a position they preferred to play in and that to insinuate this is laughable. However, because the coach has formulated his joke as a question, he has also redirected the floor back to Player 2 who responds by laughing himself and using the tag *eh*, seemingly to indicate confusion. However, he then joins into the humour exchange the coach has initiated, perhaps unwittingly, by evaluating the head coach's accusation as *harsh*. This is met with greater amounts of laughter from the gathered team. As the laughter dies down, the assistant coach tries to get the discussion back on task, by reinitiating the performance evaluation task at hand (in line 17) as he draws attention to another issue in the video footage.

How might this humour exchange be assessed, particularly the head coach's humour attempt? As this speech event is designed to draw critical attention to player faults during a match, we might assess the coach's humorous remarks as an attempt more generally to lighten the mood and mitigate any negative feeling the players might be having as they work through recordings that almost exclusively highlight their shortcomings and mistakes. Seen from this perspective, the humour may be an attempt to manage solidarity with players at a time when the coaches are performing face-threatening and potentially relationship-damaging speech acts. We pick up this point more directly in the next chapter.

However, there is additional contextual information that might add nuance to our interpretation of this humour attempt by the coach. Maz's positioning at fullback is central to understanding the joke and criticism that is being hinted at here in this extract. During my time with the team, it was clear that there was a sense of disagreement between the head coach and Maz about which position Maz should play. Maz wanted to play at first five (a game-driving position) while the coach seemed to want him to play at fullback. On this occasion, Maz is playing at fullback, and it is his decision making while playing in this fullback position that has caused the error and let the opposition score a try. The coach, in drawing attention to Maz's desire to play at first five and suggesting that he has deliberately made the mistakes to try and force the coach's hand, is arguably teasing Maz.

Teasing, while still a form of humour, can be more problematic and complex to assess when it comes to understanding the sometimes-multiple functions it performs, particularly in such a wide participation framework (i.e. with the rest of the team listening). On the one hand, the humorous exchange for those from the wider group listening along may provide entertainment and help to lighten the mood in what is a sometimes face-threatening interactional context. At the same time, the tease may also be an attempt to foster solidarity between two individuals who may have different opinions about where the player should play. Read from this perspective, the coach may be extending an olive leaf and publicly illustrating for the rest of the team that the relationship between himself and Maz is on good ground, despite the player not playing in his favoured position. Both of these functions potentially point to the construction of positive relations and indicate a lower degree of social distance between the individuals involved.

However, teasing can also perform other subtle functions that are not necessarily solidarity oriented. In this case, one of those may be to subtly and indirectly put Maz in his place, hierarchically. Maz has openly expressed a personal desire to play in a position that the coach does not want him to play in and by teasing him the coach may be attempting to manage this difference of opinion in his favour. By challenging the player's motivations for making the mistakes, or even that he had motivations for making the mistake, the coach may be enacting a powerful identity over the player, one that claims the right to hold people accountable, even if these accountability acts are dressed up and performed indirectly through acts of humour. Seen from this perspective, teasing can be viewed less as a solidarity device and more as another tool in the repertoire of power mechanisms that coaches draw on to enact their control over the players, be it individual players or the wider group (Boxer & Cortés-Conde, 1997; Miller, 1986).

In Extract 5 we see another humour exchange between the head coach and the players that arguably amounts to teasing. This one is also interesting to reflect on in light of the key issue of this chapter – how coach–player solidarity works – as it also shows the coach's authority potentially being undermined through humour directed back at him by a player in the team. This extract, which we will unpack across two parts, provides us with an example to mine for evidence of how this situation, where the coach is the butt of the joke, plays out and what signals are sent about coach–player social distance and solidarity in the process.

In this extract, the head coach is winding down a training session he has run with the backs (a subgroup of the team) and is providing some final remarks about the upcoming match. Of particular interest is the exchange between lines 8 and 23, where the head coach (Tane) tries to recall the name of a strategic play and when he struggles, he humorously threatens another player to remember and recall it or lose his position in the team (in line 12). However, in line 20, the coach then finds himself on the receiving end of the same humorous sequence, with another player in the team challenging the coach to recall the strategy name.

1.	Tane:	so if they only go um ++ ten wing then ++ then ++ then it's probably going to be on that way
2.		but we've gotta make sure that we beat the halfback getting round
3.		if he does and if the halfback comes round we've gotta still be aware to call shooter and go back that way
4.		so when I watched the [opposition team name] game on the weekend um the halfback always stays here and once the halfback goes we'll go round and cover
5.		which means on Sunday we'll probably we'll probably go shooter
6.		or==
7.	Maz:	==we can even get the half back to (unclear)
8.	Tane:	**yeah + so what did we call that last year**
9.		{2.0}
10.		**BJ you were in the team**
11.	BJ:	**yeah** {puts ball to his head to mimic thinking}
12.	Tane:	**come on + you wanna stay in the team**
13.	Players:	{loud laughter}

14.	BJ:	**um (fuck) I can't /remember**
15.	Maz:	**/TBH**
16.	BJ:	**aye yeah T==**
17.	Leaf:	**==nah was it**
18.	BJ:	**nah I can't remember**
19.	Tane:	**the pressure**
20.	Timmy:	{*to the coach*} **what is it Tane**
21.	Players:	{*loud laughter*}
22.	Tane:	**I'll get back to you**
23.		**wasn't it Rams?**
24.	Maz:	no that was moneyball wasn't it
25.	Leaf:	was it
26.	Tane:	Rams was oh Rams was off the deck eh
27.		I'll go back to your um your backline menu that Flynn did for us
28.		um /so + so there's\ those options
		[…]

Extract 5(A): [training session data] talk from the closing segment of a training drill

The origin of this humour sequence is in line 8 when the coach asks the wider group for the name of a strategy the team used last year to help combat what is perceived to be the opposition's attack strategy. After a period of silence, he then selects a particular player (BJ) to offer an answer and justifies his reason by saying that BJ was in the team (and in the half back position) and should therefore be able to recall it. In line 11, BJ acknowledges that he should know (*yeah*) at which stage Tane humorously suggests that if the player wants to remain in the team, he needs to recall the strategy name. This is met by loud laughter from the assembled group of backs who signal that they interpret this remark to be humorous and not a real threat.

In line 14, the player admits that he cannot recall the name of the strategy. Others jump in with suggestions, but the strategy name still alludes BJ who has been tasked with remembering it. In line 19, Tane then takes his teasing sequence further, evaluating the player's inability to recall the strategy when put on the spot as perhaps being a sign of not being able to handle *the pressure*. This move extends the teasing further and continues to threaten the face of the player being targeted by the tease. However, at this point, in line 20, another player, Timmy, one who is very experienced, jumps in and directs the question back to the coach, asking him to recall it (*what is it Tane?*). This is met with even louder laughter from the assembled group. This louder laughter in line 21 may reflect an understanding that the action by Timmy in this exchange flouts the social norms of player–coach relations by claiming the power to hold the coaches accountable. Timmy also uses the coach's first name which suggests a degree of familiarity and a less formal exchange.

While it is viewed and interpreted as humour, through his humour attempt, Timmy has temporarily undermined or reduced the coach's position of authority, and any association with being untouchable, in a very public way. The conditions set by the coach when suggesting that the player who could not recall the strategy name was unable to handle *the pressure* have now potentially been shifted to him, and make his inability to recall the strategy name potentially face-threatening for Tane. The coach joins in the laughter and defers answering to another time (*I'll get back to you*) which is an admission that he does not know but also a power move that suggests he can defer answering. He does put forward a potential answer (in line 23), but this is hedged with uncertainty markers, namely a **negatively constructed Y/N interrogative** that favours a no answer. All of these moves (to defer answering, join in with the laughter and pose a heavily hedged answer) help the coach to navigate the face-threat that has now shifted to him. It may also threaten the coach's expert identity, as the member of the team with the greatest claims to expert knowledge (which we reviewed in Chapter 4). As this sequence draws to a close, the exchange continues as players and the coach correct one another and then negotiate a plan to find out the name of this strategy.

This sort of humour exchange perhaps reflects the closest illustration of equal footing (or no social distance) being enacted between coaches and players in our data. Not only do we see players (or a player) claiming the same rights as coaches to both issue humour attempts in front of the wider group, but we also see this player claiming the right to challenge the hierarchically more powerful coach and hold him accountable. This action essentially constructs a more equal floor, and a more equal footing, where accountability and jostling are bidirectional social processes between coaches and players.

Such practices hint at a high degree of solidarity being constructed between the coach and the players at this moment in time. In this sequence, the coach has had his power and rights to not be challenged by subordinates undermined. While on the one hand this may be read negatively as disrespectful, it can also be seen as a moment through which solidarity is being performed through a shared joke that interactionally (and temporarily) establishes the individuals as equals. Additionally, the shared laughter after both of these jokes perhaps indicates that those gathered do not perceive anything malicious in the underlying speech acts being performed. The presence of laughter and jocular insults has also been a feature identified in previous research as functioning to enhance solidarity (Daly et al., 2004; Hay, 1994; Kuiper, 1991).

However, as this extract continued, we saw moves by the coach to potentially reassert his authority over the players and redress any undermining of this power that may have resulted from the earlier humorous exchange. In Extract 5B, a continuation of the above extract, we see the coach bringing the interaction to a close (line 51) and telling them they have a bit of downtime while they wait for the next training drill to start. In doing so, he teases the other group of players (the forwards), who the backs are waiting for and who are not in earshot, by humorously referring to them as *idiots*, a move that arguably attempts to build bonds with the assembled players (or backs). However, as everyone starts walking away, the coach reinitiates his search for the strategy name and again holds BJ accountable (lines 53 to 56).

		[...]
48.	Tane:	let's let's not be afraid to call our moves and go through with our skills like Maz was saying ++ okay==
49.		==let's back our skills to get our + our um ourselves away or backdoor on ourselves
50.		{3.0}
51.		**a bit of downtime until we wait for these idiots**
52.		{everyone starts walking away}
53.		**BJ**
54.	BJ:	**yo**
55.	Head coach:	**think of what that term was**
56.	BJ:	**yep**
57.		{some players laugh}

Extract 5(B): [training session data] talk from the closing segment of a training drill

In line 53, we see the coach call out to BJ, as he is walking away, and in line 55 direct him to find out the name of the strategy. BJ agrees and as everyone is walking away some players gathered near BJ laugh again and tease him. Importantly, this action by the coach in line 55 is performed loud enough for the assembled playing group to hear. This activates a wider participation framework (than just Tane, and BJ) and opens up the potential for the coach's action to be functioning on multiple levels. In other words, the coach may be performing additional social actions beyond merely asking the player to find out the name for a strategy. He may also be communicating to the rest of the group at the same time, perhaps attempting to reassert some of the authority that may have been watered down by the establishment of more equal relations in the humour exchange that occurred immediately before this one. Viewed from this perspective, the action performed by the coach in line 55 might reflect a more general discomfort with the idea of establishing more equal relations and may reflect an attempt to publicly reassert or repair his authority in front of the group. By publicly and explicitly repairing this asymmetrical power dynamic, through a directive to the player, the coach indicates to the players that normal service has resumed and the more typical power dynamic between the coach and his players has been re-established after a temporary redefinition of their relationship.

The sequences surveyed above provide an in-depth illustration of how humour worked in coach–player interactions in our team and give us data upon which to further unpack the relational dynamics of solidarity between coaches and players. On the basis of the evidence presented above, we do see humour being exchanged between coaches and players. However, that humour is initiated by coaches and can take the form of teasing of the players by the coach. Additionally, we might also conclude that attempts by players to establish an equal footing with coaches, and engage in their own jostling and teasing of the coaches, may be viewed as more problematic by the coaches, perhaps on the basis that it (uncomfortably) reduces hierarchical distance between coaches and players and establishes a more familiar relational dynamic than we have seen established in other chapters of this book. We pick up and unpack this point further when we wrap up our account of coach–player solidarity in the last section of this chapter.

Establishing shared attitudes: Letting the players in

However, before we do bring this chapter to a close, we will highlight one final feature we feel can inform a discussion of how solidarity works between coaches and players. In our data, we found evidence of some coaches expressing often quite explicit personal attitudes, particularly towards the opposition immediately before the match. Extract 6 comes from the build-up to a match. In this extract, one of the assistant coaches is wrapping up the drill and debriefing the players before they head into the changing sheds to finalize their preparations for the start of the match. He provides some final advice and warnings to the players regarding the opposition and the need to execute fast line speed against them. However, before he closes the interaction, he arguably **changes his interactional footing** and shares an assessment of the opposition that reveals how he himself feels about them (see lines 10–11 in particular).

1. Terry: there's something I wanna say (unclear) just what I said before
2. as much as I'm not over the new rules yet one thing these cunts will try and do is choke you when you carry

3.		so make sure you carry nice and fucking bullseye get that leg drive
4.		just get rid of the fucking threads okay
5.		and defensively okay + I'm not talking about defensive ruck as a system fucking work hard==
6.		==if line speed was that easy every fucking cunt would do it
7.		line speed comes from working off the ball to get your fucking line in place
8.		get (unclear) get your mates THEN you can get your speed
9.		so fucking work hard off the ball to bring that
10.		**the last thing for those of you who might be fucking new and don't know it that's fucking (opposition name) there**
11.		**I don't give a fuck if it's pre-season in season or grand fucking final we hate those cunts**
12.	Player?:	yeah
13.	Terry:	just fucking take that in with you as well alright {*coach walks away from the players and leaves the captain to pick up the thread of the communication*}
14.	Player?:	alright boys
15.	Seb:	bring it in boys
16.		HEY HEY!
17.	Players:	HO!

Extract 6: [match day data] talk from the closing segment of a pre-match warm-up drill

The emotive language (swear words) used by Terry to describe the opposition (as *cunts*) and to express feelings of *hate* towards them does stand out, particularly in relation to other settings, extracts and language features we have surveyed in previous chapters. As a message, the utterances of the coach here arguably attempt to rally the team and encourage similar attitudes by those he is addressing and can therefore be seen as direct attempts to foster shared feelings and togetherness within the team. However, indirectly, they also build solidarity between the coach and the players. In the process of making these assessments, the coach is putting on record very personal and expressive remarks about other people and entrusts those listening with this new personal knowledge he has disclosed to them. This sharing of personal attitudes has been noted as a feature of relationships that have a high degree of solidarity (Drasovean & Tagg, 2015; J. Harwood, 2016).

With reference to swearing more generally, the frequent use of swear words in interaction in male sports teams has also been noted by other researchers as a solidarity device (Wilson, 2011). While swear words can convey content-level meanings, they do make meanings on a more pragmatic or relational level, for example, helping the speaker to express to their audience the intensity of their message level. However, at a deeper relational level, their use may also function symbolically to signal or reconstruct association with a group or groups of people (i.e. men or rugby players) who are seen to ritually use them. While evidence suggests that the amount of swearing between men and women is not that different (Bayard & Krishnayya, 2001), associations with and observations of frequent swearing in the environment of a men's sports team have been noted as attempts to performing masculinity. Therefore, the frequent and ritual use of swearwords in our team, particularly strong ones that are de-semanticized and ritually deployed across a range of interactional contexts, may reflect a more ritual performance of solidarity along gender and professional identity lines.

Returning to the extract, the use of the pronoun *we* is also significant here as it helps the coach to construe an ingroup (those assembled and listening) and an outgroup (the opposition). The *we* in *we hate those cunts* is somewhat ambiguous but, at the same time, quite powerful. It may be referring to everyone in the region that our team represents, it may be referring to everyone who has previously played for the team before, it may be referring just to those present and listening, or it may be referencing all of these groups and connecting them together into a single, large ingroup. The coach is also arguably establishing himself as a member of this ingroup and, in the process, establishes a bond between himself and the players on the basis of a shared dislike for this particular opposition. The coach also establishes another group of individuals – those who are *new* and *those who don't know yet* – and, in essence, initiates them into this ingroup by establishing one of the key conditions upon which this group is built (their dislike for this particular opposition). Through this interactional sequence of utterances, the coach invites these new players to adopt this position towards the opposition in order to see themselves as part of the *we*.

While the above is perhaps more likely to be understood as a motivational technique, the coach's actions and message design work here can simultaneously be read as an attempt to establish solidarity between himself and the players. By directly expressing how he feels, the coach is sharing and letting the players see his personal beliefs and attitudes, putting on record and trusting players with his very critical and sometimes explosive assessments of another group of people. Sharing of this kind is frequently seen in close relationships, such as those between friends, which are typically defined along low-social distance and high-solidarity lines. However, here, in this professional context, by volunteering and disclosing these very personal feelings of others, the coach is momentarily establishing a more personal or closer relationship with the players.

Wrapping up: Social distance in the coach–player relationship

In this chapter, we have looked again at interactions between the coaches and players, but this time we have analysed the linguistic practices for evidence of solidarity and social distance between coaches and players, particularly efforts by the coaches (as dominant speakers in team settings) to foster solidarity with their players.

In the above analysis, we have highlighted a range of features in the coaches' language that could be functioning to foster solidarity between themselves and their players within the professional activities they are engaged in. These features include the encoding of their talk with informal language that, in this formal workplace context, may be viewed as an attempt to reduce the formality of the situation and by extension the formality of the relations between the coaches and the players. We also highlighted efforts by some of the coaches to mitigate their directives (a practice we will pick up on further in the final findings chapter) and to draw on implied directives when engaged in sequences of talk designed to educate players. Such a practice may work as a solidarity-fostering device if we view it as an attempt to (temporarily and/or strategically) obfuscate the asymmetrical power relationship typical between coaches and players. In situations where there is less power distance between individuals, there is arguably greater solidarity as speakers attempt to construct themselves more as equals. In educational settings there may be strategic value in having lower degrees of power distance, as experts make themselves more approachable to players to make dialogue on issues being experienced more comfortable.

We also surveyed humour sequences in our data in the interactions between coaches and players. Humour has long been understood to reflect and construct bonds of solidarity between those sharing a joke. However, in reality, humour is much more intricate and complex and there are different kinds of humour that may establish more or less solidarity between individuals. In our data, teasing was a feature of the humour patterns identified in coach–player interactions and these practices are arguably another mechanism within the coach's armoury for performing their powerful identities and powerful roles. We also saw evidence of what happens when the tables are turned and a player teased the coach. In this instance, we saw what was arguably an attempt by the coach to reassert that power difference in the wake of this humour sequence in which their authoritative position in the team had been temporarily undermined or challenged.

Finally, we saw examples of one coach (Terry) sharing what were personal, expressive and very revealing assessments of another group of players that, if seen in other contexts (like the media), might be deemed to be very controversial. Such sharing of personal attitudes and feelings has long been associated with close relationships, and it may be this association that led us to interpret these linguistic practices as fostering solidarity with the players and not only performing motivational functions. Letting people in and letting them see how you see the world is a very personal action and implies a level of trust that these personal opinions will be kept in confidence or interpreted as genuine attempts to share and bond. It is these associations that point to meanings of solidarity in this expressive sharing of personal attitudes.

The above discussion highlights specific ritual and interesting linguistic practices in a range of contextual situations in our data and unpacks how these practices can be seen to function to foster solidarity between coaches and players. However, when it comes to assessing these findings together, for broader conclusions about how solidarity works in coach–player relations, we have a more complex picture. On the one hand, on the basis of the evidence presented in this chapter, we can argue that maintaining solidarity with their players is or was a concern for coaches in our team. In other words, coaches did make linguistic adjustments to their talk and/or engaged in a range of linguistic practices that attempt, signal or establish more familiar bonds with others in the course of their everyday authentic interactions.

However, at the same time, the evidence we have reviewed above does show that these solidarity-fostering practices are still being performed in situations where coaches are enacting power over the players. In other words, we found little evidence of the purpose of talk diverging from task-oriented to relationally oriented aims (i.e. discussion of topics away from rugby, small talk sequences). So, while solidarity may be being oriented to by the coach in and through actions such as informal language, mitigating directives, engaging in joke sequences and sharing personal assessments of the opposition, these acts are performed within a wider frame of task-oriented activity that marks relations between coaches and players as professional and distant in terms of power. As a result, any notions of solidarity along equality lines, such as the anecdotal claims of friendship, were not evident in our team. Relationships are strictly business, and what we see is more of an attempt by coaches to make themselves more approachable through stylistic patterning of their messages as they engage in their everyday purposeful, professional and powerful linguistic practices.

In cases where the talk between coaches and players did diverge from the more professional, task-oriented nature towards a more wholly relational nature, as in the joke-telling sequence in Extract 5 above, there were also efforts by the coach to redress threats to his power over players and protect his authority over the group. This suggests that any solidarity that is formed between coaches and players may be deemed, by coaches at least, as needing to develop *within* the wider, overarching and asymmetrical power distance that frames the professional relationship between these two groups within the team (if this is indeed possible). What might be visible through this analysis of solidarity in action, then, is the construction of professional distance between the coaches and the players. Certainly, the expression and performance of togetherness and belonging we saw in the previous chapter between members of the playing group, as they bonded before battle, was not evident in the interactions between coaches and players. The fact that the coaches are absent from those interactions is perhaps also telling with respect to coach–player solidarity, as they remove themselves from the moments when solidarity within the team is expressed in its most direct and explicit ways.

The relational dynamics and discussion presented in this chapter may reflect and reconstruct an understanding that *coaches can be friendly with players but not friends*. In other words, when drawing on many of these resources, coaches do so to help project a more relatable persona while engaged in the process of enacting their authority over the players. At the same time, these practices suggest that the activity the group (both coaches and players) are engaged in is predominantly a task-oriented one. While there are some markers of a more relational environment being constructed in the extracts above (particularly Extract 5), the coaches overwhelmingly established, through their talk and ownership of talk, business- or task-oriented relations concerned mostly with achieving tangible outcomes than building close *personal* relationships. Such practices, then, may reflect and reconstruct an overarching value of the cultural environment of high-performance sport that relationships in sports teams are first and foremost a professional, goal-oriented phenomena.

In the next and final findings chapter, we stay with the topic of coach–player solidarity and this time study patterns in coach–player interactions where critical feedback and acts of criticism were being deployed. Criticism, theoretically at least, presents a threat to solidarity between those individuals involved, i.e. the criticizer and the target for criticism. Therefore, a close analysis of the way these sequences of talk are managed promises to provide further evidence for our discussions of how solidarity works in our professional New Zealand rugby team.

9

Criticism and solidarity between coach and players

Variation in critical feedback practices

Introduction

In the final findings chapter, we continue to look at the issue of solidarity between coaches and their players by studying the way solidarity was or was not attended to in recognizable episodes of critical feedback in our data. Acts of critical feedback or criticism are interesting to look at with respect to relationships and particularly with respect to solidarity, because criticism is, at least theoretically, a threat to interpersonal solidarity. When an individual criticizes another, the act can threaten the positive face of the person they are criticizing, which, in turn, can damage feelings of solidarity between the criticizer and the target for the criticism. The degree of face and solidarity loss may extend further for the target of the criticism if that criticism is delivered in a room full of people.

Linguists have shown how speakers may navigate this threat by refraining from issuing any criticism in a situation where it might be expected, or by attempting to modify the strength of the act of criticism so as to make it more tolerable for the target of criticism (P. Brown & Levinson, 1978; Goffman, 2006; J. Holmes, 1984; J. Holmes & Marra, 2004; Lim & Bowers, 1991; Schnurr et al., 2007; Spencer-Oatey, 2008). However, alternatively, speakers may, for any number of reasons, not manage the threat at all and engage in face-threatening behaviour (Bousfield, 2008; Bousfield & Locher, 2008; Culpeper, 2011; File, 2017). In our data, there was observable variation in the way criticism of players was performed in and across different situations by coaches. In some situations, coaches took care and could be seen to linguistically minimize the threat of their acts of criticism, drawing on very indirect methods of shaping their critical feedback for players. In other situations, we saw evidence of very direct acts of criticism which were in some cases actually boosted in what might be seen as a direct threat to solidarity.

In this chapter, we draw attention to this variation and mine the situations or contexts in which direct and indirect practices of criticism in coach–player interactions were deployed for insights about coach–player solidarity. In particular, we aim to locate features of these different situations that might explain the variable practices we see. In the analysis that follows, we move from the most indirect to the most direct forms of criticism that we found in the coach–player interactions in our data, presenting illustrations of critical in a range of contexts and unpacking potential explanations for a coach's efforts (or lack of effort) to protect the positive face of the player that is subject to critical feedback.

Leaving criticism unsaid: Withholding praise as a form of criticism

In our data we found some evidence of coaches refraining from critical feedback altogether in situations where it was theoretically justified or relevant. In Extract 1, we illustrate a situation where this strategy was particularly evident: while the team were engaged in training drills in training sessions. In this extract, the forwards are engaged in a repetitive scrummage drill where pairs (a prop and a lock) are practising their scrum connections by trying to coordinate their efforts to push more effectively against a scrum machine. Extract 1 contains three sequences from this training drill that occurred one after the other as different pairs performed the drill one after the other. As can be seen, there are differences in the way praise is used in Sequences 1 and 3 and the way it is withheld in Sequence 2.

{Coach 1 approaches players who have just done the task and provides feedback}
{Group 1 assembles to do the task}

Sequence 1

1. **Red**:   CROUCH +++ BIND +++ SET {players engage and push, then hold}
2.   AND {as players push}
3.   stay straight

CRITICISM AND SOLIDARITY BETWEEN COACH AND PLAYERS

4.		AND *{as players push}*
5.		yep
6.		break
7.		nice
8.	**Players**:	nice boys *{other players clap and offer positive feedback}*

{Group 2 assemble to do the task, talking and organising themselves for the task}

Sequence 2

8.	**Jase**:	are you left shoulder
9.	**Abel**:	yep
10.	**Jase**:	do you wanna go with him
11.	**Abel**:	nah I'll just go here
12.	**Jase**:	oh yeah
13.		{4.0} *{as players get into position}*
14.	**Red**:	CROUCH +++ BIND +++ SET *{players engage and push, then hold}*
15.		and *{as players push}*
16.		{1.0}
17.		break
18.		{1.0}
19.		break

{player 1 walks towards Coach 2 and appears to ask for feedback}
{Group 3 get ready to do the task}

Sequence 3

20.	**Red**:	CROUCH +++ BIND +++ SET *{players engage and push, then hold}*
21.		YEAH there you go
22.	**Players**:	IN *{as players push}*
23.		nice
24.	**Players**:	IN *{as players push}*
25.	**Red**:	break
26.		yeah nice boys
27.		nice NAME

Extract 1: [training session data] talk during a live training drill (with the forwards)

Each sequence above follows a ritual pattern, in terms of both the physical actions and the way the interaction plays out. Each pair assembles to do the drill, sometimes briefly speaking to each other about the way they will approach it. They are then given the go-ahead to do the drill by the coach who counts them in using the ritual scrum preparation phrase (*crouch, bind, set*). While the players do the drill, the coach encourages them to continue pushing using the word *and* (lines 2, 4 and 15) to help them both coordinate their pushes and indicate that they should keep going. He then tells them to stop, using the directive *break*. At this stage, and in Sequences 1 and 3, we see public displays of positive feedback being issued to those players who have just completed the drill from both the coaches and the surrounding players upon successful completion of the drill.

In Sequence 2, we see this praise stage withheld by both the players and the coach. For those watching on, including the researcher, it is obvious that the players involved in Sequence 2 have not been able to complete the drill appropriately. Their backs are bent in an unsafe position, they have not been able to coordinate their pushing efforts and, importantly, the scrum machine they are pushing has not really moved. The fact that their backs are bent in an unsafe position is what likely leads to the call from the coach to stop the drill (through the directive *break* in lines 17 and 19). Upon completion of the drill, the coach and players withhold praise, a move that is marked in comparison to the other sequences illustrated here and other instances of this training drill.

This action to withhold praise could be seen as an indirect way to perform critical feedback. By withholding positive feedback, when it is ritually due or expected in an interactional sequence, coaches and players signal that the drill was not performed properly, and that praise is therefore not warranted. In not filling this **praise** slot, the group indicate that the drill performance as not good enough, but they do so in a very indirect fashion, choosing not to go on record and give critical feedback (or feedback of any kind for that matter) in a situation where it is, by all accounts, justified or appropriate.

Withholding of praise, as a strategy for delivering (or implying) criticism, then, may help coaches and players to perform the dual demands of holding players accountable and encouraging correctness in drill performance, while at the same time attempting to manage face threats that are likely to already be felt by the players from their public failure to perform a drill. Any decision to go on record and offer further critical feedback to the players may compound these threats and damage face further.

The other alternative, to simply offer praise and words of encouragement, was also not taken up in this sequence, and this may similarly be explained with respect to the potential for face-threat. Praise for an errant performance, particularly when it has been given to players who correctly performed the drill, may also come across as patronizing (to those in Sequence 2), a move which may in its own right be deemed face-threatening in this particular professional context. It may also be a contravention of the high-performance ideals professional sports teams often set for themselves, to only accept high standards and never accept mediocrity. In short, there must be some form of consequence for an errant performance and withholding praise when it is due was the most indirect way this is accomplished in our data.

The setting in which this strategy is being used might also be significant for understanding when and why this more indirect strategy for delivering critical feedback is used by coaches. The fact that this indirect strategy occurred in training sessions may reflect an understanding that training sessions are a place where players can try things out, push their limits and fail in an effort to improve and get better, and that mistakes do not necessarily need a public evaluation by the coach, particularly if they impinge on player confidence. In other words, the indirect strategies deployed in this episode of critical feedback may be an attempt to not kick the player when they are already down.

Putting critical feedback on record: Implying and mitigating acts of criticism in match evaluation settings

Despite some evidence of the above strategy in our data, coaches would more frequently put on record critical feedback of players, predominantly by offering what could be read as corrective or critical accounts of player performances. However, in the majority of these instances, where acts of critical feedback were clearly being performed, there was an effort by the coaches to modify the force of these acts. We found a significant amount of evidence of this practice in two settings in particular and we illustrate these below, starting with match evaluation sessions.

Implied criticism in match evaluation sessions

One setting where we saw a significant amount of critical feedback was the match evaluation session, usually held immediately before the first training session after a match. Extract 2, which we have already reviewed in our Chapter 4 discussion of the functions of questions, comes from a match evaluation session and shows the coach engaged in the process of delivering critical feedback to the players. Unlike in Extract 1, some form of recognizable critical feedback in this context was put on record, usually as a passage of play was being shown to the players and reviewed. However, the coaches did appear to mitigate the strength of this critical feedback by drawing on a range of linguistic and interactional resources designed to soften the critical stance being articulated on the passage of play in question. One of those resources was to **imply criticism** through what was, by and large, a descriptive account of the players' actions.

1.	**Tane**:	okay so if we have a look here ++ you know that's +++ that's just one
2.		step in and moving
3.		so that's almost gonna be a + that's almost going to be a voluntary tackle
4.		so if that happens ++ and I've got no problem with this + got no
5.		problem with this
6.		but ++ if it happens where where should the penetration come from
7.	**Salu**:	the tip support
8.	**Tane**:	yeah ++ so these guys should be you know if this guy's standing still
9.		then these guys need to be penetrating and getting the tips on out there
10.		okay + cos if you have a look ++ being there + you know these guys
11.		are all in
12.		here's a little bit of a gap that we can get into ++ okay

Extract 2: [team meeting data] talk from a match evaluation session

In this particular case, we see that the technical decisions of two players (when involved in the ruck) are being highlighted for critical attention by the coach (lines 1 to 3). The issue appears to be either how many or which players are committing themselves to the ruck. Some players who have already set the defensive line have suddenly entered the ruck in an attempt to disrupt the opposition's ball. However, in doing so, they have left gaps in the defensive line, and the coach appears to be drawing attention to which players can perform this disruptive action and which need to remain in the defensive line.

Technical details aside, it is clear in Extract 2 that the coach is engaged in the process of providing a critical account of their actions in this passage of play. However, we need to draw on our understanding of the match evaluation activity that the group are engaged in to help us make this determination, as the coach's actual acts of criticism are only **implied** in what is a *descriptive* analysis (or running commentary) of the sequence of play. The majority of the acts being issued in this extract are descriptions (or statements) of what people are doing and are not doing, and the coach is relying on players to understand that these descriptive remarks (that are free from any strong critical markers) are performing important critical feedback functions for addressing issues.

There are a range of subtle markers in the design of the coach's speech actions that perhaps provide some interpretive support for understanding the remarks of the coach as being critical in nature. Of these markers, perhaps the clearest indication that the coach's talk is critical in nature is the sequence pre-empted by the expression *I've got no problem with this* (lines 4 to 5) and the subsequent question asking players what *should* have been done (in line 6). The former phrase suggests that while the coach does not have a problem with one aspect of the decision making by players, he does have reservations about a subsequent aspect of play. The use of *should* in the question that follows this sequence signals that everything said prior should be read as a critical account and that the coach thinks there is a more suitable or appropriate approach to executing this passage of play. He also follows this up with an explicit account of what *needs to* be done (in line 9) which can also be read as speech actions aiming to correct or direct player behaviour. The use of tokens like *problem*, the modal *should* and the semi-modal *need to* in this performance evaluation context also helps to establish it as an episode of problem talk and establish an obligation or necessity on the players to correct their actions in line with the coach's assessments.

However, in comparison to practices we saw in other contexts, which we discuss later in this chapter, the practices or actions of the coach in extracts like this still reflect an indirect approach to delivering criticism in these performance evaluation settings. Unlike in Extract 1, the coach does put on record their dissatisfaction with a particular passage of play but does so indirectly through a descriptive account of what is being done, what is not being done and what should or needs to be done. He does not provide any directly negative assessments of individuals or the passage of play, nor does he engage in other related acts associated with criticism, like assigning blame or eliciting face-threatening admissions of guilt. There are also a series of mitigators sprinkled around the sequence that potentially function to help create a more indirect tenor. The use of the adverb *almost* in line 3, when criticizing the player's failure to recognize a voluntary tackle, or the use of *a little bit* in line 12 to report on the opportunity the players missed to locate a gap in the opposition's defensive line, mitigates the strength of any criticism being implied in and through the coach's descriptive account of player actions.

Criticism that is implied and/or that has been modified or downgraded in strength was a frequent practice in these match evaluation sessions and can be read as an attempt by the coach to manage threats to solidarity between himself and individual players in the team that might emerge as significant in sequences of critical feedback. In the next section, we look at another linguistic practice that, arguably, also functions to this end.

Strategically using pronouns to minimize face threat to individuals

Another interesting linguistic feature in match evaluation sessions was the coach's frequent use of the collective pronoun *we* when shaping their acts of critical feedback. In Extract 3, the head coach (Tane) is again using a video clip to draw attention to the positioning of players in the offensive line (the lateral support). In this extract the coach is drawing attention to an issue he has observed where some players, when engaged in attack, have not stayed *lateral* and have overrun the line making quick passing through the backline harder.

1.	**Tane**:	um we just need to be careful with our lateral support
2.		so here {*playing video clip of sequence of play*} see how we've overrun-we've overrun it
3.		we did this a couple of times
4.		so we've just gotta make sure um (.) we can stay lateral
5.		but at some time before he gets tackled we might need to go back in and and um and get in behind in terms of that support
6.		so that was that was an example +++ um {*clicks to the next video*}
7.		[...]

Extract 3: [team meeting data] talk from a match evaluation session

Again, the acts of criticism are implied in the coach's contribution to this feedback sequence. In line 1, the coach shapes the first utterance of this sequence on lateral support as more of a **warning** about the need to *be careful* and remain lateral as an offensive line. The use of the phrase *we just need to be careful* implies that the coach has a problem with this aspect of play, but by shaping it as a warning he may again be trying to reduce the directness of any criticism that is being implied.

However, the use of *we* in shaping these actions is also doing a considerable amount of important face and solidarity management work in these episodes of critical feedback, by protecting guilty individuals and encouraging collective ownership of the problem (and the solutions) being discussed by the coach. In this interactional setting, because the players can see themselves and others in the video clip being played, they can see who is at fault. Those players identified are also in the room at the same time and the sequence of talk arguably subjects them to the potential for face loss amongst members of the group. The use of *we* in this regard (instead of, for example, *you* in directing criticism to a specific individual) may be an acknowledgement of this potential face threat for the individual or individuals featured in the clip and an attempt to help manage it by extending the critical feedback more broadly and generally across the wider group. In other words, by construing the target of the criticism as the whole playing group, the coach spreads the culpability and lack of knowledge in this area to a larger group of individuals (N. Harwood, 2005), protecting affected individuals from the face loss of being verbally singled out. Moves like this in these critical performance evaluation interactions can be read as strategic attempts by the coach to protect against threats to their own solidarity with particular individuals in the team or the solidarity these individual players have with other members of the team.

Managing confidence levels: Mitigating criticism before the match

Another situation where we saw efforts by the coach to reduce the force of acts of critical feedback was in the lead-up to a match, during the team's pre-match drills. Extract 4 was recorded during a pre-match warm-up routine with the backs and comes as the head coach (Tane) has called the players into a huddle to reflect on a recently completed drill. It becomes clear in the extract that the coach has seen two issues he wishes to raise with the players: reaction speed once the team have turned over the ball (line 1) and the level of the team's basic skills (line 6). In this extract, we see familiar measures taken by the coach to soften the force of any implied criticism.

1. **Tane**:   so just watching that ++ we're a little bit slow to react in our in our turnovers or whether we had the ball
2.   so the work off the ball is gonna be key to us
3.   the faster we can get into position and the faster we can react to what is in front of us
4.   if it's a turnover or we're on D + then the better we're gonna be + okay
5.   so get that enthusiasm up

6.	last thing the skills have to go up another level against this team + okay==
7.	==this is the tester for us
8.	see if we're + we're making progress and um inroads into the season + okay
9.	so our skill our skill level and our physicality and our tackle +++ alright
10.	if you get all those things and we just enjoy ourselves (like we have) like we have in the last two weeks ++ alright
11.	{claps} (let's go) boys {then walks away}

Extract 4: [match day data] talk from the closing segment of a pre-match warm-up drill

In lines 1 to 5, the coach raises and assesses the team's reaction speed in the pre-match drill as an issue. In line 1, he issues what is a recognizable act of critical feedback, critiquing the team's reaction speed once they have turned over the ball and are transitioning from defence to attack. However, this more direct act of criticism is modified through the **attenuating device** *a little bit* which may function to reduce the force of the coach's remarks for the benefit of the overhearers.

In line 6, we see the coach pick up a second topic for critical attention – the general skill level (passing, catching, timing, etc.). However, like Extracts 2 and 3 above, criticism is largely implied in descriptive observations and accounts of player action. He also states that the players' skill level needs to *go up another level* in the upcoming game. While this statement could be functioning in multiple ways, it does, at least in part, appear to imply that the team's skills on display in the training drill were not up to standard. Having observed the training drill, the researcher did witness a number of dropped balls and mistimed passes which may support the reading of this action as a mitigated critique of the general skills exhibited in the pre-game warm-up drill. Additionally, we again see the use of collective pronouns *we*, *us* and *our* to spread the culpability and collective responsibility for the issues being critiqued and the solutions being issued. As suggested above, these acts may be attempts by the coach to soften or hide, at least linguistically, any individual blame implied or inferred for criticism of the aspects of play being discussed.

While the strategies in Extract 4 are similar to those we have reviewed in earlier extracts, the context is different and it is worth reflecting on whether these mitigation strategies help to serve particular solidarity protection purposes in this specific pre-match context. One potential explanation is that the transgression noted by the coach in this episode may be moderate in the coach's eyes, and if they had been more alarming then they may have been dealt with more directly and forcefully. However, we do not have evidence to really support this explanation as acts of critical feedback in pre-match talk of this kind were encoded in similar ways.

Another explanation might be that the timing, i.e. right before the match, is not seen as the right time for more explosive, direct and unmitigated acts of criticism, perhaps because of the potential for such acts to impact the confidence of the players and feelings of solidarity within the group at a time when confidence needs to be high. Players were also clearly quite nervous and focused in the build-up to this particular match. Our team are about to play an opposition that are considered to be the best professional team in the country, and they were noticeably more quiet and pensive on the bus trip from the airport and in the hotel before the match. With the additional tension in the air in the lead-up to a match, the coach may be attempting to provide critical feedback in ways that help to get a key message across while at the same time negotiate an already tense atmosphere.

Boosting criticism: Clamping down on attitude issues

In the above sections of this chapter, we have illustrated the efforts of coaches to manage potentially face-threatening situations in which critical feedback was being delivered. We have also unpacked the situations in which these strategies were used for finer-grained explanations and insights about how and why we get these attempts to manage face and protect solidarity between coaches and players. Part of the reason we pursued this agenda in this chapter was because we also found evidence in our data of coaches being more direct and, in some cases, engaging in very face-threatening exchanges of criticism with players. This variation suggests that there are situations in which solidarity between themselves and players appears to have been less of a concern for coaches and mining these situations promises to add further nuance to our understanding of the coach–player relationship. In this section, we illustrate two of these situations where we saw less mitigation of criticism.

In Extract 5, from a training session, the assistant/forwards coach (Greg) is outlining a training drill that the forwards are about to begin. In lines 1 to 5, the coach gives instructions to the players on how to complete the scrum training drill. This drill focuses on getting into a good shape, so the forwards are able to push more effectively as a unit. For this drill, some players perform the pushing exercise (the extension) and others stand on the machine (sledge) to provide resistance for the players to push against. However, it is the behaviour in line 7 that is of the most interest here. Towards the end of this extract, we see the coach deliver what could be interpreted as a more unmitigated act of criticism.

1. **Greg**: (unclear) I want lock and loosie
2. and we're just going to work on our power lines and also our strong shape okay
3. couple of extensions and that's us done
4. (and then we'll build that up) (unclear) front row alright
5. so lock loosie three guys on the machine + on the sledge sorry
6. (1.5) *{players meander and converse}*
7. COME ON ABEL OR ASH {claps loudly} LET'S GET SOME EXCITEMENT ABOUT THIS + (fucking) scrum
8. *{players close in on the machine and one of the named players gets into position}*

Extract 5: [training session data] outlining a training session drill (forwards)

In line 7, the coach issues a louder directive to the players to *come on* and approach the task more quickly, clapping loudly and asking players to get more *excited*. These acts are functioning on many levels, including to increase the urgency shown by the players towards the drill the group are engaged in. However, the louder volume and the shift in tone, from the more instructional sequences of talk immediately prior, are most likely motivated by the player's meandering and slow assembly into positions to perform the drill. From this perspective, then, these directives can also be seen to encode criticism of the players for the lack of energy and excitement being exhibited by them in getting stuck into the drill.

Increased volume on its own does not indicate that a speech act is functioning to offer a critical account of behaviour. We do, for example, see increased volume being used in training sessions to communicate across sports fields where coaches and players are spatially distant from one another. However, here, this is not the case. The players and the coach occupy the same space as they did in lines 1 to 6 when the coach was outlining the drill. The increased volume here is functioning to both increase urgency and indicate that the players are not exhibiting the required level of *excitement*. The use of the word *fucking* muttered at a quieter volume than the rest of the message is perhaps an indication of frustration on the part of the coach. It is clear from these actions that the coach expects the players to move quicker from the end of an instructional sequence (which is arguably not explicitly signalled) into the actual physical drill. Some players began talking to one another as the coach is finishing up his instructions and, although these conversations are inaudible, it is clear from the coach's behaviour in line 7 that he considers these conversations to be off-task and secondary in relevance to the training drill.

In Extract 6, we see another situation from our data where recognizable acts of criticism were boosted even further, to the extent that they were particularly face-threatening to the individual player being addressed. This extract comes from the end of a training session. In the lead-up to this extract, the head coach (Tane) has asked another player to fetch Ashton to talk about why he did not attend a personal development (PD) session and a weights session earlier in the day. After being fetched, Ashton has come back out to the training ground to where the coach is and is confronted with a series of very direct questions that ask him for his whereabouts and whether he knows where he needs to be tomorrow. As this extract develops, it becomes clear that the head coach is unhappy with the player's failure to turn up to team events earlier in the day.

1. **Tane**: do you know what the programme is tomorrow
2. **Ashton**: yep
3. **Tane**: what are you supposed to be doing tomorrow
4. **Ashton**: going to that sponsor event==
5. **Tane**: ==and then what
6. **Ashton**: training I think
7. **Tane**: when are you coming to training
8. **Ashton**: two o'clock
9. **Tane**: so so where were you this afternoon for PD
10. **Ashton**: nah I just got here for PD==
11. **Tane**: ==where were you before that for weights
12. **Ashton**: nah cos I didn't get the email so John text me
13. **Tane**: so what is whose whose email has John got
14. **Ashton**: possibly a different one
15. **Tane**: well you better go and friggin see him now and /check\
16. that he's got the right details
17. **Ashton**: /yeah\ {nods}
18. **Tane**: okay + fucking don't want any more fuck ups {said as he
19. is walking away}
20. **Ashton**: yeah

Extract 6: [training session data] having an individual chat with a player after training

There is a lot to unpack in this extract. However, it is clear from the way it unfolds that the coach is trying to seek an explanation from Ashton as to why he did not attend important team events earlier in the day. However, in performing this purpose, the coach is clearly indicating that he is disappointed with the player and engages in what is quite a face-threatening interaction for the player being addressed. For one, Ashton is confronted with what is a series of quick-fire questions that ask him to explain himself or demonstrate his understanding of the schedule. There is no greeting; rather, the coach launches straight into his agenda of trying to find out why the player was absent for important team events earlier in the day. In line 9, in particular, the coach directly asks the player where he was today during the team's PD session, implying that he was not there, that no one else knew of his whereabouts and that an explanation is needed or warranted. A similar pattern is seen in line 12 when the coach asks about his whereabouts during the team's gym and weights session.

Ashton's explanation for not turning up to the gym session is that he did not receive the email notifying him about it. This then initiates a sequence of talk where the coach enquires as to whether the team manager (John) has got the right email. However, he makes it clear through his actions that he is dissatisfied with the player whom he is holding responsible for this email issue. In line 15, we see the coach impose upon the player to go and see the team manager to confirm he has his correct email. The use of *friggin* in line 15, while a modified swear word, boosts the intensity of his directive to the player to go and confirm his email address. The use of the semi-modal *better* and the adverb *now* increases the imposition on the player, requiring him to seek out the team manager immediately and address the problem.

Additionally, as the interaction is brought to a close by the coach, he makes a further and this time very explicit assessment of the player's behaviour, referring to it as a *fuck up* (in line 18) as he states he does not want to see any more of these *fuck ups* in the future. As a further indication of his dissatisfaction, he also delivers this final line as he is walking away from the player, denying the player the chance to address him, express his apologies or show a willingness to address the issue going forward. Closing sequences are important relationally as they serve as bridges between communicative events (Markman, 2009; Schegloff & Sacks, 1973). As speakers bring interactions to a close and depart, they typically perform important relational work in order to establish favourable conditions for their next meeting. In this instance, the coach takes it upon himself to end the interaction and ends it with a pejorative assessment of the player's behaviour and a warning to not do it again. None of these actions suggest the relationship between the player and the coach is currently on positive ground for the next time they meet.

On the basis of the evidence presented in this extract, it may be fair to argue that solidarity between the coach and Ashton is of very little concern. The coach has arguably used the interaction to intimidate Ashton and hold him accountable for what is perceived laziness or an unprofessional showing on his part. Throughout our time with the team, it became apparent that there were general question marks about this particular player's overall commitment (particularly concerning his gym work and associated weight gain and healthy eating issues). This additional knowledge may have been brought to the interaction by the coach as he designed and shaped this more direct episode of critical talk. However, more broadly, the findings presented in Extracts 5 and particularly in Extract 6 suggest that coaches do not always mitigate acts that can be read as criticism and will boost them in ways that threaten positive face and arguably withhold or deny players any solidarity with the coach. We unpack the variation in practice we have seen from the coaches below as we wrap up the findings of this chapter.

Wrapping up: Is coach–player solidarity conditional?

The goals of this final findings chapter have been slightly different. We have taken a very specific linguistic action – communicative acts that can on one level be recognized as criticizing or critical in nature – and explored how these acts were designed in various coach–player interactional contexts. While criticism and giving critical or corrective feedback are important in coaching, it does, hypothetically, present a challenge to relations of solidarity. Those giving critical feedback may pay attention to this threat by shaping their feedback acts in particular ways to protect against potential face loss for individuals and damage to the coach–player relationship.

Through our analysis, we located differing degrees of strength in the shaping of acts of criticism and tried to account for (or explain) the variation we have seen by looking at features of the different (interactional) contexts in which these choices were made. On the basis of the evidence surveyed in this chapter, we can argue that solidarity with their players does appear to be an important issue for coaches when giving critical feedback. Across the different interactional contexts we have illustrated above, there was, by and large, a significant effort taken by coaches to manage the face-threatening nature of acts designed to draw negative attention to player actions and performances. Coaches would deploy a range of strategies to manage potential face-threats to players from choosing not to put any critical remarks on record in situations when criticism was warranted, engaging in largely descriptive accounts of poor performance that only imply that they are engaged in criticizing, limiting the extent to which their own emotions or negative emotions towards the players were encoded, and littering their sequences of critical feedback with a series of modifiers designed to lower the strength of any criticism that is being drawn from their remarks.

These efforts were pervasive across a number of contexts and construct a coach concerned with maintaining the positive face of his players. This suggests that while coaches did not shy away from giving critical feedback, they did balance this need to give corrective feedback with the need to protect individuals' confidence levels, their positive face in the team and with that solidarity between themselves and their players. From this we can conclude that solidarity with their players is a concern for our coaches and one they did attempt to strategically manage in and through a range of message design actions and decisions.

However, while there was a lot of evidence in our data of the careful and considered execution of acts of criticism, there were some exceptions to this where we found evidence of situations where criticism of players was not mitigated and even boosted. In mining these situations, an observable feature that varied in these contexts was the topic or target of the criticism. In these less mitigated episodes of critical feedback, the coaches were targeting issues where players had exercised what was perceived by the coach to be a lack of energy and engagement in the business of the team (as in Extract 4) or when a player can be seen to have dropped his own professional standards, particularly concerning off-field commitment to the wider team programme (as in Extract 5).

In our search for more clarity about how coach–player solidarity works, we can draw on these distinctions in the way criticism was shaped. There was clearly variation in the way coaches approached the act of shaping criticism when there was a technical or tactical issue and when there was of an attitudinal or commitment issue. With less attention paid to the positive face-wants of those players not showing an appropriate level of commitment to the cause, we could argue that players actually need to earn solidarity with coaches and that is contingent upon their commitment to the cause. Their technical and tactical flaws are navigated more carefully by coaches, potentially in an attempt to maintain their broader confidence levels in their abilities and any claims to professional identity as a rugby player in the process. However, if they do not show a degree of commitment to the activities at hand or to attending team events, then they are (temporarily) denied their belonging to the team and any professional respect or solidarity they might wish to acquire from the coach.

These findings suggest that solidarity may be a strategic resource deployed by coaches to further their control and governance over the players. If solidarity, as it appears to be in our team, is primarily contingent on players demonstrating to the coach that they are willing to show the commitment needed to belong, then solidarity is arguably something that is being afforded to players by the coach rather than being built together with them.

We put this claim forward very tentatively. However, from what we have seen in this chapter, there is evidence that coach–player solidarity works in quite different ways to player–player solidarity, and the coach's practices in our data that can be interpreted as solidarity oriented are actually rooted in the more influential and overarching asymmetrical power relations between coaches and players that we have seen throughout the findings chapters of this book. This, as we will discuss in the final chapter of this book, is a central premise that underlies the organization of relationships – the way they work – in high-performance sports teams.

In the final chapter of this book, we will attempt the difficult task of bringing together the findings we have illustrated and discussed in our analysis chapters and trying to make sense of them. Our primary goal, as we laid out earlier in the book, is to survey all of the findings presented in this book and ask the question of how relationships are working in our team at a higher level and with the benefit of empirical findings from an array of more micro-level analyses of different practices, dyads and contexts. To discuss relationships at this broader level, we will attempt to pinpoint, in the evidence, unspoken, taken-for-granted cultural knowledge and belief systems that underlie and govern how relationships work in high-performance sports teams and that were being talked into being in the interactions of our team.

10

Widening the linguistic lens

Identifying cultural belief systems underlying how relationships work in professional sports teams

Introduction

In this book we have presented a series of illustrations, analyses and discussions of how various role-relationships are actually working in a professional New Zealand rugby team. Through this more performative analysis of relationships, we have been able to shine a light on the everyday practices that reflect and construct taken-for-granted relational dynamics of power and solidarity in this team. In line with a linguistic lens, our pursuit of this research agenda was to provide empirical illustrations and evidence of relationships in action in this professional context and add more theoretical diversity to the study of relationships in sports teams.

In this final chapter, we attempt to bring together the different illustrations, analyses and discussions we have undertaken in the previous chapters and consider (or reimagine) them at a broader level. Our goal is to identify some of the underlying cultural patterns that are being reflected and (re)constructed *in* and *across* the linguistic practices of coaches, the captain and players in our data. Here we are essentially pulling the smaller pieces of the relationship puzzle we have offered in our findings chapters together in order to offer what might be termed a broader **cultural portrait** of how relationships (particularly relations of power and solidarity) work in our team and present this portrait for further investigation and reflection in other high-performance sporting contexts. Being able to engage in such a process is one of the benefits of dedicating a book-length treatment to a topic of this kind. It provides an opportunity to consider findings not only in their individual social and interactional contexts but also across the broader cultural context, by cross-referencing the findings from the individual chapters to account for the sometimes-complex cultural belief systems that underlie interpersonal interactions we have analysed in this book.

In what follows, we present six of these broader cultural ideas or principles that emerged from this reimagining of the local-level analyses of relationships (of power and solidarity lines) in action in our team. These six cultural principles (in summary form) are as follows:

1 **Relationships in our team are predominantly transactional in nature**. People are there primarily to do a job, and this is a clear cultural idea that is evident in the interactional practices and patterns we see between the individuals of the team.

2 **Leader–follower relations permeate all social interactions in our team**. In all settings we studied, people organized themselves into very obvious leader–follower relational dynamics, suggesting this was seen as the way that relationships were or needed to be structured in this professional context.

3 **Across all the relational dynamics in our team, the coach is undoubtedly the king**. Coaches maintain a tight control over the decisions, actions and standards of their subjects. Their hierarchical position in the team is claimed, respected and unquestioned.

4 **Social structures were their flattest on the field where teamwork was at its most necessary**. Social structures did flatten on the pitch when the coach was absent, suggesting that playing group relationships are less sharply stratified hierarchically and may need to be if the playing group are to create the conditions for a fluid exchange of information needed to achieve performance goals.

5 **Having people in control is valued but having controlling people is less so**. While the prominence of leader–follower dynamics in our data meant that someone was always in control, there was also a large amount of indirect language use that may suggest people did not want to come across as too controlling in their relations with others.

6 **Solidarity with others was conditional and subject to gate-keeping practices**. Despite solidarity being perceived as a central tenet of sports teams, it was not necessarily always given or afforded to members of the team but needed to be earned. This raises interesting questions about the interrelationship between solidarity and power in understanding the culture of relating in high-performance sports teams.

These six principles are by no means an exhaustive list; rather, they are the beginning of a conversation we hope will continue as more research is carried out. They reflect patterns that were easy to locate across the practices of our team and, for that reason, could arguably be seen as influential and taken-for-granted ways of being and doing that have cultural significance to the professional domain of high-performance sport. We will introduce and discuss each of these cultural principles in the remainder of this chapter, revisiting the linguistic evidence that helped us to arrive at these broader-level claims about how relationships work.

We will also spend some time, when discussing these cultural principles, with the more abstract task of trying to account for *why* they are being oriented to or constructed in our team. In these discussions, we will draw on features of our specific team context to help us put forward claims about what might underlie the cultural principles we see our particular New Zealand rugby team orienting to. We wrap up this chapter and the book overall with a discussion of the benefits and limitations of our linguistic lens on relationships. Suggestions for future research are raised throughout the different sections of this final chapter.

Cultural principle 1: Relationships in our team are predominantly transactional in nature

One of the most obvious broader-level trends across our data set was the finding that relationships in our high-performance sports team were by and large business-oriented or transactional in nature, particularly between the coaches and the players. All of the data we collected from our time with the team and surveyed here showed the team engaged almost exclusively in purposeful, business-oriented activities designed to perform some function in pursuit of the overall professional goals of the team. This pervasive pattern construed relationships more towards the transactional end of the transactional–relational relationship scale. Shaping relationships around transactional goals is a frequent finding in other discourse analytical works carried out in other professional contexts and therefore is not a surprising one here (Koester, 2006, 2010) and is, on the one hand, largely unsurprising, as the context we have examined is, in essence, a workplace where people have gathered to pursue professional activities and goals.

However, other studies of other workplace contexts have shown how workplace teams can orient more towards the relational end of the continuum in some interactional settings, perhaps to accomplish more relational goals such as building closer bonds with one another. The interactional practice of small talk, built into official workplace interactions, is one example of a more relationally oriented goal being pursued in and through workplace interaction, where the talk functions less to achieve transactional aims and more to achieve relational bonds. The biggest concentration of more relationally or solidarity-oriented features we found in our data came from the pre-match huddles as the captain shaped the interaction in ways that emphasized the assembled players belonging and togetherness (see Chapter 7). Beyond this, language was rarely put to work for exclusively relational purposes or was performed in a very subtle way. In some cases where more relationally oriented sequences of talk were engaged in, some discomfort arose, as in the case of humour attempts in coach–player interactions (reviewed in Chapter 8), suggesting that such practices may conflict with beliefs held (at least by those in power) about how relationships should work in this team.

There are some important caveats to this claim that need mentioning here; the data we collected did not account for situations in which individuals would meet and interact with one another in their free time or in settings outside of the business of the team. Our recording method of attaching the camera to the researcher, in order to create the least amount of distraction for our participants, may have also inadvertently been influential. By strapping the camera on the researcher, we perhaps missed more subtle and unstructured interactions between members of the team that may have been less transactional and more relational in nature.

We did observe some settings where there was less of an orientation to professional team matters. One of those was on the sidelines during training sessions while some individuals waited for their turn to perform a training drill. Another was the team bus or in airport lounges on the way to and from matches. At these times, players would engage in more relationally oriented interactions, largely by talking about their personal lives and topics away from the business of the team. The topic of rugby was still a frequent one, but other topics such as family, girlfriends, shared acquaintances and current events (particularly in rugby) were also discussed. There were also a lot more conversationalists and freer turn-taking communication in these interactions as multiple individuals joined in with these more relationally oriented interactions. Recordings of these interactions were not made, and this is certainly a limitation of the current study and an important consideration for future research in this space. The decision to not record these interactions was based on the level of discomfort the researcher had about doing so. However, data from these interactions is likely to have expanded our understanding of solidarity practices in particular and may have altered the shape of the claim we have made in this first cultural principle.

Yet, these points considered, the orientation to transactional goals and the backgrounding of purely relational goals was a pervasive feature in the data we did collect. Our data show that as soon as the team entered one of the two primary professional sites (the team's training base or the venue for match days), their behaviour (and perhaps expectations on their behaviour) became very clearly transactional in nature, and talk always had a specific and by-and-large recognizable transactional purpose to accomplish. This underlying pattern arguably shapes relationships in quite structured and restricted ways.

Additionally, there was policing of this more transactional orientation to the team's behaviour which further implied the importance of this overarching cultural value to relationships in high-performance sports teams. As noted above, some talk of a more relational kind did take place during training sessions, usually between individuals waiting for their turn on the sidelines. However, pejorative assessments about this practice or talk between players on the sidelines were uttered directly to the researcher by a coach on two occasions during different training sessions ('do you think you could sort that out in your communication training'). These remarks were made in such a way that it was clear talk of this kind was not seen as beneficial or positive and was rather seen as being in contradiction to the more transactionally oriented activities of and expectations on the group. In this regard, talk of a more relational kind between the players was seen as off-task and as a sign of a lack of focus, rather than valued as an opportunity for those individuals involved to use talk to build bonds with one another. The fact that this more relationally oriented kind of talk was pushed to the fringes of more structured interactional events is further evidence to support the claim that people in our team, at their core, are there to accomplish transactionally oriented outcomes together.

This finding is an interesting one to reflect on considering how frequently we hear of successful teams having strong bonds with one another (Carron et al., 2002). For such a frequently cited value of high-performance sports teams, the limited evidence of these bonds being actively constructed by members of our team does raise interesting questions about when and how these strong, close bonds with one another are fostered and whether this is a strategic goal teams actively pursue and create space for in the course of their everyday activities. With respect to our team and working from our data set, we would argue that such bonds are either secondary in relevance to accomplishing transactional goals and therefore pushed to the fringes or left to individuals to address, or that strong bonds are seen as tied up in the actual accomplishment of the team's transactional goals and outcomes. In other words, what unites and brings members of teams together is the degree of success they accomplish in pursuit of their workplace goals and a shared alignment of what counts as success and actually achieving this success.

One final point to explore in laying out this claim here is the relationship between this valuing of transactionally oriented relations and features of the specific team context in which our data comes from. One key point to note about our context was that the data were collected during a preseason campaign, which, on the one hand, might explain this more preferred orientation to transactional relations we see across the team's interactional contexts. This preseason campaign was also unique in that it had been condensed by another allied professional team needing the facilities for the final stages of their professional competition. A predominant orientation to more transactional tasks and activities may have been seen as a solution to this contextual constraint of a shorter lead-in, and this may in part explain the patterns we see and may need considering when we interpret these patterns more broadly.

Another point to raise here concerns the gender of the team. The language of males, it has been suggested, prioritizes information exchange outcomes over more relationally oriented ones. This premise, that talk that is not rich in information is not worthwhile, has been found to influence male patterns in talk and is a factor that is said to limit males and their ability to maintain personal relationships (Tannen, 1992, p. 16). While it is important not to generalize without making reference to the specific demands of the context at hand (A. F. Freed & Greenwood, 1996), we might argue, again tentatively, that this wider sociocultural principle surrounding talk by men may also be signalled in the more transactionally oriented behaviour we have seen in our team.

All in all, from the linguistic evidence surveyed across the chapters of this book, the orientation to largely transactional relationships between individuals is arguably a central tenet underlying how relationships are working in this cultural environment. Specific efforts to oil relations between individuals in the team appear to be pushed to the fringes of other more-structured, transactionally oriented communicative activities, restricted to specific interactional events (in our case, the pre-match huddle) or are left to the players themselves to pursue outside of the bounds of their professional activities. On this basis, we would argue that relationships in sports teams are by and large built upon and around a shared orientation to transactional, workplace activity and accomplishments. This overarching claim about how relationships work will be threshed out further as we move through other sections of this chapter, particularly when discussing Cultural Principle 5 below, where we modify this overarching claim somewhat.

Cultural principle 2: Leader–follower relations permeate all social interactions in our team

The second overarching principle that emerges across the linguistic evidence is that leader–follower relationship dyads were always evident in the team's interactions; in other words, someone (usually quite obvious) was always in control. In all social interactions in our data, we were able to easily locate leader–follower relationship structures being constructed, with leadership rights and responsibilities most often being distributed in quite a clear and unambiguous fashion to ranking members of the interaction. This was most evident in the structured and respectful affordance of floor rights to those individuals with notionally powerful roles in the team's structure. The situation when this was perhaps the most diverse was on the pitch during a match. In these cases, while the influence of the captain over interactions and team governance was still very evident, more people from within the playing group adopted a leadership role in interactions. We unpack this point more later in the chapter (see Cultural Principle 4). However, by and large, it was clear in the data that leader–follower relations were a significant organizing principle oriented to by our team in their patterns of interaction.

One of the most pervasive ways this leader–follower cultural value was evident was through a predominantly monologic approach to running team interactions. The team's interactional spaces were largely enacted through the establishment of extensive performance rights for powerful individuals, like the coaches or the captain. In many of the coach-led training interactions, for example, the coaches did *all* of the talking and in some cases, no one else spoke. In many other cases, when they did speak, it was simply to acknowledge the instructions they had been given, a move which can be read as actively constructing a follower identity. However, even in situations where multiple speakers would contribute to an ongoing interaction, powerful individuals (coaches, in particular) would exercise significant influence over what other speakers contributed and when they contributed.

Again, we might expect to see evidence of this principle in what is a professional, working context. Most, if not all, multi-personnel workplaces are known to have chains of command. Establishing a chain of command is often viewed as a way an institution can coordinate the interpersonal activity of its members as they work together to pursue the institution's wider goals.

The fact that our team's relationships, as we noted above, were transactional in nature in part helps to explain or understand this prevalence of leader–follower relations in our data. Because the bulk of the activity in our team was oriented towards achieving transactional goals, the coordination of individuals in achieving these transactional outcomes becomes an important issue for the members of the group to negotiate. In our team, this appeared to be addressed through the clear and unambiguous orientation to leader–follower relational dynamics in the course of accomplishing the team's transactional goals. In other words, the method of working together towards institutional goals seen in our data is very evidently structured, with a small number of individuals claiming rights to drive the agenda, positioning the remainder of individuals as followers in the process.

This quite rigid orientation to leader–follower dynamics in our team bears some deeper reflection and consideration here. On the one hand, this dynamic reflects and reconstructs a meta message or cultural understanding (or perhaps an appreciation) that relationships in teams work best when there is a single leader coordinating the efforts of everyone else. Who that leader is may shift from interaction to interaction, but a leader emerges, usually one who has the institution's backing. Whether such an approach is appropriate or indeed whether other methods are possible are not questions we can unpack here with our more performative evidence. Yet, there has certainly been a movement towards having more empowered players in sports teams that might question such a cultural value. There is anecdotal evidence in professional sports teams of an increasing belief in inclusive power structures that involve all individuals in the governance of the team, in some cases making the coach redundant (Jones, 2019; Schofield, 2017).

However, an inclusive team governance structure was not something we saw being widely oriented to in our data and for such a cultural principle to become common practice in our team, quite different ritual interactional dynamics would be required, particularly if this principle were to be genuinely enacted. Teams would also need to consider and, to some extent, come to embrace the risks and implications for the coordination of the team's playing actions that might come from a greater orientation to more open power structure. The data in our context show an orientation to the belief that an uncomplicated, stricter organization of the team's governance structure is more suitable, by encouraging a ranking individual or individuals to take control over the decision making and coordination of the group in a particular interactional context.

Again, in critically assessing this claim, it is important to consider the specific context in which our claims emerge, particularly the pre-season timing of the observations and recordings our analyses are based on. Considering the team were in the early stages of coming together, perhaps the clearer orientation to leader–follower relations across the team's interactional spaces reflects more of a practical response strategy to getting everyone onto the same page. Alternatively, it may actually reflect a deeper belief system that leader–follower relations are normative in this wider cultural and professional context. Because the team are new to one another and are in the early stages of shaping their culture, the practices we see in our data perhaps reflect and construct deeper, more generalized understandings of how relationships commonly pattern into leader–follower dynamics in this cultural context. If so, then it would suggest that the rigid leader–follower dynamic is a significant feature of how relationships work in sports teams, and one that is providing an important frame of reference for the individuals in our specific team as they aim to settle in and get on with others in this new setting.

Leadership and followership are relational notions (Clifton, 2012; Schnurr, 2013; Schnurr et al., 2020). People position themselves vis-à-vis others in accordance with their perceptions of the degree of influence they have or can exercise over others in a given context. Some studies have shown leader–follower relations in sports teams, albeit amateur sports team contexts, to be a fluid phenomenon, in which leadership and followership identities and relationships are sometimes hard to pin down (Stavridou, 2022). However, in our data, leader–follower dynamics were constructed in quite clear and structured ways. Individuals oriented to either a leadership or followership position in a particular interactional context and enacted their position in clear and unambiguous ways. Such a finding perhaps encodes a cultural principle that relationships in sports teams work best when the bulk of individuals in the team submit themselves to the will of the powerful, for the benefit of achieving coordination and cohesion in their joint actions. These findings may also reflect or even explain other cultural values of high-performance sports teams such as the importance of team discipline, following orders and showing respect for rank. At the very least, they suggest that the interactional and relational dynamics ritually enacted in our team predominantly serve the purposes of those in power and reduce access to power to a select few individuals.

Cultural principle 3: The coach is king

What was also obvious across the interactional settings of our team was that the coaches were undoubtedly the kings. In the linguistic evidence we presented above, the coaches both claimed and were afforded extensive and, in many cases, exclusive rights to govern the team, both operationally and epistemically (through their knowledge or perspective on events, happenings, occurrences, etc.). They also took the bulk of the responsibility for holding the membership accountable – an action through which their own interpretations of the (performance) standards required of the group were foregrounded.

The primary way this power was exercised was through the uneven rights coaches had to the interactional floor. The performance rights in the team's largely monologic interactions (referenced above) were almost exclusively afforded to the coach in settings where the coach was co-present. Players exercised respect for the powerful position that the coaches maintained over the group, typically by speaking only when called upon or by remaining silent when coaches addressed them and not challenging their rights to the floor or their instructions, assessments and strategic decisions. The mere presence of the coach in the room is enough for players to put their own conversations aside, establish a team-wide floor and cede control of this interactional floor to the coach. Even in settings where the players were physically distant from the coaches, the coaches were still able to extend their reach by joining into interactions and influencing behaviour via water carriers and physios through intercom/audio transmission channels.

In accounting for this cultural value, we would argue that it reflects and reconstructs a shared cultural understanding and appreciation within our team (or perhaps sports teams more broadly) of *one* strong leader at the top of the pile. That one person, and the kingly authority that they have over others, reduces the chance of potential tension that might arise from a difference of opinion and ensures directives, assessments and other social actions go unquestioned and are accepted and acted on by subordinates. Such a structure arguably derives its basis from beliefs that the time teams are spending together is tightly controlled and being put to use in ways deemed (by the king) to be central for the achievement of the team's goals.

Why it is the coach or coaches that maintain this position as king is an interesting question to reflect on further. While it is widely accepted and understood that coaches have institutional authority in the sociocultural context of sport and high-performance sports teams (something that we have provided a great deal of evidence for in this book), the actual basis of this authority in the coach–player relationship has rarely been reflected upon. One factor may be the age difference that often distinguishes players from coaches. Coaches are typically older than players, and this age difference may be a significant influence in the construction and maintenance of leader–follower dynamics in which coaches have and exercise hierarchical status over all others in the team. Being older than those you interact with can in many contexts be the basis for greater claims to authority (Ervin-Tripp, 1972; Ide, 1982). This is certainly a feature of the coach–player interactions in our data, with four of the five coaches in the team set-up being significantly older than the players in the team.

However, there are likely to be other factors that help to establish coaches as kings in the ecosystem that is a professional sports team. One of these may be the degree of experience coaches have accumulated over their time in the game. With many coaches having played the game, they perhaps see themselves (and are accepted by players) as possessing the greater amounts of knowledge (i.e. technical expertise), experience and perspective needed to draw on to prepare the team for what to expect and how to address issues. In our team, two of the five coaches had played rugby professionally and for their national teams. One was an experienced professional player who was invited to support the coaches in the team due to a season-ending injury. Another had played rugby extensively in the region's professional team, and the last of the five coaches, while not playing professionally, had played the game extensively and had significant amounts of rugby coaching experience in the region, including at a youth development level. Four of these coaches had moved from playing into previous coaching roles before taking on the assignment of coaching this team. In the practices we have seen where some form of technical knowledge or expertise is being negotiated, coaches certainly maintained a tight control over the interaction and these sequences arguably gave coaches the platform through which to enact and reinforce their greater claims to technical expertise. Coach–player relationships, seen from this perspective, are clearly established on beliefs that those with greater amounts of experience in the game have status.

These differences in age and experience may be an important driver of the deeper cultural belief system that affords coaches the kingly authority over *their* players that we see being enacted and constructed in team interactions. However, as with previous cultural principles we have highlighted above, this sharply stratified hierarchical structure does raise questions about the suitability of such a relationship structure for achieving team goals. Players arguably have some claims to greater amounts of knowledge about the specific realities of the match that they are experiencing, based on their actual lived experiences in said match. They also show how they are capable of identifying issues when left to their own devices on the field. Yet, there is little to no evidence in our data that these experiences are treated as significant in coach–player interactional practices or integrated into problem-solving and decision-making sequences. Put another way, the experience and perspective that matters or that is constructed as significant is that of the coaches.

Regardless of whether such a structure is or was deliberately designed by our coaches or not, the interactional practices tell a very clear story: the coach as king is a taken-for-granted social structure that is hiding in plain sight in the behaviour and actions of the coaches and players. For coaches that feel discomfort with the culturally understood notion of themselves as kings in the sports team structure, a key port of call for critical reflection should be the taken-for-granted power dynamics that are being constructed in their interactional practices.

Cultural principle 4: Social structures were their flattest on the field where teamwork was at its most necessary

While leader–follower relations were a distinctive feature of the way relationships worked in our team, and coaches overwhelmingly obtained the rights to lead whenever they engaged with the players, we did find that player–player relationships were not as rigidly structured, particularly on the field during the match. Although the captain of the team was a regular contributor in these on-field interactions, sometimes performing the will of the coaches, in our data we saw an increase in the number of contributors to on-field talk and the amount of competition for the floor. Speakers who did not speak or who were not invited to speak in other settings were frequently seen taking turns and performing directives and evaluation in on-field talk.

From this evidence, we have concluded that player–player relationships are less hierarchically structured than coach–player relations. The reason for this flatter structure may lie in a belief that while on the field, the team need to rely on its multiple individuals if they are to achieve their goal of winning the match at hand. If a sharply stratified social structure, of the kind we see in coach–player interactions, were being constructed and oriented to on the field by the players, we might see individuals leaving the problem solving to those with notionally powerful roles in the team, perhaps out of respect for the leaders to be able to notice and assess whether a particular issue needs the attention of the group, and issues not being brought to the attention of the group. With the captain often head down in a ruck, the issues other players are experiencing are likely to escape his attention and some reliance on others to feed into the wider problem-solving process is likely to be required. Fostering a flatter hierarchical structure within the playing group might support such a process by encouraging a shared approach to on-field problem solving.

This need and/or understanding may ultimately be driving the more open floor in player–player interactions, as the group attempt to collaborate to do teamwork. In such a structure, players temporarily adopt a leadership role in order to be able to direct the team and temporarily construct the rest of the team as followers in the process. At the core of the relational dynamic in playing groups, then, may lie a wider preference for or belief in the flexibility of leadership and followership identities, patterning in various ways according to the situation at hand. In some situations, leaders, even those who have institutionally powerful leadership roles in the team (i.e. the captain), may find themselves being positioned as followers by others (and needing to accept this positioning as a follower), while another individual seeks to perform a leadership role by drawing the group's awareness to an issue they have noticed or are experiencing and by coordinating the efforts of others to help address it. This principle illustrates the integrated nature of relationships, leadership and teamwork and shows how in playing groups, at least, flatter social structures may emerge out of an understanding of the need to share leadership responsibilities in the interests of accomplishing greater and more cohesive teamwork.

However, while players did create a shared interactional space that welcomed the contributions of players regardless of their notional roles in the team, there were still subtle distinctions in the way contributions were shaped by players without an official institutional role or title in the team. Players without official roles would shape their actions more indirectly, perhaps in an attempt to hide some of the force behind them – force that might be more associated with the rights of leaders with official titles. This perhaps indicates that a social structure *is* being constructed amongst the players in the team, but that this social structure reconstructs respect for hierarchy but not at the expense of restricting access to the interactional floor. These more subtle practices also suggest that in this professional culture there is a pervasive respect for those with institutional titles in a team's structure that is honoured as the team work together to ensure their success on the field during the match.

However, what these findings from the player–player on-field interactions suggest about how relationships work more broadly in sports teams is that the process of relating, particularly along power lines, is not a static one but a dynamic one. Across the different contexts we have surveyed in this book, leader–follower dynamics pattern variably and in response to cultural understandings of the specific interactional context that the group is occupying. As that context shifts, individuals that are present in an interaction will engage in a process of negotiating themselves into leader–follower dyads, as the context dictates, demands or permits it. This more dynamic, time and place modelling of relationships in sports teams is clearly much messier and because of this it may be seen as a less attractive way of approaching relationships for practitioners. However, the data we have reviewed across this book suggests that the relational dynamics they construct do shift or vary quite considerably according to the context, and that this variation in the relational dynamics may be important for organizing the interpersonal response required for a specific activity or issue that is being faced by the group.

Cultural principle 5: Having people in control is valued but having controlling people is less so

It is clear from the above principles that asymmetrical power and control are significant factors that shape the relationships of members of our sports team. The leader–follower dynamics that were prevalent in our data suggest that it was important for there to always be some**one** in control – pulling the strings, coordinating the team, raising spirits, moderating efforts. However, when we look closer at *how* this power was wielded or how the acts of power were performed or encoded in language, we did notice a significant amount of indirect language, implied speech acts and mitigated action being drawn on to perform leadership duties. There were, of course, cases where more direct speech acts were performed, and we could tentatively argue that the head coach, certainly in comparison to his assistants, did appear to draw on more direct ways of shaping his speech actions. However, indirect language was certainly a feature of the performance of leadership identities in our team, and this poses some interesting more nuanced questions about how relationships are working.

This design feature of leadership talk may suggest that the leaders in the team were attempting to perform control acts in ways that helped them to come across as less controlling or, at the very least, indicated a wariness of appearing too controlling. With respect to relations in the team, this may function to construct (the illusion or impression of) greater unity between the members by attempting to reduce differences in status that are likely to be signalled when certain individuals perform powerful acts over others. In shaping acts of power and control in more indirect ways, a speaker can redress some of the social distance between themselves and their addressees by not accentuating their authority over others.

There may be multiple reasons why such a practice is being oriented to and reconstructed as a cultural principle in our team. With respect to the leader–follower dynamic, this behaviour may be an attempt to build greater togetherness between oneself and one's subordinates when engaged in everyday professional activities. By shaping acts of power in more indirect ways, a powerful individual can protect themselves from accusations of being overbearing or denying players their agency, and establish a more relaxed working atmosphere. Viewed from this perspective, the construction of a less controlling leadership identity by an individual adopting a powerful role may be an active attempt to establish closer bonds with those the speaker is leading, and feelings of trust and togetherness that can be associated with closer bonds. By symbolically signalling ways to reduce the impression of boundaries that typically exist between leaders and followers, a leader may be able to encourage more of a view (illusory or not) that the group are equals and all in this together.

The context from which our data comes may also hold some clues that can help to account for or explain this pattern in leader speech in our data. New Zealand has long been fabled as an egalitarian culture, where tall poppy syndrome thrives and can loom large over interpersonal and group relations (J. Holmes et al., 2017; Woodhams, 2019). With this in mind, perhaps what we are seeing in some of this more indirect leadership language is an orientation to this broader cultural value of egalitarianism in New Zealand culture. While leadership is valued, and leaders do emerge in the interactions in our data, their orientation to more indirect language may be an attempt to balance this leadership responsibility with the more interpersonal goal of respecting and indicating respect for those being positioned as followers.

Having people in control is clearly valued and/or expected in our professional sports team and appears to be a very evident cultural practice in the interactional data we have analysed in this book. We cannot deny that power and authority are defining features of the coach–player relationship, with ample sociolinguistic evidence of this fact presented and discussed throughout the chapters of this book. However, at the same time, the expression and performance of strong leadership identities that enhance the social distance between leaders and followers are not always evident, and these are perhaps reserved for situations when a stronger hand is deemed necessary (see discussion of coaches addressing attitude issues in Chapter 9, for example). More pervasively, leaders performed their leadership identity in more indirect ways perhaps to rebalance the higher degrees of social distance that can ordinarily characterize relations between leaders and their followers. Maintaining camaraderie and being friendly is one of Lakoff's (1973) key rules about social relationships, and camaraderie can, stereotypically at least, be threatened by the social distance being constructed between superiors and subordinates. In taking this action, leaders may be engaging in what has been referred to by linguists as more relational leadership practice (Fairhurst & Uhl-Bien, 2012; J. Holmes & Marra, 2004; Mirivel & Fuller, 2017) by attempting to orient to both their leadership tasks and the additional goal of establishing strong working relations of trust and approachability with their subordinates at the same time.

Cultural principle 6: Solidarity with others was conditional and subject to gate-keeping practices

Finally, the evidence presented in this book points to solidarity in our team being a somewhat complex phenomenon. The importance of high degrees of solidarity (or related concepts like togetherness, belonging and unity) is valued in professional sports teams. However, in the data we have analysed, solidarity appears to be a complex achievement, especially across different relational dyads in the team. In particular, there appears to be subtle differences in the nature of solidarity between different dyads (i.e. the coach–player versus the player–player dyad) with coaches shaping their interactions with players in ways that allow them to maintain some social distance. This may reflect goals by coaches to ensure players do not see them as equals or as friends or any other categorization that may ultimately impinge on the degree of overall authority they appear to want or need over players.

However, the cultural principle we found the most interesting, and one that we derived from across the findings presented in this book, was that solidarity was not necessarily given to all members freely on entry to the team but appeared to be conditional on individuals being able to demonstrate, to leaders in the team, that they deserved to belong. There were times when belonging and togetherness were perhaps more freely allocated, particularly in the player-led pre-match team huddles as the team were about to embark on a match. At these times, a position in the team appeared to be (verbally) granted to all and actively constructed in the practices of speakers. However, there were other times when individuals or groups of individuals were temporarily and symbolically denied solidarity, especially when their commitment to the wider cause was called into question. These symbolic gestures were typically performed by the captain or the coaches and suggested that solidarity, particularly solidarity with individuals who had authority in the team, was being actively used to exercise control over the group.

From a player perspective, solidarity with the coaches is an important concern, considering it is the coaches who, at least in our team context, have the final say over whether a player is signed and/or selected to play. Finding ways to connect with the coaches is arguably going to help a player's chances, and this makes maintaining solidarity with coaches a key concern. Coaches are likely to be aware of this and may be using solidarity as a carrot to help with their wider enactment of power and control over individuals in the team. For example, individuals deemed to be behaving in ways that demonstrated, above all, a poor attitude or degree of commitment to the cause were temporarily denied solidarity with the coaches. Their behaviour was called out publicly or in smaller groups, and they were denied the respect that other members and the wider group enjoyed. To be allowed back into the comfort of the group, that individual or group of individuals need to demonstrate they belong or deserve to belong.

It may be this principle that distinguishes professional sport from the more social or causal version, where making all people, regardless of ability and level of commitment, feel comfortable and welcome is seen, stereotypically at least, as a more central principle. In professional sport, belonging and solidarity may be more of a contingent phenomenon and can be actively denied to individuals if they are deemed to show signs that they are not committed to the cause of the group. In this regard, solidarity and power may interact in culturally complex ways in a professional sporting context. It may be that solidarity and belonging to the group, particularly for individual members in the group, are subject to approval by powerful members of the institution. Solidarity and belonging, then, could be seen as further mechanisms of control, wielded by individuals in the team with institutional power and authority, to hold the group accountable and coordinate/establish desirable behaviours and attitudes.

From this perspective, far from being a given, solidarity could be temporarily denied to individuals to explicitly encourage discipline, with those lacking in discipline being denied solidarity, particularly with the team's gatekeepers. This suggests that solidarity in professional sports teams, at least in part, works as an incentive, by requiring individuals who want to belong to these professional institutions to lay claim to that right to belong by performing in line with expected standards.

Wrapping up: What can readers do with the findings of this book?

As mentioned at the beginning of this chapter, these six principles discussed above are by no means meant as an exclusive list of the cultural premises underlying relationships and relating in high-performance sports teams. They are also not put forward as a rigid and definitive account of the cultural premises that govern relating in high-performance sport more generally. Rather, they are empirically informed claims about the culture of relating in our high-performance sports team that emerged in the everyday interactional and relational behaviour and practices of the members of that team and should be read as a point of departure for further reflection, research and discussion. Readers may have identified their own broader principles from the empirical illustrations of relationships in action, and there is undoubtedly going to be variation in underlying cultural principles of relating across different teams that we hope additional research in this space might reveal. However, what we hope is that by abstracting the principles presented above, we have given the research and practitioner communities (in particular) a point of departure to ground or anchor discussions about interactional practices in professional sports teams, the relational dynamics ordinary practices can construct, the cultural principles and belief systems these dynamics reflect and (re)construct, and the interconnection between these three layers.

With this intention in mind, we hope this book and the artefacts (empirical illustrations, linguistic mechanisms, relational dynamics, cultural principles) presented and discussed within will help guide and drive practitioners' own reflective actions regarding the ways they want relationships to work in their own contexts. By drawing on the chapters of this book, practitioners have a set of tools, illustrations and discussions to help them identify ritual, everyday interactional and linguistic practices in their own context, consider the relational dynamics of power and solidarity these practices (re)construct, and probe the deeper cultural principles that underlie these everyday interactional and relational practices.

For the research community, the findings presented in this book offer some largely missing empirical evidence into **the process of relating** in professional sport. The notions of power and solidarity, and how these dimensions of human relationships work in the specific context of a professional sports team, have been thoroughly unpacked in this book using real, ritual interactional contexts where issues of power and solidarity are in play. It is hoped that these illustrations and discussions of power and solidarity in action help provide the research community with evidence upon which to develop theory and develop further, perhaps interdisciplinary, research questions about relationships and relating in this professional domain. With power and solidarity being a target for a range of researchers interested in relationships in sports teams, it is hoped that the empirical evidence presented here has raised questions for readers, questions that can fruitfully drive future studies of relationships and relating in this domain.

Assessing the value of our linguistic lens: Limitations and looking forward

Through the empirical and theoretical contributions presented in the chapters of this book, we also set out to make a methodological contribution: illustrating the value of a linguistic lens for generating insights about relationships in professional sports teams. One final task in this chapter, then, is to provide a general assessment of this linguistic lens. We will consider what this linguistic lens has allowed in terms of insights into the wider research on relationships in sports teams and identify where the limitations lie in the work we have carried out through this theoretical and methodological toolkit. We would like to briefly highlight three general points or claims.

1 *We have added accounts of what sports professionals are actually doing when 'relating' in high-performance sports teams to the much larger number of accounts of what sports professionals say they do and value.*

The accounts we can provide through discourse analysis depart from the view that relationships are performed or enacted in social interaction. By approaching the study of relationships from this perspective, we have conceptualized them as social accomplishments between two or more people and have tried to look at what people are actually doing *together* as they accomplish social interaction and particular relational dynamics of power and solidarity in the course of their everyday tasks and activities. In the process, we have offered illustrations of the complex and culturally evident ways people negotiate their interpersonal relationship realities with one another in a high-performance sporting context.

Understandings of the actual social enactment of relationships in professional sports teams has been outweighed by studies that ask sports professionals to reflect, individually on what they do, think or feel about their relationships and the behaviour they or others exhibit. Such approaches prioritize a conceptualization of relationships as something that lies in the heads of individuals. By drawing on discourse analysis, we have aimed to add more performative insights to the wider study of this interdisciplinary topic. The result, it is hoped, is a greater appreciation amongst the research community of the ability for this toolkit to capture socialized cognition in action as members of a group negotiate themselves vis-à-vis one another and the (professional) tasks they are jointly engaged in. Ultimately, we hope this encourages more discussion across disciplinary boundaries of how to design interdisciplinary methodologies that can illuminate the social and the psychological aspects of relationships in tandem.

2 *We've illustrated how everyday, mundane linguistic and interactional practices in sports teams can be used as a valuable source of evidence for locating relational dynamics and cultural belief systems that are being constructed by members of a sports team.*

It is also hoped that this book has heightened awareness of the way language, particularly the everyday, mundane patterns of unfolding social interactions (in context), can reveal and reconstruct much more than just the information people share with one another in their encounters. It can also reveal the institution's interpersonal and cultural norms and how these both shape and are shaped by recurring and ritual interactional practices. The turn-taking patterns we presented in this book arguably reveal some of the bigger, assumed institutional structures that we might expect to see in this context. However, in drawing attention to these linguistic and interactional mechanisms, we are now able to pinpoint *how* these relational dynamics and social structures are being constructed through specific practices, and we have provided the research and practitioner community with concrete practices of language use to guide their focus when asking more dynamic questions about relating in their own or other contexts.

This contribution to social research is arguably unique to discourse analysis, as this toolkit departs from the view that social life is '*talked* into being' (Heritage, 1984). All social science research is interested in society to a larger extent. However, as a primary analytical endeavour, discourse analysts aim to heighten awareness of the role particular linguistic choices and practices play in the everyday reconstruction of society. In our specific context of professional sport, we have hopefully illustrated that actual language in use is a valuable source of naturally occurring empirical evidence for informing more abstract theoretical discussions about important societal notions like relationships, teamwork, identity and institutional culture.

3 *We've oriented our analyses towards complexity and engaged actively with contextual information in our team to try and assess and/or account for the role it may play in the shaping of language use and relationships.*

Our fine-grained linguistic accounts have also aimed to integrate context into the analysis and explanations about how and why relationships work the way they appear to work. This largely qualitative principle derives from a wider epistemological belief that features of the context may be a major source of information that the participants being studied are drawing on as they make decisions about how to behave and how they interpret or predict the behaviour of others. Therefore, they need to be central to any analytical account as well.

We have oriented towards this principle and introduced several contextual explanations for the patterns we have seen in our data. While many of our explanations have attempted to locate abstract cultural ideas and belief systems that are reflected and/or being reconstructed in the interactional practices and behaviour of members of our team, we have also integrated local contextual information, like stereotypical features of the national culture, specific sociocultural aspects of the identities of individuals involved and, importantly, the time our data was collected, to build claims. The result of this process is more complex (and perhaps more tentative) conclusions about how relationships are working and the array of potential influences that underlie and explain the practices we see for further testing and consolidation in future research. Discourse analysts rarely settle on a single explanation for patterns they see but engage in more of a far-reaching appreciation of social factors that influence linguistic practice, with claims gradually being solidified or adjusted as future studies are conducted.

While we hope the above three points are seen as useful contributions to the wider study of relationships in this professional domain, there are, of course, important limitations that need to be addressed here. Many of these limitations stem from the bigger decision to ground our analytical agenda in a case study analysis of a single team. Adopting a case-study approach is sound research practice in a discourse analytical study of this kind, as it allows researchers to provide a complex account of language in use in a specific context. However, for researchers from more essentialist and quantitative paradigms, this is likely to present as a key weakness of the claims we have presented in this book.

However, for discourse analysts, language patterns are simultaneously unique to the local context but also bear the marks, constraints and influence of history and wider cultural belief systems that form around a wider cultural group's behaviour (Fairclough, 2003a; Gee, 2018; Richards, 2006). It is general (culturally held and shared) ideas about language that discourse analysts can and do seek in and through their analyses. However, arriving at these is a long process, one that requires researchers and practitioners to build knowledge together. The analyses and claims presented in this book are intended to push the research and practitioner community forward with the task of generating and reflecting on a more general cultural portrait of relating and relationships in this professional domain. What we have presented in this book should be viewed as tentative, and we are fully prepared and open to the fact that these principles may be reshaped as further empirical research emerges on the topic of how relationships are working in professional sports teams.

More important for this author is that this linguistically informed research agenda is now seen by a wider audience as a valuable toolkit for addressing particular issues in the study of relationships in this professional domain (and perhaps beyond). Relationship research in high-performance sports teams would undoubtedly thrive from greater theoretical diversity and more interdisciplinary research discussions. However, this demands from researchers an appreciation of diversity, especially in the shaping of research questions that work within critical junctures of interdisciplinary interest that are able to provide a more holistic account of how relationships (should) work.

Concluding thoughts

In this book, we set out to address the question of how relationships work, both in the actual encounters where relationships are in play and at a more abstract level of cultural and socialized belief systems that underlie interpersonal action. Using the tools of discourse analysis, we located evidence of the way members of a professional New Zealand rugby team (coaches, the captain and the players) enacted and performed their relationships with one another in and through language in their everyday social (professional) interactions. We paid particular attention to the way power and solidarity appeared to work in and through language use in a variety of role-relationship dyads in the team. In doing so, we were able to provide empirical illustrations of relations of power and solidarity as they were being enacted and shaped by members of a professional New Zealand rugby team and locate specific linguistic practices that shaped these relations. These empirical accounts served as empirical evidence for the more abstract cultural ideas that appear to underlie relating in the team that were discussed in this chapter.

It is hoped that these illustrations and empirically informed accounts of relationships in action help to provide researchers interested in this interdisciplinary topic with some explicit visibility into the actual performance of relationships in sports teams. For practitioners, it is hoped that the chapters of this book provide greater guidance for discussing and unpacking questions and issues at the interface between language, relationships and culture in their own contexts.

In the process of fulfilling our research agenda, we have also demonstrated what we believe to be the value of a linguistic lens and what it is these tools offer researchers interested in the wider topic of relationships in high-performance sports teams. Such a lens may prove useful for addressing relationship management issues going forward, especially if, as trends suggest, a critical focus continues to centre on the relational practices of coaches and athletes in high-performance sporting cultures (BBC Sport, 2017a; C. Hope, 2019a, 2019b, 2021; Roan, 2016). An emphasis on how language and interactive practices establish relational dynamics may usefully be applied to identify and diagnose the ritual practices that need to change if particular relational dynamic and cultural changes are desired. For example, if greater athlete power and control are desired, what practices and interpretive processes are going to need to change to support the development of such a culture?

In concluding this book, while some progress towards understanding how relationships work in a high-performance sporting culture has been made here, this book has merely scratched the surface. There is much more work to be done, and it is hoped that the findings presented in this book are only the starting point of a more extensive body of research that unpacks, illustrates and assesses how relationships are actually working in high-performance sports teams.

Appendix 1

Technical rugby terms explained

The following terms and attempted definitions are by no means a complete list of rugby's technical terminology, nor do they provide complete coverage of the technical rugby terms found in the extracts of this book. However, they are core terms that are frequent in the data extracts and are ones that having some knowledge of might help facilitate deeper understanding of the data extracts.

Forwards	A sub-group of eight players in the team including the following positions:
Prop	Two players in the team play this position. Amongst other duties, they are responsible for providing stability in the scrum and supporting the locks by lifting them in the lineouts. They wear the numbers 1 and 3 on their jerseys.
Hooker	One player in the team plays this position. Amongst other duties, they are responsible for throwing the ball into the lineouts. They wear the number 2 on their jersey.
Front row	A collective term for the two props and the hooker.
Lock	Two players in the team play this position. They are usually the tallest in the team. Amongst other duties, they are responsible for jumping to grab the ball during a lineout. They wear the numbers 4 and 5 on their jerseys.
Loosies/loose forward	Two players in the team play this position. Amongst other duties, they are responsible for trying to secure turnovers from rucks. They wear the numbers 6 and 7 on their jerseys.
Number 8	One player in the team plays this position. They are at the back of the scrum and control the ball once it has reached the back of the scrum. They wear the number 8 on their jersey.

APPENDIX 1

Backs	A sub-group of seven players in the team including the following positions:
Half back	One player in the team plays this position. They do a lot of passing of the ball to the backline to feed sequences of attacking play by the backs. They also do a lot of kicking. They wear the number 9 on their jersey.
First five/fly half	One player in the team plays this position. They are often the key driver and decision maker when it comes to strategy and what the team will do when they have the ball. They do a lot of strategic attacking and defensive kicking. They wear the number 10 on their jersey.
Centre	Two players in the team play this position. They are in the centre of the back line. They wear the numbers 12 and 13 on their jerseys.
Wing	Two players in the team play this position. They are usually amongst the fastest players in the team and take a lot of responsibility for finishing off tries. They wear the numbers 11 and 14 on their jerseys.
Fullback	One player in the team plays this position. They are the last line of defence. They wear the number 15 on their jersey.
Set piece	A set piece is a specific event in the game of rugby that usually happens when the play has broken down and needs to be restarted. Set piece plays provide a structured way for the play to restart.
Scrum	One of the set pieces in rugby. Scrums usually happen when play breaks down after a player drops the ball forward. It involves both team's forwards forming units and pushing against one another to compete for the ball.
Lineout	Another set piece in rugby. Lineouts usually happen when the ball has gone over the sideline and out of play. It involves both team's forwards forming two lines and jumping to compete for the ball as it is thrown in from the sideline.
The hit	The moment when both opposition scrums combine and start to push against one another.
Sled	A training aide. This machine helps to mimic an opposition's scrum by providing weighted resistance for the forwards to form a scrum and push against.
Ruck	When players tackle one another as the game is taking place a ruck can sometimes form. This is where a player has been tackled and they have fallen to the ground and look to present the ball to another waiting member of their team.
Maps	A detailed outline (or map) of the strategy or strategic plays the team will execute.

APPENDIX 1

Sideline	The outer lines of the rugby field where the players and staff who are not playing sit and watch the match or training session.
Penalty goal	One of the point-scoring opportunities in rugby. When teams are awarded a penalty on the field for an infringement by the opposition, they might elect to kick a penalty goal if the goalposts are in the kicker's range. A penalty goal is worth three points.
Try	The biggest point scoring opportunity in rugby. A try is scored when a member of a team puts the ball down on or behind the opposition's try line.
Try line	The line that teams must place the ball behind if they are to score a try.
Conversion	The kicker in each team (usually the first-five) gets to attempt a conversion after the team score a try. The conversion is worth two points and requires the kicker to kick the ball between the goalposts.
Twenty-two	A significant line on the rugby field that is 22 metres out from each team's try line.
Stoppage	A short break in play. Stoppages can happen after a number of events during the match including after a try has been scored (while a conversion is being attempted) or when an injury has occurred.

Appendix 2

Contextual information about individuals in the team

Pseudonym	Nickname	Playing position	Age (at time of recording)	Ethnic background	Provincial caps	Higher-level caps	Additional notes
Jason	Jase	Prop	19 y 11 m	NZ Polynesian	6	0	Known coaches through school
Harvey	Hook	Hooker	20 y 3 m	NZ Maori	14	14	
Tamati	Tee	Hooker	19 y 1 m	NZ Polynesian	0	0	Previous experience with coaches
Chase	Cherry	Lock/loose forward	21 y 3 m	NZ European	26	0	
Jayden	Jay	Prop	18 y 10 m	Polynesian	0	0	Previous experience with coaches
Sebastian	Seb	Loose Forward	24 y 6 m	NZ Polynesian	25	0	
Flynn	Fly	Midfield/Wing	20 y 8 m	South African	10	13	Previous experience with coaches (U16s)
Timothy	Timmy	Wing	28 y 3 m	NZ European	29	0	3 seasons with the team, some previous experience with coaches
Kingston	Kingy	Midfield	26 y 9 m	NZ Polynesian	10	0	Previous experience with coaches

Pseudonym	Nickname	Playing position	Age (at time of recording)	Ethnic background	Provincial caps	Higher-level caps	Additional notes
Mark	Maz	First Five/Fullback	21 y 8 m	NZ Maori Polynesian	13	13	Game driver, 4th season with the squad, previous experience with coaches
Salu	Salu	Halfback/first five	29 y 9 m	NZ Polynesian	35	0	
Michael	Mickey	Lock	25 y 1 m	NZ Polynesian	6	27	
Thomas	Topper	Lock/loose forward	29 y 2 m	NZ Maori	22	0	Rugby journeyman, played for a number of clubs overseas (caps not registered here)
Phoenix	Phony	Hooker/flanker	27 y 4 m	NZ Polynesian	0	0	Wider squad member
Nixon	Nix	Loose Forward	26 y 8 m	NZ European	4	0	Previous experience with coaches
Liam	Leaf	Midfield	27 y 5 m	NZ European	56	49	Previous experience with coaches
Nikau	Nikau	Halfback	22 y 9 m	NZ Maori	7	0	
Steve	Stevie	Prop	21 y 8 m	Polynesian	6	0	Previous experience with coaches (age group)
Jesse	Jez	Loose Forward	29 y 3 m	NZ Polynesian	0	0	Previous experience with assistant coach
Sione	Sione	Midfield/winger	20 y 3 m	NZ Polynesian	3	0	
Lima	Lima	First five/fullback	21 y 3 m	NZ Maori	0	0	Previous experience with coaches

Pseudonym	Nickname	Playing position	Age (at time of recording)	Ethnic background	Provincial caps	Higher-level caps	Additional notes
Lagi	Lagi	Winger/fullback	18 y 6 m	NZ Polynesian	0	0	Previous experience with coaches (coached school)
Rangi	Rangi	First five-eighth	19 y 8 m	NZ Polynesian	0	0	
Ashton	Ash	Lock/loose forward	19 y 2 m	NZ Maori Polynesian	0	0	Previous experience with coaches (age group rep)
Terence	Beef	Prop	29 y 1 m	White North American	11	0	Visiting player, signed from overseas
Manu	Manu	Midfield	19 y 9 m	NZ Polynesian	0	0	
Abel	Abel	Lock/loose forward	23 y 6 m	NZ Polynesian	0	0	
Henare	Hendy	Prop	Unknown	NZ Polynesian	19	0	All caps for a lower division
Grayson	Grayson	Prop	Unknown	Unknown	15	0	14 caps for a lower division
Brian	BJ	Half back	Unknown	NZ European	2	0	
Aaron	Azza	Hooker	21 y 7 m	NZ European	17	0	
Fletcher	Fletch	Prop	Unknown	NZ Maori	19	0	All caps for a lower division

References

Aarons, D., & Mierowsky, M. (2017). How to do things with jokes: Speech acts in standup comedy. *The European Journal of Humour Research*, *5*(4), 158. https://doi.org/10.7592/EJHR2017.5.4.aarons

Alasuutari, P. (1995). *Researching culture: Qualitative method and cultural studies*. Sage.

Alvesson, M., & Karreman, D. (2000). Varieties of discourse: On the study of organizations through discourse analysis. *Human Relations*, *53*(9), 1125–1149.

Asmuß, B. (2015). Multimodal perspectives on meeting interaction: Recent trends in conversation analysis. In J. A. Allen, N. Lehmann-Willenbrock, & S. G. Rogelberg (Eds.), *The Cambridge Handbook of Meeting Science* (pp. 277–304). Cambridge University Press. https://doi.org/10.1017/CBO9781107589735.013

Australian Associated Press. (2018). New Zealand women's football coach resigns amid alleged 'toxic culture.' *The Guardian*. http://www.theguardian.com/football/2018/jul/31/new-zealand-womens-football-coach-resigns-amid-alleged-toxic-culture

Azadfada, S., Besmi, M., Doroudian, A. A. (2014). The relationship between servant leadership and athlete satisfaction. *International Journal of Basic Sciences and Applied Research*, *3*(8), 528–537.

Balaguer, I., González, L., Fabra, P., Castillo, I., Mercé, J., & Duda, J. L. (2012). Coaches' interpersonal style, basic psychological needs and the well- and ill-being of young soccer players: A longitudinal analysis. *Journal of Sports Sciences*, *30*(15), 1619–1629. https://doi.org/10.1080/02640414.2012.731517

Bayard, D., & Krishnayya, S. (2001). Gender, expletive use, and context: Male and female expletive use in structured and unstructured conversation among New Zealand university students. *Women and Language: WL*, *24*(1), 1–15.

BBC Sport. (2017a). GB rowing coaching culture 'hard' but falls short of bullying, says review. *BBC Sport*. http://www.bbc.co.uk/sport/rowing/38826722

BBC Sport. (2017b, January 27). David Weir: GB wheelchair coach Jenni Banks 'belittled' me at Rio Paralympics. *BBC Sport*. http://www.bbc.co.uk/sport/disability-sport/38770498

Beeching, K. (2006). Sociolinguistics: The study of speakers' choices. *Journal of Sociolinguistics*, *10*(2), 278–282. https://doi.org/10.1111/j.1360-6441.2006.0327i.x

Bell, A. (1984). Language style as audience design. *Language in Society*, *13*(2), 145–204.

Bell, A., & Gibson, A. (2011). Staging language: An introduction to the sociolinguistics of performance. *Journal of Sociolinguistics*, *15*(5), 555–572. https://doi.org/10.1111/j.1467-9841.2011.00517.x

Bell, A., & Johnson, G. (1997). Towards a sociolinguistics of style. *University of Pennsylvania Working Papers in Linguistics, 4*(1), 2.

Bellinger, D. C., & Gleason, J. B. (1982). Sex differences in parental directives to young children. *Sex Roles, 8*(11), 1123–1139.

Bennie, A., & O'Connor, D. (2012). Coach-athlete relationships: A qualitative study of professional sport teams in Australia. *International Journal of Sport and Health Science, 10*, 58–64.

Biber, D. (1988). *Variation across speech and writing*. Cambridge University Press.

Biber, D. (Ed.). (1999). *Longman grammar of spoken and written English*. Longman.

Blommaert, J. (2007). Sociolinguistics and discourse analysis: Orders of indexicality and polycentricity. *Journal of Multicultural Discourses, 2*(2), 115–130.

Bousfield, D. (2008). *Impoliteness in interaction*. John Benjamins Publishing Company.

Bousfield, D., & Locher, M. A. (Eds.). (2008). *Impoliteness in language: Studies on its interplay with power in theory and practice*. Mouton de Gruyter.

Boxer, D. (2002). *Applying sociolinguistics: Domains and face-to-face interaction*. John Benjamins Publishing Company.

Boxer, D., & Cortés-Conde, F. (1997). From bonding to biting: Conversational joking and identity display. *Journal of Pragmatics, 27*(3), 275–294. https://doi.org/10.1016/S0378-2166(96)00031-8

Boyd, M., & Rubin, D. (2006). How contingent questioning promotes extended student talk: A function of display questions. *Journal of Literacy Research, 38*(2), 141–169. https://doi.org/10.1207/s15548430jlr3802_2

Brawley, L. R., Carron, A. V., & Widmeyer, W. N. (1987). Assessing the cohesion of teams: Validity of the Group Environment Questionnaire. *Journal of Sport Psychology, 9*(3), 275–294.

Brown, G., & Yule, G. (1983). *Discourse analysis*. Cambridge University Press.

Brown, P., & Levinson, S. (1978). Universals in language use: Politeness phenomena. In E. N. Goody (Ed.), *Questions and politeness: Strategies in social interaction* (pp. 56–289). Cambridge University Press.

Brown, R., & Gilman, A. (1960). *The pronouns of power and solidarity. Style in language*, 252–281.

Bubel, C. (2006). *The linguistic construction of character relations in TV drama: Doing friendship in Sex and the City* [Doctoral dissertation]. Saarbrücken University.

Buchstaller, I. (2006). Social stereotypes, personality traits and regional perception displaced: Attitudes towards the 'new' quotatives in the U.K. *Journal of Sociolinguistics, 10*(3), 362–381. https://doi.org/10.1111/j.1360-6441.2006.00332.x

Bull, P., & Fetzer, A. (2006). Who are we and who are you?: The strategic use of forms of address in political interviews. *Text & Talk, 26*(1), 3–37.

Burke, M. (2001). Obeying until it hurts: Coach-athlete relationships. *Journal of the Philosophy of Sport, 28*(2), 227–240. https://doi.org/10.1080/00948705.2001.9714616

Candela, A. (1998). Students' power in classroom discourse. *Linguistics and Education, 10*(2), 139–163. https://doi.org/10.1016/S0898-5898(99)80107-7

Carron, A. V., Bray, S. R., & Eys, M. A. (2002). Team cohesion and team success in sport. *Journal of Sports Sciences*, *20*(2), 119–126.

Carter, R., Goddard, A., Reah, D., Sanger, K., & Bowring, M. (Eds.). (2001). *Working with texts: A core introduction to language analysis* (2nd ed.). Routledge.

Chimbwete-Phiri, R., & Schnurr, S. (2017). Negotiating knowledge and creating solidarity: Humour in antenatal counselling sessions at a rural hospital in Malawi. *Lingua*, *197*, 68–82. https://doi.org/10.1016/j.lingua.2017.03.003

Chovanec, J. (2016). Eavesdropping on media talk: Microphone gaffes and unintended humour in sports broadcasts. *Journal of Pragmatics*, *95* (Supplement C), 93–106. https://doi.org/10.1016/j.pragma.2016.01.011

Clayman, S. (2012). Turn-constructional units and the transition-relevance place. *The Handbook of Conversation Analysis*, 151–166.

Clayman, S., & Heritage, J. (2002). *The news interview: Journalists and public figures on the air*. Cambridge University Press.

Clifton, J. (2012). A discursive approach to leadership: Doing assessments and managing organizational meanings. *Journal of Business Communication*, *49*(2), 148–168. https://doi.org/10.1177/0021943612437762

Clifton, J., Van De Mieroop, D., Sehgal, P., & Aneet, Dr. (2018). The multimodal enactment of deontic and epistemic authority in Indian meetings. *Pragmatics*, *28*(3), 333–360. https://doi.org/10.1075/prag.17011.cli

Cotterill, S., Cheetham, R., & Fransen, K. (2019). Professional rugby coaches' perceptions of the role of the team captain. *The Sport Psychologist*, *33*(4), 276–284. https://doi.org/10.1123/tsp.2018-0094

Coulthard, M. (Ed.). (1992). *Advances in spoken discourse analysis*. Routledge.

Coupland, N. (1980). Style-shifting in a Cardiff work-setting. *Language in Society*, *9*(1), 1–12. https://doi.org/10.1017/S0047404500007752

Culpeper, J. (2011). *Impoliteness: Using language to cause offence*. Cambridge University Press.

Daly, N., Holmes, J., Newton, J., & Stubbe, M. (2004). Expletives as solidarity signals in FTAs on the factory floor. *Journal of Pragmatics*, *36*(5), 945–964. https://doi.org/10.1016/j.pragma.2003.12.004

Davis, L., & Jowett, S. (2010). Investigating the interpersonal dynamics between coaches and athletes based on fundamental principles of attachment. *Journal of Clinical Sport Psychology*, *4*(2), 112–132.

Drasovean, A., & Tagg, C. (2015). Evaluative language and its solidarity-building role on TED.com: An appraisal and corpus analysis. *Language@Internet*, *12*. http://www.languageatinternet.org/articles/2015/drasovean

Drew, P., & Heritage, J. (Eds.). (1992). *Talk at work: Interaction in institutional settings* (Vol. *8*). Cambridge University Press.

Duda, J. L. (2013). The conceptual and empirical foundations of Empowering Coaching™: Setting the stage for the PAPA project. *International Journal of Sport and Exercise Psychology*, *11*(4), 311–318. https://doi.org/10.1080/1612197X.2013.839414

Dynel, M. (2014). Participation framework underlying YouTube interaction. *Journal of Pragmatics*, *73*, 37–52. https://doi.org/10.1016/j.pragma.2014.04.001

Edelsky, C. (1981). Who's got the floor? *Language in Society*, *10*(3), 383–421. https://doi.org/10.1017/S004740450000885X

Eggins, S. (2004). *An introduction to systemic functional linguistics* (2nd ed.). Continuum.
Eggins, S., & Slade, D. (1997). *Analysing casual conversation*. Cassell.
Ervin-Tripp, S. M. (1987). Sociolinguistic rules of address. In B. Mayor & A. K. Pugh (Eds.), *Language, communication and education* (pp. 162–168). The Open University.
Fairclough, N. (1985). Critical and descriptive goals in discourse analysis. *Journal of Pragmatics*, *9*(6), 739–763. https://doi.org/10.1016/0378-2166(85)90002-5
Fairclough, N. (1992). *Discourse and social change*. Polity Press.
Fairclough, N. (2001). *Language and power* (2nd ed.). Longman.
Fairclough, N. (2003a). *Analysing discourse: Textual analysis for social research*. Routledge.
Fairclough, N. (2003b). *Analyzing discourse: Textual analysis for social research*. Routledge.
Fairhurst, G. T., & Uhl-Bien, M. (2012). Organizational discourse analysis (ODA): Examining leadership as a relational process. *The Leadership Quarterly*, *23*(6), 1043–1062. https://doi.org/10.1016/j.leaqua.2012.10.005
File, K. A. (2017). 'That was a bit daft though, wasn't it?' Strategic use of impoliteness in a post-match interview. In A. Bczkowska (Ed.), *Impoliteness in media discourse* (pp. 107–125). New York, NY : Peter Lang Edition.
File, K. A. (2018). 'You're Manchester United manager, you can't say things like that': Impression management and identity performance by professional football managers in the media. *Journal of Pragmatics*, *127*, 56–70. https://doi.org/10.1016/j.pragma.2018.01.001
File, K. A. (2019). Managing impressions and relationships when speaking to the sports media. In D. Collins, A. Cruickshank, & G. Jordet (Eds.), *Routledge handbook of elite sport performance* (1st ed., pp. 258–266). Routledge. https://doi.org/10.4324/9781315266343-29
File, K. A., & Wilson, N. (2017). Adapting self for private and public audiences: The enactment of leadership identity by New Zealand rugby coaches in huddles and interviews. In D. Van De Mieroop & S. Schnurr (Eds.), *Identity struggles. Evidence from workplaces around the world* (pp. 317–333). John Benjamins Publishing Company.
Freed, A., & Ehrlich, S. (Eds.). (2010). *'Why do you ask?': The function of questions in institutional discourse*. Oxford University Press.
Freed, A. F., & Greenwood, A. (1996). Women, men, and type of talk: What makes the difference? *Language in Society*, *25*(1), 1–26. https://doi.org/10.1017/S0047404500020418
French, P., & Local, J. (1983). Turn-competitive incomings. *Journal of Pragmatics*, *7*(1), 17–38. https://doi.org/10.1016/0378-2166(83)90147-9
Frey, L. R. (1996). Remembering and 're-membering': A history of theory and research on communication and group decision making. In R. Hirokawa & M. Poole (Eds.), *Communication and group decision making*. Sage. https://doi.org/10.4135/9781452243764
García-Calvo, T., Leo, F. M., Gonzalez-Ponce, I., Sánchez-Miguel, P. A., Mouratidis, A., & Ntoumanis, N. (2014). Perceived coach-created and peer-created motivational climates and their associations with team cohesion and athlete satisfaction: Evidence from a longitudinal study. *Journal of Sports Sciences*, *32*(18), 1738–1750. https://doi.org/10.1080/02640414.2014.918641

REFERENCES

Gee, J. P. (2018). *Introducing discourse analysis: From grammar to society*. Routledge.

Giles, H. (Ed.). (2016). *Communication accommodation theory: Negotiating personal relationships and social identities across contexts*. Cambridge University Press.

Goffman, E. (1970). *Strategic interaction*. Blackwell.

Goffman, E. (1976). Replies and responses. *Language in Society*, 5(3), 257–313.

Goffman, E. (1979). Footing. *Semiotica*, 25(1–2), 1–30. https://doi.org/10.1515/semi.1979.25.1-2.1

Goffman, E. (1981). *Forms of talk*. Blackwell.

Goffman, E. (2006). On face-work: An analysis of ritual elements in social interaction. In A. Jaworski & N. Coupland (Eds.), *The discourse reader* (2nd ed., pp. 299–310). Routledge.

Goldberg, J. A. (1990). Interrupting the discourse on interruptions. *Journal of Pragmatics*, 14(6), 883–903. https://doi.org/10.1016/0378-2166(90)90045-F

Groom, R., Cushion, C. J., & Nelson, L. J. (2012). Analysing coach–athlete 'talk in interaction' within the delivery of video-based performance feedback in elite youth soccer. *Qualitative Research in Sport, Exercise and Health*, 4(3), 439–458. https://doi.org/10.1080/2159676X.2012.693525

Gumperz, J. J. (1982). *Discourse strategies*. Cambridge University Press.

Gumperz, J. J. (1999). On interactional sociolinguistic method. In S. Sarangi & C. Roberts (Eds.), *Talk, work and institutional order* (pp. 453–471). Mouton de Gruyter.

Gumperz, J. J. (2015). Interactional sociolinguistics a personal perspective. In D. Tannen, H. E. Hamilton, & D. Schiffrin (Eds.), *The handbook of discourse Analysis* (pp. 309–323). John Wiley & Sons, Inc. https://doi.org/10.1002/9781118584194.ch14

Halldorsson, V., Thorlindsson, T., & Katovich, M. A. (2017). Teamwork in sport: A sociological analysis. *Sport in Society*, 20(9), 1281–1296. https://doi.org/10.1080/17430437.2017.1284798

Halliday, M. A. K., & Matthiessen, C. M. I. M. (2014). *Halliday's introduction to functional grammar* (4th ed.). Routledge.

Harwood, J. (2016). Communicative predictors of solidarity in the grandparent-grandchild relationship: *Journal of Social and Personal Relationships*. https://doi.org/10.1177/0265407500176003

Harwood, N. (2005). 'We do not seem to have a theory … The theory I present here attempts to fill this gap': Inclusive and exclusive pronouns in academic writing. *Applied Linguistics*, 26(3), 343–375. https://doi.org/10.1093/applin/ami012

Hay, J. (1994). Jocular abuse patterns in mixed-group interaction. *Wellington Working Papers in Linguistics*, 6, 26–55.

Heath, S., & Langman, J. (1994). Shared thinking and the register of coaching. In D. Biber & E. Finegan (Eds.), *Sociolinguistic perspectives on register* (pp. 82–105). Oxford University Press US.

Heritage, J. (1984). *Garfinkel and ethnomethodology*. Polity.

Heritage, J., Robinson, J.D. (2011). 'Some' versus 'Any' medical issues: encouraging patients to reveal their unmet concerns. In: Antaki, C. (Ed.), *Applied Conversation Analysis* (pp. 15–31). Palgrave Advances in Linguistics. Palgrave Macmillan, London. https://doi.org/10.1057/9780230316874_2.

Heuzé, J.-P., Raimbault, N., & Fontayne, P. (2006). Relationships between cohesion, collective efficacy and performance in professional basketball teams: An examination of mediating effects. *Journal of Sports Sciences*, *24*(1), 59–68. https://doi.org/10.1080/02640410500127736

Hodge, K., Henry, G., & Smith, W. (2014). A case study of excellence in elite sport: Motivational climate in a world champion team. *The Sport Psychologist*, *28*(1), 60–74. https://doi.org/10.1123/tsp.2013-0037

Holmes, J. (1984). Modifying illocutionary force. *Journal of Pragmatics*, *8*(3), 345–365. https://doi.org/10.1016/0378-2166(84)90028-6

Holmes, J. (2013). *An introduction to sociolinguistics* (4th ed.). Routledge.

Holmes, J. (2014). Doing discourse analysis in sociolinguistics. In J. Holmes & K. Hazen (Eds.), *Research methods in sociolinguistics: A practical guide* (pp. 177–193). Wiley Blackwell.

Holmes, J., & Chiles, T. (2010). 'Is that right?' Questions and questioning as control devices in the workplace. In A. Freed & S. Ehrlich (Eds.), *'Why do you ask?': The function of questions in institutional discourse* (pp. 187–210). Oxford University Press.

Holmes, J., & Marra, M. (2004). Relational practice in the workplace: Women's talk or gendered discourse? *Language in Society*, *33*(3), 377–398.

Holmes, J., & Schnurr, S. (2006). 'Doing femininity' at work: More than just relational practice1. *Journal of Sociolinguistics*, *10*(1), 31–51. https://doi.org/10.1111/j.1360-6441.2006.00316.x

Holmes, J., & Stubbe, M. (2003). *Power and politeness in the workplace: A sociolinguistic analysis of talk at work*. Pearson.

Holmes, J., Marra, M., & Vine, B. (2012). Politeness and impoliteness in ethnic varieties of New Zealand English. *Journal of Pragmatics*, *44*(9), 1063–1076. https://doi.org/10.1016/j.pragma.2011.11.006

Holmes, J., Marra, M., & Lazzaro-Salazar, M. (2017). Negotiating the tall poppy syndrome in New Zealand workplaces: Women leaders managing the challenge. *Gender and Language*, *11*(1), 1–29. https://doi.org/10.1558/genl.31236

Holmes, T. (2019, January 22). Matildas coach sacked after players revealed they were afraid to ask for help. *ABC News*. https://www.abc.net.au/news/2019-01-22/matildas-environment-of-stress-and-fear/10734412

Hope, C. (2019a, January 3). *Bellamy steps down as Cardiff U18 coach pending club investigation*. Mail Online. https://www.dailymail.co.uk/sport/sportsnews/article-6553247/Craig-Bellamy-steps-Cardiff-U18-coach-pending-club-investigation-bullying-allegations.html

Hope, C. (2019b, March 6). Peter Beardsley no longer employed by Newcastle after investigation. *Mail Online*. https://www.dailymail.co.uk/sport/sportsnews/article-6777565/Peter-Beardsley-no-longer-employed-Newcastle-investigation-alleged-racism-bullying.html

Hope, C. (2021, March 14). *Cardiff suspend academy manager amid fresh bullying probe*. Mail Online. https://www.dailymail.co.uk/sport/sportsnews/article-9361293/Cardiff-City-suspend-academy-manager-James-McCarthy-amid-fresh-bullying-probe.html

Hope, N. (2017, November 13). Dan Keatings: 'The climate of fear is real in British Gymnastics.' *BBC Sport*. http://www.bbc.co.uk/sport/gymnastics/41976299

REFERENCES

Hultgren, A. K. (2011). 'Building rapport' with customers across the world: The global diffusion of a call centre speech style1. *Journal of Sociolinguistics*, *15*(1), 36–64. https://doi.org/10.1111/j.1467-9841.2010.00466.x

Hutchby, I. (2014). Communicative affordances and participation frameworks in mediated interaction. *Journal of Pragmatics*, *72*, 86–89. https://doi.org/10.1016/j.pragma.2014.08.012

Hyland, K., & Paltridge, B. (Eds.). (2013). *Continuum companion to discourse analysis*. Bloomsbury Academic.

Hymes, D. (1967). Models of the interaction of language and social setting. *Journal of Social Issues*, *23*(2), 8–28. https://doi.org/10.1111/j.1540-4560.1967.tb00572.x

Hymes, D. (1972). On communicative competence. In J. B. Pride & J. Holmes (Eds.), *Sociolinguistics: Selected readings* (pp. 269–293). Penguin.

Hymes, D. H. (1974). *Foundations in sociolinguistics: An ethnographic approach*. University of Pennsylvania Press.

Ide, S. (1982). Japanese sociolinguistics politeness and women's language. *Lingua*, *57*(2–4), 357–385.

Ingle, S. (2017a, February 19). Toni Minichiello set to be warned over swearing at female athlete. *The Guardian*. https://www.theguardian.com/sport/2017/feb/19/toni-minichiello-set-to-be-warned-over-swearing-at-female-athlete-british-athletics

Ingle, S. (2017b, March 10). British Cycling's reputation in tatters after scathing review is leaked. *The Guardian*. https://www.theguardian.com/sport/2017/mar/10/british-cycling-dave-brailsford-reputation-in-tatters-review

Ingle, S. (2017c, October 9). British Bobsleigh's head coach said 'black drivers do not make good bobsleigh drivers.' *The Guardian*. http://www.theguardian.com/sport/2017/oct/09/british-bobsleigh-head-coach-lee-johnston-black-drivers

Ingle, S. (2017d, October 9). Inside British Bobsleigh: A toxic culture which left athletes afraid to speak up | Sean Ingle. *The Guardian*. http://www.theguardian.com/sport/2017/oct/09/british-bobsleigh-toxic-culture-uk-sport-winter-olympics-2018

Jackson, B., Grove, J. R., & Beauchamp, M. R. (2010). Relational efficacy beliefs and relationship quality within coach-athlete dyads. *Journal of Social and Personal Relationships*, *27*(8), 1035–1050. https://doi.org/10.1177/0265407510378123

Jaspers, J. (2012). Interactional sociolinguistics and discourse analysis. In J. P. Gee & M. Handford (Eds.), *The Routledge handbook of discourse analysis* (pp. 135–146). Routledge.

Jaworski, A., & Coupland, N. (Eds.). (2006). *The discourse reader* (2nd ed.). Routledge.

Jefferson, G. (1988). On the sequential organization of troubles-talk in ordinary conversation. *Social Problems*, *35*(4), 418–441. https://doi.org/10.2307/800595

Jewitt, C. (Ed.). (2014). *The Routledge handbook of multimodal analysis* (2nd ed.). Routledge.

Johnstone, B. (2008). *Discourse analysis* (2nd ed.). Blackwell Publishing.

Jones, E. (2019, November 17). Eddie Jones: Players follow blindly even when they are badly led. *The Sunday Times*. https://www.thetimes.co.uk/article/eddie-jones-players-follow-blindly-even-when-they-are-badly-led-672rpdttv

Jowett, S., & Cockerill, I. M. (2002). Incompatibility in the coach-athlete relationship. In Cockerill (Ed.), *Solutions in sport psychology* (pp. 16–31). Cengage Learning EMEA.

Jowett, S., & Cockerill, I. M. (2003). Olympic medallists' perspective of the athlete–coach relationship. *Psychology of Sport and Exercise*, *4*(4), 313–331. https://doi.org/10.1016/S1469-0292(02)00011-0

Jowett, S., & Ntoumanis, N. (2004). The coach–athlete relationship questionnaire (CART-Q): Development and initial validation. *Scandinavian Journal of Medicine & Science in Sports*, *14*(4), 245–257.

Kádár, D. Z., & Bax, M. M. H. (2013). In-group ritual and relational work. *Journal of Pragmatics*, *58*, 73–86. https://doi.org/10.1016/j.pragma.2013.03.011

Kassing, J. W., & Infante, D. A. (1999). Aggressive communication in the coach-athlete relationship. *Communication Research Reports*, *16*(2), 110–120. https://doi.org/10.1080/08824099909388708

Knowler, R. (2017). Crusaders centre Jack Goodhue forced to learn gift of the rugby gab. *Stuff.* http://www.stuff.co.nz/sport/rugby/super-rugby/95186309/crusaders-centre-jack-goodhue-forced-to-learn-gift-of-the-rugby-gab

Koester, A. (2006). *Investigating workplace discourse*. Routledge, Taylor & Francis Group.

Koester, A. (2010). *Workplace discourse*. Continuum.

Koshik, I. (2002). Designedly incomplete utterances: A pedagogical practice for eliciting knowledge displays in error correction sequences. *Research on Language & Social Interaction*, *35*(3), 277–309. https://doi.org/10.1207/S15327973RLSI3503_2

Kozub, S., & McDonnell, J. (2000). Exploring the relationship between cohesion and collective efficacy in rugby teams. *Journal of Sport Behavior; Mobile, Ala.*, *23*(2), 120–129.

Kuiper, K. (1991). Sporting formulae in New Zealand English: Two models of male solidarity. In J. Cheshire (Ed.), *English around the world* (pp. 200–210). Cambridge University Press. https://doi.org/10.1017/CBO9780511611889.014

Lafrenière, M.-A. K., Jowett, S., Vallerand, R. J., Donahue, E. G., & Lorimer, R. (2008). Passion in sport: On the quality of the coach–athlete relationship. *Journal of Sport and Exercise Psychology*, *30*(5), 541–560. https://doi.org/10.1123/jsep.30.5.541

Lakoff, R. (1973). Language and woman's place. *Language in Society*, *2*(1), 45–79. https://doi.org/10.1017/S0047404500000051

Landmark, A. M. D., Gulbrandsen, P., & Svennevig, J. (2015). Whose decision? Negotiating epistemic and deontic rights in medical treatment decisions. *Journal of Pragmatics*, *78*, 54–69. https://doi.org/10.1016/j.pragma.2014.11.007

Lee, Y., Kim, S.-H., & Joon-Ho, K. (2013). Coach leadership effect on elite handball players' psychological empowerment and organizational citizenship behavior. *International Journal of Sports Science & Coaching*, *8*(2), 327–342.

Liddicoat, A. (2022). *An introduction to conversation analysis* (3rd ed.). Bloomsbury Academic.

Lim, T.-S., & Bowers, J. W. (1991). Facework solidarity, approbation, and tact. *Human Communication Research*, *17*(3), 415–450. https://doi.org/10.1111/j.1468-2958.1991.tb00239.x

Lipovsky, C. (2008). Constructing affiliation and solidarity in job interviews. *Discourse & Communication*, *2*(4), 411–432. https://doi.org/10.1177/1750481308095938

Locher, M. A. (2010). Relational work, politeness, and identity construction. In D. R. Matsumoto & American Psychological Association (Eds.), *APA handbook of interpersonal communication* (pp. 111–138). American Psychological Association.

Locher, M. A. (2013). Relational work and interpersonal pragmatics. *Journal of Pragmatics, 58*, 145–149. https://doi.org/10.1016/j.pragma.2013.09.014

Locher, M. A., & Watts, R. J. (2005). Politeness theory and relational work. *Journal of Politeness Research. Language, Behaviour, Culture, 1*(1), 9–33. https://doi.org/10.1515/jplr.2005.1.1.9

Love, R. (2021). Swearing in informal spoken English: 1990s–2010s. *Text & Talk, 41*(5–6), 739–762. https://doi.org/10.1515/text-2020-0051

Lyle, J. (2002). *Sports coaching concepts: A framework for coaches' behaviour*. Routledge.

Markman, K. M. (2009). 'So what shall we talk about': Openings and closings in chat-based virtual meetings. *Journal of Business Communication, 46*(1), 150–170. https://doi.org/10.1177/0021943608325751

Marra, M., Vine, B., & Holmes, J. (2008, July). Heroes, fathers and good mates: Leadership styles of men at work. In *Proceedings of the Australian and New Zealand Communication Association Conference 2008* (pp. 1–15).

McEnery, T. (2006). *Swearing in English: Bad language, purity and power from 1586 to the present* [Electronic resource]. Routledge. https://ebookcentral.proquest.com/lib/warw/detail.action?docID=182243

Metge, J., & Laing, P. (1984). *Talking past each other: Problems of cross cultural communication*. Victoria University Press.

Meyerhoff, M. (1994). Sounds pretty ethnic, eh?: A pragmatic particle in New Zealand English. *Language in Society, 23*, 367–388.

Miller, P. (1986). Teasing as language socialization and verbal play in a white working class community. *Language Socialization across Cultures, 3*, 199.

Mirivel, J. C., & Fuller, R. (2017). Relational talk at work. In B. Vine (Ed.), *The Routledge handbook of language in the workplace* (pp. 216 and 227). Routledge.

Nanouri, K., Tseliou, E., Abakoumkin, G., & Bozatzis, N. (2022). 'Who decided this?': Negotiating epistemic and deontic authority in systemic family therapy training. *Discourse Studies*, 146144562110374. https://doi.org/10.1177/14614456211037450

O'Connor, D., Larkin, P., Robertson, S., & Goodyear, P. (2021). The art of the question: The structure of questions posed by youth soccer coaches during training. *Physical Education and Sport Pedagogy*, 1–16. https://doi.org/10.1080/17408989.2021.1877270

O'Connor, M., & Macfarlane, A. (2002). New Zealand Maori stories and symbols: Family value lessons for western counsellors. *International Journal for the Advancement of Counselling, 24*(4), 223–237. https://doi.org/10.1023/A:1023368729169

O'Halloran, K. L., & Smith, B. A. (Eds.). (2011). *Multimodal studies: Exploring issues and domains*. Routledge.

Ostermann, A. C. (2003). Localizing power and solidarity: Pronoun alternation at an all-female police station and a feminist crisis intervention center in Brazil. *Language in Society, 32*(3), 351–381. https://doi.org/10.1017/S0047404503323036

Pescosolido, A. T., & Saavedra, R. (2012). Cohesion and sports teams a review. *Small Group Research, 43*(6), 744–758. https://doi.org/10.1177/1046496412465020

Poczwardowski, A., Barott, J. E., & Jowett, S. (2006). Diversifying approaches to research on athlete–coach relationships. *Psychology of Sport and Exercise*, *7*(2), 125–142.

Poutiainen, S. (2015). Interpersonal Ideology. In K. Tracy, T. Sandel, & C. Ilie (Eds.), *The international encyclopedia of language and social interaction* (1st ed., pp. 1–6). Wiley. https://doi.org/10.1002/9781118611463

Power. (2015). In A. Stevenson & C. Lindberg (Eds.), *New Oxford American Dictionary* (3rd ed.). Oxford University Press.

Prapavessis, H., & Carron, A. V. (1997). Sacrifice, cohesion, and conformity to norms in sport teams. *Group Dynamics: Theory, Research, and Practice*, *1*(3), 231.

Puchta, C., & Potter, J. (1999). Asking elaborate questions: Focus groups and the management of spontaneity. *Journal of Sociolinguistics*, *3*(3), 314–335.

Richards, K. (2006). *Language and professional identity: Aspects of collaborative interaction*. Palgrave Macmillan.

Roan, D. (2016). Shane Sutton: Jess Varnish's sexism allegations upheld by British Cycling. *BBC Sport*. http://www.bbc.co.uk/sport/cycling/37804761

Roan, D. (2017, March 23). British Swimming: Bullying claims by Paralympians are investigated. *BBC Sport*. http://www.bbc.co.uk/sport/disability-sport/39368319

Rosaldo, M. Z. (1982). The things we do with words: Ilongot speech acts and speech act theory in philosophy. *Language in Society*, *11*(2), 203–237. https://doi.org/10.1017/S0047404500009209

Rubin, G. B. (2016). *Negotiating power through tag questions in crisis negotiations* [PhD Thesis]. Georgetown University.

Rylander, P. (2015). Coaches' bases of power: Developing some initial knowledge of athletes' compliance with coaches in team sports. *Journal of Applied Sport Psychology*, *27*(1), 110–121. https://doi.org/10.1080/10413200.2014.954065

Sacks, H., Schegloff, E. A., & Jefferson, G. (1974). A simplest systematics for the organization of turn-taking for conversation. *Language*, *50*(4), 696–735. https://doi.org/10.2307/412243

Sagar, S. S., & Jowett, S. (2012). Communicative acts in coach–athlete interactions: When losing competitions and when making mistakes in training. *Western Journal of Communication*, *76*(2), 148–174. https://doi.org/10.1080/10570314.2011.651256

Salmela, M. (2015). Collective emotions as 'the glue' of group solidarity. In A. Laitinen & A. B. Pessi (Eds.), *Solidarity: Theory and practice* (pp. 55–87). Lexington Books.

Schegloff, E. A. (1995). Discourse as an interactional achievement III: The omnirelevance of action. *Research on Language & Social Interaction*, *28*(3), 185.

Schegloff, E. A., & Sacks, H. (1973). Opening up closings. *Semiotica*, *8*(4), 289–327.

Schiffrin, D. (1994). *Approaches to discourse*. Blackwell Publishers.

Schiffrin, D. (1996). Interactional sociolinguistics. In S. McKay & N. H. Hornberger (Eds.), *Sociolinguistics and language teaching* (pp. 307–328). Cambridge University Press.

Schnurr, S. (2009). Constructing leader identities through teasing at work. *Journal of Pragmatics*, *41*(6), 1125–1138. https://doi.org/10.1016/j.pragma.2008.10.002

Schnurr, S. (2013). *Exploring professional communication: Language in action*. Routledge.

Schnurr, S., File, K. A., Clayton, D., Wolfers, S., & Stavridou, A. (2020). Exploring the processes of emergent leadership in a netball team: Providing empirical evidence through discourse analysis. *Discourse & Communication*, 1750481320961658. https://doi.org/10.1177/1750481320961658

Schnurr, S., Marra, M., & Holmes, J. (2007). Being (im)polite in New Zealand workplaces: Māori and Pākehā leaders. *Journal of Pragmatics*, *39*(4), 712–729. https://doi.org/10.1016/j.pragma.2006.11.016

Schofield, D. (2017, June 5). Eddie Jones: I want to make myself redundant by letting England players take control. *The Telegraph*. http://www.telegraph.co.uk/rugby-union/2017/06/05/eddie-jones-want-make-redundant-letting-england-players-take/

Schulze, R. (2014). Representing inequality in language: Words as social categorizers of experience. In H. Pishwa & R. Schulze (Eds.), *The expression of inequality in interaction: Power, dominance, and status* (pp. 17–48). John Benjamins Publishing Company.

Searle, J. R. (1969). *Speech acts: An essay in the philosophy of language* (Vol. *626*). Cambridge university press.

Searle, J. R. (1985). *Expression and meaning: Studies in the theory of speech acts*. Cambridge University Press.

Sinclair, J., & Coulthard, M. (1992). Towards an analysis of discourse. In M. Coulthard (Ed.), *Advances in spoken discourse analysis* (pp. 1–34). Routledge.

Smith, M. J., Figgins, S. G., Jewiss, M., & Kearney, P. E. (2018). Investigating inspirational leader communication in an elite team sport context. *International Journal of Sports Science & Coaching*, *13*(2), 213–224.

Solidarity. (2015). In A. Stevenson & C. Lindberg (Eds.), *New Oxford American Dictionary* (3rd ed.). Oxford University Press.

Spencer-Oatey, H. (2008). Face, (Im)politeness and Rapport. In H. Spencer-Oatey (Ed.), *Culturally speaking* (2nd ed.). Continuum.

Spencer-Oatey, H. (2011). Conceptualising 'the relational' in pragmatics: Insights from metapragmatic emotion and (im) politeness comments. *Journal of Pragmatics*, *43*(14), 3565–3578.

Spencer-Oatey, H. (2015). Rapport management model. In K. Tracy, T. Sandel, & C. Ilie (Eds.), *The international Encyclopedia of language and social interaction* (1st ed., pp. 1–6). Wiley. https://doi.org/10.1002/9781118611463

Stavridou, A. (2022). *Challenging traditional understandings of leadership and followership through discourse: A sociolinguistic case study of a basketball team*. University of Warwick.

Stevanovic, M., & Svennevig, J. (2015). Introduction: Epistemics and deontics in conversational directives. *Journal of Pragmatics*, *78*, 1–6. https://doi.org/10.1016/j.pragma.2015.01.008

Tannen, D. (1992). *That's not what I meant!: How conversational style makes or breaks your relations with others*. Virago.

Tannen, D. (1993a). *Framing in discourse*. Oxford University Press on Demand.

Tannen, D. (1993b). What's in a frame? Surface evidence for underlying expectations. *Framing in Discourse*, *14*, 56.

Tannen, D. (2004). Interactional sociolinguistics. In U. Ammon, N. Dittmar, K. Mattheier, & P. Trudgill (Eds.), *Sociolinguistics / Soziolinguistik* (pp. 76–88). De Gruyter Mouton.

Thornborrow, J. (2014). *Power talk: Language and interaction in institutional discourse*. Routledge. https://doi.org/10.4324/9781315839172

Turman, P. D. (2003). Coaches and cohesion: The impact of coaching techniques on team cohesion in the small group sport setting. *Journal of Sport Behaviour*, *26*(1), 86–104.

Turman, P. D. (2008). Coaches' immediacy behaviors as predictors of athletes' perceptions of satisfaction and team cohesion. *Western Journal of Communication*, *72*(2), 162–179. https://doi.org/10.1080/10570310802038424

Vine, B. (2004). *Getting things done at work: The discourse of power in workplace interaction*. John Benjamins Publishing Company.

Vine, B., Holmes, J., Marra, M., Pfeifer, D., & Jackson, B. (2008). Exploring co-leadership talk through interactional sociolinguistics. *Leadership*, *4*(3), 339–360.

Walsh, K. (2018, May 15). *Mo Salah opens up on Jurgen Klopp 'friendship' at Liverpool*. Liverpool Echo. https://www.liverpoolecho.co.uk/sport/football/football-news/mohamed-salah-opens-up-friendship-14659580

Wang, J. (2006). Questions and the exercise of power. *Discourse & Society*, *17*(4), 529–548. https://doi.org/10.1177/0957926506063127

Wells, G. (1993). Reevaluating the IRF sequence: A proposal for the articulation of theories of activity and discourse for the analysis of teaching and learning in the classroom. *Linguistics and Education*, *5*(1), 1–37. https://doi.org/10.1016/S0898-5898(05)80001-4

Wilson, N. (2009). The discourse of deputies: Communicating co-leadership in a rugby club. *Te Reo*, *52*, 73–98.

Wilson, N. (2010). Bros, boys and guys: Address term function and communities of practice in a New Zealand rugby team. *New Zealand English Journal*, *24*, 33–54.

Wilson, N. (2011). *Leadership as communicative practice: The discursive construction of leadership and team identity in a New Zealand rugby team* [Doctoral dissertation]. Victoria University of Wellington.

Wolfers, S., File, K. A., & Schnurr, S. (2017). 'Just because he's black': Identity construction and racial humour in a German U-19 football team. *Journal of Pragmatics*, *112*, 83–96. https://doi.org/10.1016/j.pragma.2017.02.003

Woodhams, J. M. (2019). Egalitarianism and politics in New Zealand. *Political Identity in Discourse*, 67–101. https://doi.org/10.1007/978-3-030-18630-2_3

Yates, L. (2010). Speech act performance in workplace settings. In A. Martínez-Flor & E. Usó-Juan (Eds.), *Language learning & language teaching* (Vol. *26*, pp. 109–126). John Benjamins Publishing Company. https://doi.org/10.1075/lllt.26.07yat

Index

Aarons, D. 37
Alasuutari, P. 49
Alvesson, M. 14, 55
analytical process 25–7, 56
    authentic interactions 26, 28–36
    contextual information 27, 52–4
    cultural belief systems 27, 55–6
    language patterns, social actions in 26, 36–49
    power and solidarity, relational dynamics of 26–7, 49–52
    sense-making and 49
Asmuß, B. 48
asymmetrical power relations (coaches & players) 59, 76–8, 80, 93, 95, 172, 191
authentic interactions (data) 26, 57
    data set of interactions 28–9
    limitations in data set 29, 31–2
    primary unit of analysis 34–6
    transcribing language and social interaction 32–4
    type and amount 30–1
Azadfada, S. 1

Balaguer, I. 78
Bax, M. M. H. 148
Bayard, D. 171
Beeching, K. 1
Bell, A. 14, 147
Bellinger, D. C. 160
belonging and togetherness 13, 17, 50, 135, 140, 148, 174, 196, 208. *See also* pre-match team talks (belonging and togetherness)
Bennie, A. 1
Bergmann Drewe 155
Biber, D. 37, 41, 157

Blommaert, J. 1, 12
Bousfield, D. 175
Bowers, J. W. 175
Boxer, D. 2, 162, 165
Boyd, M. 80, 82
Brawley, L. R. 3
British Cycling (accusations of bullying) 4
Brown, G. 1, 12, 45
Brown, P. 1, 175
Brown, R. 16–17
Bubel, C. 94
Buchstaller, I. 14
Bull, P. 141
bullying 4–5
Burke, M. 1

Candela, A. 82
captain 2, 9, 21, 54, 57, 64–5, 95, 97, 204
    captain-player dyad 9
    captain-player role-relationships 20
    institutional role of 131–2
    interactional responsibilities of 110–12
    invitation to address group by 98–101
    power sharing 109, 114
Carron, A. V. 3, 197
Carter, R. 34
chief problem-solver, coach as 80, 84–8, 93
Chiles, T. 79
Chimbwete-Phiri, R. 17
Chovanec, J. 34
claiming interactional rights 101–6
Clayman, S. 45, 74
Clifton, J. 48, 201

coach(es) 9, 57, 65, 77, 114, 145, 171, 194, 201–3, 208
  animating directives from 107–10
  bullying, racism, sexism and discrimination (reports of) 4–5
  as chief problem-solver 80, 84–8, 93
  coach-captain dyad 9
  coach-captain(-player) relationship 97
  coach-captain relationship 109, 114 (*see also* power sharing)
  coach-captain role-relationships 20
  coach-player dyad 9, 207
  coach-player role-relationship 57, 80
  coach-player solidarity 21, 155–6, 165, 169, 174, 176, 190–1 (*see also* criticism)
  control over players (*see* control over players by coaches)
  as educator 80–3, 93
  as motivator 80, 90–3
  and players 1, 20–1, 28, 59, 71, 77–8, 80, 95, 173
  positioning of/by 41, 86, 93, 182
  as sheriff 80, 88–90, 93
coach-player interactions 21, 59, 60, 69, 71, 79, 85, 92, 132–3, 154, 202
  amount of talk 61
  closing 60–1
  directives 66
  explicit directives 66
  humour 169, 196
  initiating 60–1
  performance evaluations 85, 87
  questions and question tags 61–2, 79, 92
coach-player relationship 59, 69, 76, 78–9, 92, 94, 97, 132, 155, 185, 202–4
  power 59
  relational dynamics of 78, 155
  social distance in (*see* social distance)
  solidarity 155–6, 173
Cockerill, I. M. 1
cohesion 3, 129, 148
contextual information 27, 52–4, 131, 164, 212, 218–20

control over players by coaches 20, 59
  controlling player contributions 62–5
  in decision-making sequences 69–71
  interactional mechanisms of 76–8
  legitimizing 64–5
  offering floor 64
  in performances evaluation 72–6
  talk to instruct 65–9
Cortés-Conde, F. 162, 165
Cotterill, S. 97
Coulthard, M. 12, 82
Coupland, N. 1, 14
criticism 175, 190
  attenuating device 184
  boosting 185–9
  confidence levels, managing 183–5
  direct and indirect practices of 176
  implied 179–82
  pronouns to minimize 182–3
Culpeper, J. 175
cultural belief systems 27, 55–6, 191, 194, 203, 209, 212–13
cultural knowledge systems 8, 19, 21, 53, 55, 191
cultural principles 2, 18, 21, 194, 201–3, 209
  about leader-follower relations 194, 198–201
  about people in control 194, 205–7
  about social structures 194, 203–5
  about solidarity with others 194, 207–9
  about team relationships, transactional nature 194–8

Daly, N. 17, 167
Davis, L. 1, 3
designedly incomplete questions/utterances 80–3
  directives 107, 113, 152
  explicit directives 66
  hiding and mitigating 159–61
  implied directives 160–1, 172
  indirect strategies for realizing directives 131
discourse analysis 11, 210–11, 213
  social actions in language patterns 36–49
  theoretical tools of 2, 11–15

Drasovean, A. 170
Drew, P. 1, 8, 45
Duda, J. L. 3, 78
Dynel, M. 34

Edelsky, C. 123
educational role-relationship 83
educator, coach as 80–3, 93
Eggins, S. 156–7, 159
Ehrlich, S. 94
empirically illustrating of relationships in action 1–2, 55, 193, 209, 213
Ervin-Tripp, S. M. 202
expert power 16, 42, 50, 68
    coaches and players 68
    to direct team 126–9
    through questions 92–5

Fairclough, N. 1, 12, 14, 16, 34, 55, 213
Fairhurst, G. T. 207
Fetzer, A. 141
File, K. A. 3, 41, 175
Freed, A. F. 94, 198
French, P. 123
Frey, L. R. 15
Fuller, R. 12, 207

García-Calvo, T. 3
Gee, J. P. 1, 12, 14, 55, 213
Gibson, A. 14
Giles, H. 14
Gilman, A. 16–17
Gleason, J. B. 160
Goffman, E. 10, 34, 109, 175
Goldberg, J. A. 105
Greenwood, A. 198
Groom, R. 3, 20
Gumperz, J. J. 10, 45

Halldorsson, V. 17
Halliday, M. A. K. 41
Harwood, J. 170
Harwood, N. 183
Hay, J. 167
Heath, S. 79
Heritage, J. 1, 8, 45, 100, 211
Heuzé, J.-P. 3

high-performance sports teams 2, 77, 79, 94, 174, 191, 195, 213. *See also* New Zealand rugby team (*The Rhinos*)
    context of 8, 78, 163, 193, 211
    cultural belief systems of 27, 55–6, 163
    cultural values of 113, 174, 197, 201, 209
    interpersonal ideology in 21
    relational culture/context of 20, 194, 209
Hodge, K. 78
Holmes, J. 2, 11–13, 16, 50, 65, 79, 94, 155, 158, 175, 206–7
Holmes, T. 5
Hope, C. 5, 214
Hope, N. 4
Hultgren, A. K. 14
Hutchby, I. 34
Hyland, K. 1, 12
Hymes, D. 10

Ide, S. 202
identity 27, 143, 159, 199
    expert 107, 118, 167
    leadership and followership 65, 201, 204, 206–7
implied directives 160–1, 172
indirect strategies for realizing directives 131
Infante, D. A. 1
informal language and leadership 156–9
Ingle, S. 4
institutional roles 105, 131, 162
    as captain 131–2
    coaches 162
    leadership role 101, 204
intensifiers 130
interactional dynamics 2, 10, 18–19, 49–52, 54, 76, 200
    coaches, captains and players 57
    to relational dynamics 49–52
interactional footing 169
interactional practices 76
    claiming interactional rights 101–6
    relinquishing the floor 74
    self-selecting 74, 103–4
    shifting topic 103

interactional role/task 27, 35–6, 52–3, 77, 98, 110, 112
interpersonal functions of language 13
interpersonal ideology 2, 10, 18–19, 21, 55

Jackson, B. 1
Jaspers, J. 2, 45
Jaworski, A. 1
Jefferson, G. 10, 45
Jewitt, C. 48
Johnson, G. 14, 147
Johnstone, B. 12, 37
Jones, E. 114, 200
Jowett, S. 1, 3

Kádár, D. Z. 148
Karreman, D. 14, 55
Kassing, J. W. 1
Knowler, R. 120
Koester, A. 195
Koshik, I. 80, 82
Kozub, S. 3
Krishnayya, S. 171
Kuiper, K. 167

Lafrenière, M.-A. K. 1
Laing, P. 142
Lakoff, R. 207
Landmark, A. M. D. 42
Langman, J. 79
language 2, 6, 11, 126, 135, 211, 213. *See also* linguistic lens
  functional properties of 13
  interactional practices 135–6, 138, 151, 214
  and leadership 156–9, 161, 172
  micro-level analysis of 25
  and social interaction 23, 32–4
  and society 10, 22
  use and power/solidarity 16–17, 49–52, 135–6
language patterns, social actions in 26
  design choices of speech actions 40–2
  integrating levels of analysis 49
  non-verbal actions 48–9
  speech actions of utterance 38–40
  turn-taking patterns 45–8
  utterances, content 38

leader-follower dyads 205
leader-follower relationship 100, 194, 198–201, 203
Lee, Y. 78
Levinson, S. 1, 175
levity and humour 161–9, 172
Liddicoat, A. 1, 45
Lim, T.-S. 175
linguistic exchanges 2
linguistic lens 2, 27–8, 54, 193
  limitations and benefits 195, 210–13
  micro and macro levels 14–15
  on player-player relations 132
  on relationships 17–20
linguistic subsystems 41
Lipovsky, C. 17
Local, J. 123
Locher, M. A. 12, 50, 175
Love, R. 157
Lyle, J. 3

Macfarlane, A. 142
Markman, K. M. 188
Marra, M. 11, 50, 158, 175, 207
Matthiessen, C. M. I. M. 41
McDonnell, J. 3
McEnery, T. 157
Metge, J. 142
Meyerhoff, M. 147, 158
Mierowsky, M. 37
Miller, P. 165
Mirivel, J. C. 12, 207
motivator, coach as 80, 90–3
multiparty interactional floor 118–24, 129

Nanouri, K. 42
negatively constructed Y/N interrogative 167
New Zealand rugby team (*The Rhinos*) 1, 8–10, 25, 213
  contextual information (individuals) 218–20
  relationships in 6, 8–9, 11, 15, 17, 26–7, 49
  role-relationships 8–10, 25, 193
  social interactions 11, 25
  solidarity 152, 174
  team membership and roles 6–7, 13
  technical terminology 215–17

nodding 62, 68, 86–7
non-linguistic markers 136–8
non-verbal/non-linguistic behaviour 48–9, 136
Ntoumanis, N. 1, 3

O'Connor, D. 1, 79
O'Connor, M. 142
O'Halloran, K. L. 48
on-field huddles 106, 110, 115, 117–20, 131–3
Ostermann, A. C. 17

Paltridge, B. 1, 12
performance evaluations 94
 coach questions in 80–1
 control over players, by coaches in 72–6
 decision-making in 86–7
 setting of 79–80
performance of relationships 3
 breakdowns in 5
 bullying, racism, sexism and discrimination (reports) 5–6
 positive relationships 3
Pescosolido, A. T. 3
player(s) 8–9, 62, 69, 84, 87, 122, 136–7, 146–7, 155, 183, 185, 203
 asymmetrical power relations with 76–8
 coaches and 1, 20–1, 28, 59, 71, 77–8, 80, 95, 173
 player-player dyad 9, 207
 player-player interactions 20–1, 54, 115, 117, 120, 123–4, 126, 133, 204
 player-player solidarity 21, 191
 questions 88–92
 shared attitudes of 169–71
player-player relationships 20, 54, 117, 133, 204
 degree of experience 131
 institutional role of 131–2
 power dynamics (*see* power dynamics (player-player relations))
Poczwardowski, A. 3
Potter, J. 82
Poutiainen, S. 2, 19, 55

power and solidarity 1–2, 19, 23, 25, 55, 134–5, 210, 213
 between coaches and players 21, 173–4 (*see also* criticism)
 language use and 16–17, 49–52
 relational dynamics of 20, 26–7, 54, 57, 169, 193, 209–10
power dynamics (player-player relations) 132–4
 expert power to direct team 126–9
 and multiparty interactional floor 118–22
power sharing 97, 107, 109–15
praise, withholding of 176–9
Prapavessis, H. 3
pre-match huddles 136, 138–45, 149–50, 152–4, 196
pre-match team talks (belonging and togetherness) 110, 135, 151–4, 196, 208
 collective pronouns and familiarizers in 141–3, 152
 formalities, before and after 149–51
 involvement markers in 143, 145–7
 non-linguistic markers in 136–8, 151
 reducing potential divisions in 143–5
 repetition and mirroring in 150–1
 shared purpose and emotional pulse in 138–41
 solidarity in 135–6
 team chants in 147–9, 152
pseudo inclusive pronouns 161
Puchta, C. 82

question-response-evaluation-elaboration 82
questions 78, 79–80, 93
 designedly incomplete 80–3
 to direct attention to problems 84–8
 to establish shared knowledge 80–3
 expert power through 92–5
 to hold players accountable 88–90
 and question tags 61–2
questions-answer patterns/sequences 78, 83, 85, 94

relational culture/context 20
relational dynamics 2, 10, 18–19, 55–6, 76, 174, 193, 205, 211, 214

coach-player relations 78, 155
leader-follower 194, 199
of power and solidarity 20, 26–7, 54, 57, 169, 193, 209–10
relational functions of language 13
relationships 3, 6, 8–9, 15, 17, 26–7, 49, 114, 170, 173–4, 191, 193, 201, 206–7
in action 9–11
cultural portrait of 193, 213
dyads 3–4, 9, 198 (*see also specific relationship dyads*)
empirical illustrations of 1–2, 55
social enactment of 211
transactional nature of 194–8
Richards, K. 15, 213
Roan, D. 4, 214
Robinson, J. D. 100
role-relationships 8, 29, 53, 76, 79, 193
captain-player 20
coach-captain 20
coach-player 57, 80
dyads 213
educational 83
institutional 79
participation frameworks 34, 140
roles, professional 8–9, 25, 34, 45, 53
coach 93
in New Zealand rugby team 6–7, 13
Rosaldo, M. Z. 37
Rubin, D. 80, 82
Rubin, G. B. 94
Rylander, P. 20

Saavedra, R. 3
Sacks, H. 10, 45, 188
Sagar, S. S. 1
Salmela, M. 135, 151
Schegloff, E. A. 10, 45, 188
Schiffrin, D. 1, 45
Schnurr, S. 3, 12, 17, 162, 175, 201
Schofield, D. 78, 114, 200
Schulze, R. 16
Searle, J. R. 12, 37
shared attitudes 169–71
sheriff, coach as 80, 88–90, 93
Sinclair, J. 82
Slade, D. 156
Smith, B. A. 48

Smith, M. J. 141
social distance 17, 36, 51, 155–61, 171, 207
social interactions 4, 10–11, 13, 16, 17, 21, 29, 160
language and 23, 32–4
leader-follower relations in 194, 198–201
speech actions in 45, 48
socialized belief systems 213
society, language and 10, 22
sociolinguistics 1, 10–11, 14, 22, 41, 57, 134, 207
solidarity. *See* power and solidarity
solidarity-fostering practices 173
speech actions 12, 37, 133, 181, 206
design of 37, 40–2
directness and indirectness of 42
lexicogrammatical system 41–4
in social interaction 45, 48
of utterances 38–40 (*see also* utterances)
Spencer-Oatey, H. 12, 50, 175
Stavridou, A. 201
Stevanovic, M. 42
strategic decision-making 124–6
Stubbe, M. 16
sub-roles (of the coach) 80
as chief problem-solver 80, 84–8, 93
as educator 80–3
as motivator 80, 90–3
as sheriff 80, 88–90, 93
Svennevig, J. 42

Tagg, C. 170
taken-for-granted practices 1, 16, 20, 55, 59, 61, 66, 77, 92, 100, 114, 136, 151–2, 195, 203
Tannen, D. 55, 198
technical vocabulary 158
Thornborrow, J. 16
toxic cultures 5
transactional functions of language 13
transition-relevance places (TRP) 74–5
Turman, P. D. 3
turn-taking patterns 37, 45–8, 211

Uhl-Bien, M. 207

utterances 13, 37–9, 40, 48–9, 51–2, 80–3, 171, 182. *See also* speech actions

Vine, B. 2, 16, 45, 65, 160

Walsh, K. 155
Wang, J. 94
Watts, R. J. 50

Wells, G. 82
Wilson, N. 3, 28, 31, 41, 142, 153, 171
Wolfers, S. 3
Woodhams, J. M. 206
workplace teams 195–6

Yates, L. 37
Yule, G. 1, 12, 45

www.ingramcontent.com/pod-product-compliance
Lightning Source LLC
Chambersburg PA
CBHW050350230426

43663CB00010B/2057